16 April 1995

To: Ginny

Thank you so very much for your dedication to volunteering. It's "gems" like you that keep us going. Bullriders like you are hard to find.

Always,

Hy Bonetak

365
MAIN
COURSE
DISHES

365 MAIN COURSE DISHES

CRESCENT BOOKS
New York

First published by Ebury Press
an imprint of The Random Century Group
Random Century House
20 Vauxhall Bridge Road
London SW1V 2SA

This 1992 edition published by Crescent Books, distributed by
Outlet Book Company, Inc., a Random House Company,
225 Park Avenue South, New York, New York 10003.

Printed and bound in Italy.

ISBN 0–517–06951–2

8 7 6 5 4 3 2 1

CONTENTS

MEAT 6

POULTRY AND GAME 63

FISH AND SHELLFISH 93

VEGETARIAN DISHES 120

LIGHT MEALS 137

SALADS 166

Index 174

MEAT

This mouth-watering selection of meat-based dishes includes all types of meat and variety meats cooked in every way imaginable. From warming country casseroles to an elegant crown roast of lamb or a simply cooked, tender, juicy steak – you will be sure to find a recipe to please.

CLUB STEAKS WITH MUSTARD

SERVES 4

4 tablespoons wholegrain mustard	2 tablespoons chopped parsley
2 tablespoons all-purpose flour	2 tablespoons chopped thyme
four 6-ounce club steaks	

1 Mix together the mustard and flour, then spread on top of each steak.
2 Line a broiler pan with foil, sprinkle with the herbs and put the steaks on top. Cook under a preheated broiler for 5–15 minutes, turning frequently, until the steaks are cooked to your liking. Serve at once.

––––––––––– **TO MICROWAVE** –––––––––––
Complete step 1. Preheat a large browning skillet on HIGH for 5 minutes or according to manufacturer's instructions. Quickly put the herbs and steaks in the browning skillet and cook on HIGH for 5–7 minutes.

STILTON STEAKS

SERVES 4

1 cup crumbled Stilton cheese	pepper
2 tablespoons butter, softened	four 4–6-ounce club or fillet steaks
½–¾ cup chopped walnut pieces	

1 Put the cheese in a bowl and mash with a fork. Add the butter and walnuts and mix in. Season to taste.
2 Put the steaks on the broiler rack and season with plenty of pepper. Cook under a preheated broiler for 5–15 minutes, turning frequently, until the steaks are cooked to your liking.
3 Remove the steaks from under the broiler, sprinkle the cheese and nut mixture evenly over them and press down with a spatula. Broil for a further minute or until the topping is melted and bubbling. Serve hot.

STEAK WITH CREAM SAUCE

SERVES 4

four 6-ounce fillet steaks	1 tablespoon lemon juice
2 garlic cloves, crushed (optional)	2 tablespoons Worcestershire sauce
salt and pepper	1–2 tablespoons brandy
¼ cup butter	⅔ cup light cream
1 cup very thinly sliced button mushrooms	1 tablespoon minced parsley
¼ cup minced onion	parsley sprigs, for garnish

1 Rub the steaks with the garlic and season well.
2 Melt half the butter in a skillet and sauté the steaks over a high heat for about 2 minutes on each side to brown. If you like your steaks well done, cook for longer. Transfer to a warm serving dish and keep hot.
3 Heat the remaining butter in the skillet and quickly fry the mushrooms and onion for about 5 minutes or until tender. Add the lemon juice, Worcestershire sauce and brandy and bring to a boil.
4 Stir in the cream and minced parsley, bring almost to a boil, check the seasoning, then quickly pour over the steaks. Serve garnished with parsley sprigs.

STEAK WITH PORT

SERVES 4

1½ pounds top round steak cut into 1-inch cubes	½ pound bulk pork sausage
¼ cup wholewheat flour	⅔ cup fresh wholewheat breadcrumbs
1 medium onion, sliced	2 tablespoons chopped parsley
4 cloves	1 tablespoon currant jelly
salt and pepper	
⅔ cup port	
about 2 cups beef bouillon	

1 Toss the meat in the flour, shaking off excess, and put in a Dutch oven.
2 Add the onion and cloves and season to taste. Pour in the port and just enough bouillon to cover the meat.
3 Cover the pot and cook in a preheated oven at 325°F for about 3 hours or until the meat is tender.
4 Meanwhile, mix together the sausage, breadcrumbs and parsley and season to taste. With floured hands, form the mixture into eight balls.
5 Forty minutes before the end of the cooking time, stir the currant jelly into the pot. Add the sausage meatballs and cook, uncovered, until the sausage meatballs are cooked and brown. Skim off any excess fat and serve hot.

STRIPS OF BEEF IN WHISKY SAUCE

SERVES 4

1 tablespoon butter	⅓ cup whisky liqueur, such as Drambuie
1½ pounds club steak, cut into strips	⅓ cup heavy cream
1 large onion, chopped	salt and pepper

1 Melt the butter in a skillet. Add the beef strips and onion and sauté for 5–10 minutes or until the beef is brown and cooked to taste.
2 Stir in the liqueur and cream. Heat gently to reduce slightly. Season to taste, then serve at once.

TO MICROWAVE

Preheat a large browning skillet on HIGH for 5 minutes or according to manufacturer's instructions. Quickly put the butter, beef and onion in the browning skillet. Cook on HIGH for 5–7 minutes or until the meat is cooked to taste, stirring frequently. Stir in the liqueur and season to taste. Cook on HIGH for 1 minute, then stir in the cream and serve at once.

BEEF OLIVES

SERVES 4

4 bacon slices, finely chopped	salt and pepper
1 small onion, chopped	8 thin slices of top round of beef, (total weight about 1½ pounds)
2 tablespoons chopped parsley	1 tablespoon prepared English mustard
2 cups fresh breadcrumbs	3 tablespoons seasoned flour
¼ cup shredded beef suet	2 tablespoons butter
¼ teaspoon dried mixed herbs	2 tablespoons vegetable oil
1 small egg	2 cups beef bouillon
1 lemon	2 medium onions, sliced

1 Mix the bacon with the chopped onion, parsley, breadcrumbs, suet, herbs and egg. Add the grated rind of ½ of the lemon and 1 teaspoon juice and season to taste.
2 Put the meat between two sheets of baker's parchment and beat out with a meat mallet or rolling pin.
3 Spread mustard thinly over the meat, then divide the stuffing equally among the pieces. Roll up and secure with strong cotton or fine twine. Toss in seasoned flour, reserving excess flour.
4 Heat the butter and oil in a shallow flameproof casserole into which all the beef olives will just fit. Add the olives and cook until well browned. Remove from the pan.
5 Stir the remaining seasoned flour into the pan residue and cook for 1–2 minutes or until lightly browned. Remove from the heat, gradually stir in the bouillon and bring to a boil. Season to taste, then return the meat to the pan.
6 Scatter the sliced onions over the meat. Cover and cook in a preheated oven at 325°F for 1½ hours.

GROUND BEEF KABOBS WITH HORSERADISH RELISH

SERVES 6

1½ pounds lean ground beef	salt and pepper
2 cups grated onion	1 egg, beaten
9 tablespoons horseradish sauce	all-purpose flour, for coating
3 tablespoons chopped thyme	⅔ cup plain yogurt
4 cups fresh white breadcrumbs	½ cup minced parsley

1 Put the ground beef in a large bowl and mix in the onion, 6 tablespoons of the horseradish, the thyme and breadcrumbs. Season to taste.

2 Add enough egg to bind the mixture together and, with floured hands, shape into 18 even-size sausages. Cover and chill in the refrigerator until required.

3 Thread the kabobs lengthwise onto six oiled skewers. Cook under a preheated broiler for about 20 minutes, turning frequently.

4 Meanwhile, mix the yogurt with the remaining horseradish and the parsley. Serve the kabobs hot, with the sauce in a separate sauceboat.

―――――――――― **VARIATION** ――――――――――

For a more luxurious horseradish sauce, stir 2 tablespoons grated fresh horseradish into a whipped mixture of ⅓ cup of heavy cream and ⅓ cup dairy sour cream. Add ½ teaspoon vinegar, ½ teaspoon sugar and salt and pepper to taste.

BITKIS

SERVES 6

⅔ cup medium oatmeal	¼ cup vegetable oil
1¼ cups milk	2 tablespoons butter
2 medium onions, roughly chopped	¼ cup all-purpose flour
2 pounds lean ground beef	2 cups beef or chicken bouillon
salt and pepper	2 tablespoons tomato paste
3 tablespoons caraway seeds (optional)	1¼ cups dairy sour cream
5 tablespoons seasoned flour	parsley sprigs, for garnish

1 Soak the oatmeal in the milk overnight. Squeeze out excess milk and mix the oatmeal with the onions, ground beef and seasoning to taste.

2 Put this mixture twice through a grinder or mix in a food processor until smooth. Beat in 2 teaspoons of the caraway seeds, if using.

3 Shape in 18 round flat cakes, or bitkis. Coat with seasoned flour.

4 Heat the oil in a large skillet, add the bitkis and cook until well browned. Place in a single layer in a large shallow ovenproof dish.

5 Melt the butter in a saucepan, add the all-purpose flour and cook over low heat, stirring with a wooden spoon, for 2 minutes. Remove from the heat and gradually blend in the bouillon. Bring to a boil slowly, then simmer for 2–3 minutes, stirring. Stir in the tomato paste, sour cream and remaining caraway seeds, if using.

6 Pour the sauce over the bitkis and cook in a preheated oven at 350°F for about 1¼ hours or until cooked. Garnish with parsley.

ITALIAN-STYLE MEATBALLS

SERVES 4

2 tablespoons olive oil	1 cup fresh white breadcrumbs
1 large onion, minced	½ cup freshly grated Parmesan cheese
2 garlic cloves, crushed	1 egg, beaten
1-pound can chopped tomatoes	20 small ripe olives, pitted
2 teaspoons dried mixed herbs	vegetable oil, for deep frying
2 teaspoons dried oregano	½ cup red or white dry Italian wine
salt and pepper	
1 pound lean ground beef	

1 Heat the oil in a heavy-based saucepan, add the onion and half of the crushed garlic and sauté gently for about 5 minutes or until soft and lightly colored.

2 Add the tomatoes, half of the herbs and seasoning to taste. Bring to a boil, stirring, then lower the heat, cover and simmer for about 20 minutes

3 Meanwhile, make the meatballs. Put the ground beef in a bowl with the breadcrumbs, Parmesan, remaining garlic and herbs. Mix well, then season and bind with egg.

4 Pick up a small amount of the mixture, about the size of a walnut. Press one olive in the center, then shape the mixture around it. Repeat to make 20 meatballs.

5 Heat the oil in a deep-fat fryer to 375°F. Deep-fry the meatballs in batches for 2–3 minutes or until lightly browned, then drain thoroughly on absorbent kitchen paper.

6 Stir the wine into the tomato sauce, than add 1¼ cups water and the meatballs. Shake the pan to coat the balls in the sauce, adding more water if necessary. Cover and simmer for 15 minutes, then season and serve.

CHINESE BEEF AND VEGETABLE STIR-FRY

SERVES 4

¾ pound fillet or rump steak, sliced into very thin strips	⅓ cup sesame or vegetable oil
2 tablespoons cornstarch	1 onion, thinly sliced
¼ cup soy sauce	1 garlic clove, crushed
6 tablespoons dry sherry	1 inch piece of fresh root ginger, crushed
2 tablespoons dark soft brown sugar	2 celery stalks, thinly sliced
2 tablespoons wine vinegar	1 sweet red pepper, sliced into thin strips
salt and pepper	½ pound snow peas, halved

1 Put the steak in a bowl. Mix together the next five ingredients and season to taste. Pour over the steak, stir well to mix, then cover and leave to marinate for 1 hour.

2 Heat 2 tablespoons of the oil in a wok or large skillet. Add the onion, garlic and ginger and fry gently, stirring, for 5 minutes or until soft.

3 Heat another 1 tablespoon of the oil in the wok. Add the celery and sweet red pepper and fry, stirring, for a further 5 minutes or until tender but still crisp. Remove the vegetables from the wok with a slotted spoon.

4 Drain the steak from the marinade. Heat the remaining oil in the wok, add the steak and stir-fry over high heat for 5 minutes. Remove with a slotted spoon and set aside.

5 Add the snow peas to the wok and stir-fry over high heat for 2–3 minutes. Return the steak and vegetables to the wok, then pour in the marinade and stir until bubbling and well mixed. Taste and season. Serve immediately.

BOILED BEEF AND CARROTS

SERVES 6

3½ pounds lean brisket of beef	8 cloves
bouquet garni	2 small turnips, quartered
6 black peppercorns, lightly crushed	2 celery stalks, chopped
2 small onions, quartered	1 leek, chopped
	18 small carrots

1 Tie up into a neat shape.

2 Place the beef in a large saucepan, add just enough water to cover and bring slowly to a boil. Skim the surface, then add the bouquet garni, peppercorns, onions (each quarter stuck with a clove), turnips, celery and leek. Lower the heat and simmer very gently for about 2 hours.

3 Add the small carrots and simmer gently for a further 30–40 minutes or until the carrots are tender.

4 Carefully transfer the beef and small carrots to a warmed serving plate and keep warm.

5 Skim the fat from the surface of the cooling liquor, then strain. Boil the liquor to reduce slightly, then pour into a warmed sauceboat or pitcher.

6 Serve the beef surrounded by the carrots, with the sauce served separately.

SPICED BEEF

SERVES 6

4 pound piece corned beef	½ teaspoon dry mustard
1 medium onion, sliced	1 teaspoon ground cinnamon
4 medium carrots, sliced	juice of 1 lemon
1 small turnip, sliced	
8 cloves	
⅔ cup dark soft brown sugar	

1 Tie up the meat to form a neat shape and put in a large saucepan or Dutch oven with the vegetables.

2 Cover with water and bring slowly to a boil. Skim the surface, cover and simmer for 3–4 hours or until tender. Let cool completely in the liquid for 3–4 hours.

3 Drain the meat well, then put into a roasting pan and stick the cloves into the fat. Mix together the remaining ingredients and spread over the meat.

4 Bake in a preheated oven at 350°F for 45 minutes to 1 hour or until tender, basting from time to time. Serve hot or cold.

BEEF IN WINE WITH WALNUTS

SERVES 6

2 pounds boneless stewing beef, cut into 1-inch cubes	1 teaspoon ground allspice
⅔ cup dry red wine	2 tablespoons all-purpose flour
3 medium parsnips	⅔ cup beef bouillon
1 tablespoon corn oil	½ cup ground walnuts
1 tablespoon butter	salt and pepper
1 small onion, minced	chopped walnuts, for garnish
1 garlic clove, crushed	

1 Put the beef in a bowl with the wine and mix well. Cover and leave to marinate overnight, stirring occasionally.
2 Cut the parsnips into 2 inch lengths, about ½ inch wide. Drain the meat from the marinade, reserving the marinade. Heat the oil and butter in a large skillet, add the beef, a few pieces at a time, and cook over a high heat until browned. Transfer to an ovenproof casserole with a slotted spoon.
3 Add the onion and garlic to the skillet and sauté for 5–10 minutes or until beginning to brown. Stir in the allspice, flour, reserved marinade, bouillon and ground walnuts. Bring to a boil, stirring constantly.
4 Pour into the casserole and add the parsnips. Season lightly to taste. Cover and cook in a preheated oven at 325°F for 2½–3 hours or until the meat is really tender.
5 Serve hot, straight from the casserole, sprinkled with the chopped walnuts.

BEEF AND CHESTNUT CASSEROLE

SERVES 4

3 tablespoons corn oil	2 tablespoons mushroom ketchup
2½ pounds chuck steak, cubed	1 teaspoon dried mixed herbs
1 medium onion, sliced	salt and pepper
1 garlic clove, crushed	1-pound can whole chestnuts in salted water, drained
2 tablespoons wholewheat flour	
1¼ cups hard cider	2 tablespoons chopped fresh parsley, for garnish
1¼ cups beef bouillon	

1 Heat the oil in a large Dutch oven, add the beef in batches and fry over brisk heat until browned on all sides. Remove with a slotted spoon and set aside.
2 Add the onion and garlic to the pot, lower the heat and fry gently for 5 minutes or until soft but not colored.
3 Return the meat to the pot and stir in the flour. Cook, stirring, for 1–2 minutes, then stir in the cider, bouillon and mushroom ketchup. Bring slowly to a boil, then add the herbs and season to taste.
4 Cover the casserole and cook in a preheated oven at 325°F for 2 hours or until the beef is tender.
5 Ten minutes before the end of the cooking time, remove the casserole from the oven and add the chestnuts. Return to the oven to complete cooking. Taste and adjust the seasoning and sprinkle with the parsley before serving.

BEEF STEW WITH DUMPLINGS

SERVES 4

1½ pounds stewing steak, cut into cubes	3 medium tomatoes, quartered
1 tablespoon all-purpose flour	1 teaspoon dried mixed herbs
¼ cup drippings or lard	1 tablespoon tomato paste (optional)
3 medium onions, diced	FOR THE DUMPLINGS
2½ cups diced carrots	2 cups self-rising flour
2½–3 cups diced potatoes	pinch of salt
4 celery stalks, diced	⅓–½ cup shortening
2½ cups beef bouillon	
salt and pepper	

1 Put the meat in a plastic bag with the flour and shake until coated. Heat the drippings or lard in a large saucepan, add the meat and cook until browned. Remove the meat from the pan with a slotted spoon.

2 Add the onions, carrots, potatoes and celery to the pan and sauté for about 5 minutes or until lightly browned.

3 Remove the pan from the heat and add the bouillon, seasoning, tomatoes, herbs and tomato paste (if using). Return the meat to the pan, bring to a boil, cover, reduce the heat and simmer gently for 2 hours.

4 To make the dumplings, put the flour and salt in a bowl, add the shortening and cut in until the mixture resembles fine breadcrumbs. Gradually mix in 5–6 tablespoons water until the mixture forms a light, elastic dough. Turn onto a floured surface and knead lightly. Cut the dough into eight pieces and roll each into a ball.

5 Arrange the dumplings on top of the stew, re-cover and continue cooking for a further 20–25 minutes.

BEEF IN CIDER

SERVES 4–5

1 tablespoon corn oil	¼ cup all-purpose flour
1 pound top round steak, cut into cubes	1¼ cups hard cider
½ pound thin pork sausage links, halved	5 cloves
1 medium onion, chopped	3 beef bouillon cubes
2 celery stalks, chopped	salt and pepper
1 Gravenstein apple, cored and sliced	2 teaspoons chopped parsley, for garnish

1 Heat the oil in a large skillet, add the meat, sausages and onion and sauté for about 10 minutes or until lightly browned.

2 Add the celery and apple and sprinkle in the flour. Stir well, then add the hard cider and cloves. Crumble in the bouillon cubes and stir well again.

3 Transfer to an ovenproof casserole, cover and cook in a preheated oven at 350°F for 2–2½ hours or until the meat is tender. Season to taste and garnish with parsley before serving.

BEEF IN STOUT

SERVES 4–6

1 tablespoon butter	salt and pepper
about 1 tablespoon corn oil	2 tablespoons all-purpose flour
2 pounds top round steak, cut into 2-inch cubes	1¼ cups stout (dark beer)
4 medium onions, sliced	1 bay leaf
2 cups halved button mushrooms	1 teaspoon soft dark brown sugar

1 Heat the butter and oil in a large Dutch oven and cook the meat for 10 minutes or until browned all over. Remove the meat from the pot with a slotted spoon.

2 Add the onions and mushrooms to the pot, adding more oil if necessary, and fry for about 5 minutes or until softened. Season to taste, add the flour and stir well so that the flour absorbs the fat.

3 Return the meat to the pan, pour in the stout and add the bay leaf and brown sugar. Stir well to mix.

4 Cover and cook gently, either on the hob or in a preheated oven at 350°F for about 2½ hours or until the meat is tender.

--- **COOK'S TIP** ---

Stout gets its dark color and bitterness from the roasted malt or barley used in its brewing. It makes a delicious gravy when used in a casserole and is packed with goodness.

MEXICAN BEEF TORTILLAS

SERVES 4

2 tablespoons oil	2 cups chopped peeled tomatoes
2 onions, minced	2 fresh green chilies, seeded and finely chopped
2 garlic cloves, crushed	
½–1 teaspoon chili powder	1 teaspoon granulated sugar
1 pound lean ground beef	
2 tablespoons tomato paste	12 hot tortillas (see below)
salt and pepper	

1 Heat the oil in a heavy-based saucepan, add half the onions and garlic and fry gently for 5 minutes or until soft and lightly colored. Add the chili powder and fry for a further 1–2 minutes, stirring constantly.

2 Add the beef and sauté until browned. Add the tomato paste and stir to mix, then add salt and pepper to taste. Fry for a further 10–15 minutes, stirring occasionally.

3 Meanwhile, put the tomatoes in a blender or food processor with the remaining onions and garlic, the chilies, sugar and salt and pepper to taste. Work until quite smooth, then transfer to a sauceboat or pitcher.

4 Put a spoonful of the beef mixture on a hot tortilla and roll up. Repeat until all the beef and tortillas are used. Serve immediately, with the cold tomato sauce.

--- **COOK'S TIP** ---

To make 12 tortillas, mix 2¼ cups all-purpose flour with 1 teaspoon salt and cut in 3 tablespoons shortening. Gradually add 1 cup lukewarm water and mix to a dough. Knead lightly and shape into 12 pieces. Roll out thinly between sheets of wax paper. Cook the tortillas for about 30 seconds on each side in an ungreased skillet until speckled with brown. Stack in foil to keep hot.

BOEUF STROGANOFF
SERVES 4

HUNGARIAN GOULASH
SERVES 6

1½ pounds rump steak, thinly sliced	1 onion, thinly sliced
3 tablespoons all-purpose flour	2 cups sliced mushrooms
	⅔ cup dairy sour cream
salt and pepper	2 teaspoons tomato paste (optional)
¼ cup butter	

1 Put the steak slices between two sheets of baker's parchment and beat out with a meat mallet or rolling pin.
2 Trim the fat off the steak and discard. Cut the meat across the grain into thin strips. Coat the strips of steak in flour seasoned with salt and pepper.
3 Melt half the butter in a skillet, add the meat and sauté for 5–7 minutes or until golden brown, tossing constantly.
4 Add the remaining butter, the onion and mushrooms and sauté, stirring, for 3–4 minutes. Stir in the sour cream and tomato paste (if liked), and season well, using plenty of pepper. Heat through gently, without boiling. Transfer to a warmed serving dish and serve immediately.

3 tablespoons beef drippings or oil	1-pound can tomatoes
3 medium onions, chopped	salt and pepper
2 garlic cloves, crushed	1 sweet green or red pepper, chopped
2½ pounds chuck steak, cut into 1½-inch pieces	1¼ pounds potatoes, peeled and cut into 1-inch chunks
1 tablespoon mild paprika	
¼ teaspoon caraway seeds	2 green chilies (optional)

1 Melt the drippings or heat the oil in a Dutch oven, add the onions and garlic and cook over moderate heat for 10 minutes or until the onions are soft and golden brown, stirring occasionally.
2 Add the meat and cook over high heat, stirring constantly, until browned slightly. Add the paprika, caraway seeds, tomatoes with their juice, 1¼ cups water and salt and pepper to taste. Stir well to break up the tomatoes.
3 Bring to a boil, cover and cook in a preheated oven at 325°F for 1½ hours.
4 Remove the pot from the oven and stir in the chopped pepper and potatoes, adding the whole chilies if liked. Cover and return to the oven for a further 45 minutes or until the potatoes are tender. The goulash should be of a fairly thin consistency.
5 Remove the chilies, and taste and adjust the seasoning before serving.

BEEF AND SPINACH CURRY

SERVES 4–6

10 black peppercorns	6 garlic cloves, crushed
4 cloves	1-inch piece of fresh root ginger, finely chopped
2 bay leaves	2 pounds lean stewing beef, cut into 1-inch cubes
seeds of 6 cardamoms	
2 teaspoons cumin seeds	⅔ cup plain yogurt
1 tablespoon coriander seeds	2 pounds fresh leaf spinach, stalks removed, or two 10-ounce packets frozen spinach, thawed and drained
½ teaspoon chili powder	
1 teaspoon salt	
6 tablespoons ghee or oil	
1 large onion, minced	

1 Finely grind the dry spices and salt in a small electric mill or with a pestle and mortar.

2 Heat the ghee or oil in a large heavy-based saucepan or Dutch oven, add the onion, garlic, ginger and ground spices and cook over a moderate heat for about 5 minutes or until softened and just turning brown.

3 Increase the heat and add the meat. Cook, stirring all the time, until the meat is well browned on all sides. Add the yogurt to the pan, 1 tablespoon at a time. Cook each addition over a high heat, stirring constantly, until the yogurt is absorbed.

4 Cover the pan tightly with a lid and turn down the heat to very low. Simmer for 1½ hours or until the meat is tender, stirring occasionally.

5 Add the spinach, mix well and cook over a moderate heat for a further 5–10 minutes, stirring all the time until the liquid has evaporated. Adjust the seasoning and serve.

GROUND BEEF WITH PEAS

SERVES 4–6

2 tablespoons ghee or oil	8-ounce can tomatoes, chopped
1 medium onion, minced	1 teaspoon superfine sugar
1-inch piece of fresh root ginger, grated	2 teaspoons salt
8 garlic cloves, crushed	10-ounce packet frozen peas
2 teaspoons ground cumin	3 tablespoons chopped cilantro, parsley or mint
1 tablespoon ground coriander	2 tablespoons lemon or lime juice
1 teaspoon chili powder	1 teaspoon garam masala
½ teaspoon ground turmeric	
2 pounds lean ground beef	

1 Heat the ghee or oil in a heavy-based saucepan or Dutch oven, add the onion and cook over a high heat for about 5 minutes or until just turning brown. Lower the heat, add the ginger, garlic and spices and cook gently for 2–3 minutes.

2 Add the ground beef, chopped tomatoes with their juice, sugar and salt. Stir well until mixed and bring to a boil. Cover and simmer for 45 minutes.

3 Stir in the peas, herbs and lemon or lime juice. Cover and simmer for 15 minutes, stirring occasionally.

4 To serve, sprinkle with garam masala. Serve hot.

STEAMED BEEF AND TOMATO PUDDING

SERVES 4–6

FOR THE FILLING	½ teaspoon dried oregano
3 tablespoons olive oil	1 tablespoon mild paprika
½ teaspoon cumin seeds	½ teaspoon black pepper
1 cup chopped onion	2 beef bouillon cubes
⅔ cup diced mixed sweet red, green and yellow peppers	½ cup chopped mushrooms
1 garlic clove, crushed	FOR THE DOUGH
½ teaspoon salt	2 cups self-rising flour
1 bay leaf	¼ cup shredded beef suet
1 pound lean ground beef	¼ cup grated potato
1-pound can tomatoes	½ teaspoon salt
2 tablespoons tomato paste	½ teaspoon baking powder

1 Heat the oil in a pan, add the cumin and fry for 30 seconds. Add the onion and peppers and sauté for 5–6 minutes. Add the garlic, salt and bay leaf. Add the beef, stir well and sauté for 5 minutes. Drain the tomatoes, reserving the juice, and chop, discarding the seeds.

2 Add the tomatoes, tomato paste, oregano, paprika, pepper, bouillon cubes and tomato juice and cook for 10 minutes. Add the mushrooms, season and cook for 5 minutes.

3 To make the dough, mix the ingredients and gradually add about ⅔ cup water to bind. Roll out to a 14-inch round and cut out one quarter for the lid. Use to line a greased 6-cup pudding mold. Spoon in the meat and cover with the dough lid. Cover with greased baker's parchment and foil and steam for 1½ hours.

CURRIED BEEF AND APPLE BAKE

SERVES 4

2-ounce slice of bread, crusts removed	1½ pounds lean ground beef
1¼ cups milk	2 tablespoons raisins
3 tablespoons butter or margarine	¼ cup slivered almonds
2 medium onions, minced	1 tablespoon lemon juice
1 cooking apple, cored and chopped	salt and pepper
1 tablespoon mild curry powder	2 bay leaves
	3 eggs

1 Put the bread in a bowl, pour in the milk and leave to soak. Meanwhile, melt the butter in a saucepan, add the onions and sauté for 5 minutes or until beginning to soften. Add the apple and curry powder and fry, stirring, for a further 2–3 minutes.

2 Turn the onion mixture into a bowl and add the meat, raisins, almonds, lemon juice and salt and pepper to taste. Mix until well combined.

3 Squeeze the milk from the bread, reserving the milk, and stir the bread into the meat mixture.

4 Place the bay leaves on the bottom of a 5–cup pie dish. Fill with the meat mixture, then cover with foil. Bake in a preheated oven at 350°F for 35 minutes, then remove the foil and break up the meat mixture with a fork.

5 Whisk the eggs together with the reserved milk and pour over the meat, stirring gently to distribute the custard mixture evenly.

6 Return the dish to the oven and cook for a further 35 minutes or until the custard has set and the top browned.

BEEF 'MOUSSAKA'

SERVES 4–6

1 pound eggplants, sliced	1-pound can tomatoes
salt and pepper	1¼ cups plain yogurt
6 tablespoons vegetable oil	2 medium eggs, beaten
2 large onions, sliced	¼ teaspoon grated nutmeg
1 garlic clove, chopped	¼ cup grated Parmesan cheese
1½ pounds lean ground beef	

1 Layer the eggplant slices in a colander, sprinkling each layer with salt. Cover and leave for about 30 minutes.
2 Meanwhile, heat 2 tablespoons oil in a skillet and sauté the onions and garlic for 5 minutes. Add the ground meat and fry for 10 minutes. Add the tomatoes with their juice, season to taste and simmer for 20 minutes.
3 Drain the eggplant slices, rinse and dry well on kitchen paper towels. Heat the remaining oil in a separate large skillet and cook the eggplant slices for 4–5 minutes or until lightly browned, turning once. Add more oil, if necessary.
4 Arrange a layer of eggplant slices in the bottom of a large ovenproof dish and spoon over a layer of the meat mixture. Continue the layers until all the meat and eggplants are used, finishing with a layer of eggplant.
5 Beat the yogurt, eggs and nutmeg together, season to taste and stir in half the Parmesan. Pour over the dish and sprinkle with the remaining cheese. Bake in a preheated oven at 350°F for 45 minutes–1 hour or until golden.

BEEF AND RED BEAN GRATIN

SERVES 4

½ cup dried red kidney beans, soaked overnight	2 cups chopped tomatoes
⅓ cup butter or margarine	1 tablespoon tomato paste
1 small onion, thinly sliced	1 teaspoon chopped fresh mixed herbs or ½ teaspoon dried
½ pound lean ground beef	1 cup milk
½ cup all-purpose flour	½ cup shredded Cheddar or Monterey Jack cheese
scant 1 cup beef bouillon	¼ teaspoon prepared English mustard
cayenne	
salt and pepper	

1 Drain the beans and put in a saucepan. Cover with water and boil rapidly for 10 minutes, then boil gently for 45 minutes or until tender. Drain.
2 Melt 2 tablespoons butter in a saucepan, add the onion and beef and brown over a high heat, stirring. Stir in 6 tablespoons flour, the bouillon, cayenne, salt and pepper. Cook until very thick. Transfer to an ovenproof dish.
3 Melt another 2 tablespoons butter in the pan, add the tomatoes and cook for 10 minutes or until soft. Stir in the beans, tomato paste and herbs and simmer until reduced. Spread over the meat.
4 Melt the remaining butter in a clean pan and add the remaining flour. Cook, stirring, for 2 minutes. Remove from the heat and stir in the milk. Bring to a boil and cook, stirring, until thick.
5 Stir in half the cheese and the mustard and season. Pour the sauce over the bean layer and sprinkle the remaining cheese on top. Bake in a preheated oven at 400°F for 25 minutes or until golden brown. Serve hot.

MEAT AND POTATO PIE

SERVES 4

FOR THE FILLING
corn oil, for frying

½ pound baby onions

1 garlic clove, crushed

¼ pound button
mushrooms

1 pound beef bottom
round, cubed

4 large potatoes, peeled and
cut into small cubes

1 cup sliced carrots

1 teaspoon dried mixed
herbs

1¼ cups beef bouillon

⅔ cup red wine

salt and pepper

1 teaspoon cornstarch

FOR THE DOUGH
¼ cup shredded beef suet

1 cup self-rising flour

pinch of salt

milk, to glaze

1 Heat a little oil in a medium saucepan, add the onions, garlic and mushrooms and fry for 3 minutes. Drain and place in a 5-cup ovenproof casserole.

2 Add the meat to the pan, a few pieces at a time, and fry until browned, then add to the casserole.

3 Add the potatoes, carrots and herbs to the casserole and pour in the bouillon and wine. Season well, stir and cook in a preheated oven at 325°F for 2 hours.

4 Fifteen minutes before the end of the cooking time, blend the cornstarch to a paste with a little cold water. Stir into the casserole and continue cooking.

5 Meanwhile, to make the dough, mix the suet, flour and salt in a bowl and gradually stir in enough water to bind. Roll out the dough until large enough to cover the casserole and press the edges firmly onto the rim. Brush with a little milk to glaze. Return to the oven and cook at 400°F for about 30 minutes or until brown.

STEAK AND KIDNEY PIE

SERVES 4

salt and pepper

1¾ cups all-purpose flour

1½ pounds beef top round
or other steak, cubed

6 ounces beef kidney, cored
and chopped

½ cup butter

1–2 garlic cloves, crushed

1 large onion, chopped

¼ pound button
mushrooms

⅔ cup beef bouillon

⅔ cup brown ale

1 bay leaf

½ teaspoon dried thyme

1 tablespoon
Worcestershire sauce

1 tablespoon tomato paste

milk, to glaze

1 Season ¼ cup of the flour, then toss the steak and kidney in the flour, shaking off and reserving any excess.

2 Melt 2 tablespoons of the butter in a large saucepan and lightly fry the garlic, onion and mushrooms for 3 minutes. Add the steak, kidney and reserved seasoned flour and cook for 5 minutes or until lightly browned.

3 Gradually stir in the bouillon, ale, bay leaf, thyme, Worcestershire sauce and tomato paste. Cover and simmer for 1¼ hours. Spoon into a 8-cup pie dish.

4 Put the remaining flour and a pinch of salt in a bowl. Cut in the remaining butter. Gradually add about ¼ cup cold water and mix to form a dough.

5 Roll out the dough to 2 inches wider than the pie dish. Cut an 1-inch wide strip from the outer edge. Brush the rim of the dish with water and press the dough strip in place around it. Brush with water and cover with the dough lid. Garnish with dough leaves, brush with milk and bake in a preheated oven at 400°F for 30–45 minutes or until the crust is golden brown.

MEAT LOAF WITH ONION SAUCE

SERVES 4

2 tablespoons butter	1 tablespoon chopped fresh mixed herbs or 1 teaspoon dried
2 medium onions, finely chopped	
1 teaspoon mild paprika	salt and pepper
1 pound lean ground beef	1 egg, beaten
1½ cups fresh breadcrumbs	2 tablespoons wholewheat flour
1 garlic clove, crushed	1¼ cups fresh milk
4 tablespoons tomato paste	

1 Grease a 4-cup loaf pan, then line the base with greased baker's parchment. Melt half the butter in a skillet. Add half the onions and cook for 5 minutes or until soft. Add the paprika and cook for 1 minute, stirring. Remove from the heat.

2 Add the beef, breadcrumbs, garlic, tomato paste and herbs to the onions and season to taste. Stir thoroughly until evenly mixed, then bind with the beaten egg.

3 Spoon the mixture into the loaf pan, level the surface and cover tightly with foil. Stand the pan in a roasting pan and pour in water to a depth of 1 inch. Bake in a preheated oven at 350°F for 1½ hours.

4 Meanwhile, melt the remaining butter in a saucepan. Add the rest of the onion and cook for 10 minutes or until soft but not colored, stirring occasionally. Add the flour and cook for 1–2 minutes, stirring. Remove from the heat and add the milk, stirring constantly. Simmer for 2–3 minutes or until thick, stirring constantly. Simmer very gently for a further 2–3 minutes. Season to taste.

5 To serve the meat loaf, turn out onto a warmed plate and peel off the parchment. Serve with the hot onion sauce.

BEEF WELLINGTON

SERVES 8

3 pound fillet of beef	6 ounces smooth liver pâté
pepper	14-ounce packet frozen puff pastry, thawed
1 tablespoon oil	
3 tablespoons butter	1 egg, beaten, to glaze
2 cups sliced button mushrooms	

1 Trim and tie up the fillet at intervals so it retains its shape. Season to taste with pepper. Heat the oil and 1 tablespoon of the butter in a large skillet, add the meat and fry briskly on all sides. Press down with a wooden spoon while frying to seal well. Transfer to a roasting pan.

2 Roast the beef in a preheated oven at 425°F for 20 minutes, then set the beef aside to allow it to cool. Remove the twine.

3 Meanwhile, melt the remaining butter in the skillet and fry the mushrooms for about 5 minutes or until soft. Leave until cold, then blend with the pâté.

4 On a lightly floured surface, roll out the pastry to a large rectangle measuring about 13 x 11 inches and about ¼ inch thick.

5 Spread the pâté mixture down the center of the pastry. Place the meat on top. Brush the pastry edges with egg. Fold the pastry edges over lengthwise. Place on a baking sheet with the pastry join underneath and fold the ends under the meat.

6 Decorate with leaves cut from the pastry trimmings, brush with the remaining egg and bake in a preheated oven at 425°F for 50–60 minutes, depending on how well done you like your beef, covering with foil after 25 minutes. Allow to rest for 10 minutes before serving.

VEAL SCALLOPS IN MUSHROOM SAUCE

SERVES 4

four 6-ounce veal scallops	1 small onion, chopped
2 slices of cooked ham, halved	1 cup sliced button mushrooms
¼ cup butter	¼ cup all-purpose flour
1 celery stalk, chopped	1¼ cups milk
1 dessert apple, peeled, cored and chopped	salt and pepper
	2 tablespoons fromage frais
¼ cup shredded Cheddar cheese or Monterey Jack	celery leaves, for garnish

1 Put each scallop between two sheets of dampened baker's parchment and beat until thin with a meat mallet.

2 Place a ham slice on each scallop.

3 Melt 1 tablespoon of the butter in a large skillet, add the celery and apple and fry lightly for 3–4 minutes. Stir in the cheese.

4 Place some of the stuffing on each scallop and roll up, securing with wooden toothpicks or fine twine.

5 Melt the remaining butter in the pan. Add the veal rolls and cook over a high heat until browned on all sides, then reduce the heat and cook for 10 minutes. Remove from the pan, place on a warmed serving plate and keep hot.

6 Add the onion and mushrooms to the pan and cook for about 5 minutes or until softened. Stir in the flour and cook for 2 minutes, then gradually add the milk, stirring continuously, until the sauce thickens, boils and is smooth. Simmer for 1–2 minutes. Season to taste.

7 Stir the fromage frais into the sauce, pour over the scallops and garnish with celery leaves. Serve at once.

ESCALOPES FINES HERBES

SERVES 4

four 4-ounce veal scallops	½ cup dry white wine
salt and pepper	2 tablespoons chopped herbs (parsley, chervil, tarragon and chives)
3 tablespoons all-purpose flour	
2 tablespoons butter or margarine	4 tablespoons heavy cream
	lemon wedges, to serve

1 Place the veal scallops between two sheets of dampened baker's parchment and beat until thin with a rolling pin or meat mallet.

2 Season the flour with a little salt and pepper and use to coat the scallops.

3 Melt the butter or margarine in a large skillet, add the scallops and fry over a high heat for 1–2 minutes on each side or until browned. (You may have to fry in two batches, depending on the size of the skillet.) Lower the heat and continue to cook for a further 4 minutes on each side or until tender. Transfer the veal to a warmed serving dish, cover and keep hot.

4 Add the white wine to the skillet and bring slowly to a boil, stirring to scrape up any sediment left in the pan. Stir in the herbs and cream and season to taste. Simmer very gently for about 5 minutes or until slightly thickened.

5 Pour the sauce over the scallops and serve immediately, with lemon wedges.

VEAL COBBLER

SERVES 4–6

2 tablespoons butter	2 cups sliced button mushrooms
1 large onion, minced	2 tablespoons dairy sour cream
1 garlic clove, crushed	
2 pounds lean stewing veal, cut into 1-inch cubes	chopped parsley, for garnish
2 tablespoons mild paprika	FOR THE TOPPING
salt and pepper	2 cups self-rising flour
1 sweet red pepper, cut into rings	pinch of salt
	¼ cup butter
1 sweet green pepper, cut into rings	⅔ cup milk
1-pound can chopped tomatoes	milk, to glaze

1 Melt the butter in a flameproof casserole, add the onion and garlic and sauté for 5 minutes. Add the pie veal and cook for a further 5–7 minutes or until evenly browned.

2 Stir in the paprika, season and cook for a further 2 minutes. Add the pepper rings, tomatoes and mushrooms. Stir well and cook for 5 minutes. Cover and cook in a preheated oven at 375°F for 1½–2 hours.

3 Meanwhile, make the topping. Sift the flour and salt into a bowl, add the butter and cut in until the mixture resembles fine breadcrumbs. Gradually mix in the milk to form a smooth, soft dough. Roll out to ½ inch thick and cut into rounds using a 2-inch cutter.

4 Remove the casserole from the oven and carefully position the biscuits around the edge of the dish. Brush with milk to glaze, then cook, uncovered, for a final 30–35 minutes. Pour the sour cream over the casserole, avoiding the biscuits, and sprinkle with parsley.

SAUTÉED VEAL WITH ZUCCHINI AND GRAPEFRUIT

SERVES 4

1 pound piece of veal rump or fillet	1 pound zucchini, thinly sliced
2 grapefruit	a few saffron strands
3 tablespoons olive oil	salt and pepper

1 Cut the veal into wafer-thin slices. Place between two sheets of dampened baker's parchment and beat out with a rolling pin or meat mallet.

2 With a potato peeler, pare the rind off one of the grapefruit. Cut into thin matchstick strips. Squeeze the juice from the grapefruit and reserve.

3 With a serrated knife, peel the remaining grapefruit as you would an apple, removing all skin and pith. Slice the grapefruit flesh thinly and set aside.

4 Heat 2 tablespoons of the oil in a large skillet. Add a few slices of veal and sauté for about 2–3 minutes or until well browned on both sides. Transfer to a warmed serving dish, cover and keep warm while sautéeing the remainder.

5 Heat the remaining oil in the pan, add the zucchini and sauté for 2–3 minutes or until beginning to brown. Add the strips of grapefruit rind, the saffron strands and 6 tablespoons of the reserved grapefruit juice.

6 Bring to a boil, then lower the heat and simmer for 4–5 minutes or until the liquid is well reduced. Stir in the thinly sliced grapefruit and heat through.

7 Season to taste, pour over the veal and serve.

FRICASSÉE OF VEAL

SERVES 6

SPICED VEAL WITH PEPPERS

SERVES 4

2 pounds boneless stewing veal	salt and pepper
1 pound carrots	¼ cup butter
1 medium onion, sliced	½ cup all-purpose flour
1 tablespoon chopped fresh thyme or ½ teaspoon dried	2 egg yolks
⅔ cup dry white wine	⅔ cup light cream
	chopped parsley, for garnish

1 Cut the veal into 1½–inch cubes, discarding any skin or fat. Put the meat in a saucepan, cover with cold water, bring to a boil and cook for 1 minute. Strain the meat and rinse under cold running water to remove all scum. Rinse out the pan thoroughly and replace the meat.

2 Cut the carrots into finger-size pieces and add to the pan with the onion, thyme, wine and 4 cups water. Season to taste. Bring slowly to a boil, cover and simmer gently for about 1¼ hours or until the veal is quite tender.

3 Strain off the cooking liquid, make up to 3 cups with bouillon, if necessary, and reserve. Keep the veal and vegetables warm in a covered serving dish.

4 Melt the butter in a saucepan, stir in the flour and cook gently for 1 minute, stirring. Remove from the heat and gradually stir in the strained cooking liquid and season well. Bring to a boil, stirring all the time, then simmer for 5 minutes.

5 Mix the egg yolks with the cream. Remove the sauce from the heat and stir in the cream mixture. Return to the heat and warm gently, without boiling, until the sauce becomes slightly thicker. Adjust the seasoning and pour over the meat. Serve garnished with parsley.

1¼ pound boneless stewing veal	½ teaspoon ground turmeric
1 tablespoon oil	½ teaspoon ground cumin
2 medium onions, thinly sliced	½ teaspoon chili powder
2 small sweet red peppers, thinly sliced	¼ teaspoon ground cloves
1 garlic clove, crushed	2 cups chopped tomatoes
½ teaspoon ground ginger	1¼ cups plain yogurt
	salt and pepper

1 Trim the veal of fat and cut into chunky cubes.

2 Heat the oil in a large saucepan. Add the onions, peppers, garlic and spices and fry for 1 minute. Stir in the chopped tomatoes.

3 Turn the heat to very low and add the yogurt very gradually, stirring well between each addition.

4 Add the veal and season to taste. Cover and simmer gently for 30 minutes.

5 Uncover the pan and cook the veal for a further 30 minutes or until it is tender and the liquid has reduced. Stir occasionally to prevent the meat sticking to the pan. Taste and adjust the seasoning before serving.

VEAL IN MARSALA

SERVES 6

six 3-ounce veal scallops	1½ cups sliced button mushrooms
salt and pepper	6 tablespoons Marsala
all-purpose flour, for coating	6 tablespoons chicken bouillon
¼ cup oil	1 teaspoon arrowroot
¼ cup butter	lemon wedges, to serve
1 onion, minced	

1 Trim each scallop to remove any skin. Place well apart between two sheets of dampened baker's parchment and beat out until very thin, using a meat mallet or rolling pin.
2 Season the flour, add the veal and toss until coated. Heat the oil and butter in a large deep skillet, add the veal and cook until well browned on all sides.
3 Push the veal to the side of the pan and add the onion and mushrooms to the remaining fat. Cook until browned. Add the Marsala and bouillon, bring to a boil and season lightly.
4 Cover the pan and cook gently for 5–10 minutes or until the veal is quite tender. Transfer to a warmed serving dish, cover and keep warm.
5 Mix the arrowroot to a smooth paste with a little water. Stir into the pan juices off the heat, then bring slowly to a boil, stirring all the time. Cook for 1 minute, adjust the seasoning and spoon over the veal. Serve with lemon.

VEAL SCALLOPS

SERVES 4

four 4-ounce veal scallops	2 teaspoons all-purpose flour
5 tablespoons butter	salt and pepper
1 small onion, chopped	pinch of ground mace
¾ cup dry white wine	FOR THE GARNISH
1¾ cups veal bouillon	crisp bacon rolls
1–2 teaspoons mushroom ketchup	button mushroom caps
about 1 tablespoon lemon juice	lemon twists
	parsley sprigs

1 Cut each scallop into two pieces and place between two sheets of dampened baker's parchment. Beat until thin with a rolling pin or meat mallet.
2 Melt 4 tablespoons of the butter in a skillet, add the veal and cook for about 2 minutes on each side. Transfer to a warmed plate and keep warm.
3 Add the onion to the butter remaining in the pan and cook for about 3 minutes or until softened but not browned, stirring frequently. Stir in the wine, bring to a boil and cook until almost evaporated. Stir in the bouillon, mushroom ketchup and lemon juice, return to a boil and simmer until reduced to 1 cup.
4 Work the flour into the remaining butter, then gradually whisk into the mixture to thicken it slightly. Season with salt, pepper and mace, taste and add more mushroom ketchup and lemon juice if necessary.
5 Arrange the scallops, overlapping each other, on a warmed oval serving platter. Spoon some of the sauce down the center of the scallops, garnish and serve the remaining sauce separately.

VEAL AND KIDNEY PIE

SERVES 6

2 pounds stewing veal, cut into 1-inch cubes	6 tablespoons all-purpose flour
juice of 1 lemon	2 tablespoons light cream
1¼ teaspoons dried tarragon	FOR THE DOUGH
	1 cup wholewheat flour
salt and pepper	2 cups all-purpose flour
½ pound lamb kidneys	1 cup butter or margarine
¾ pound leeks	1 egg, beaten, to glaze
3 tablespoons butter or margarine	

1 Place the veal in a saucepan with 4 cups water, 1 tablespoon lemon juice and 1 teaspoon tarragon. Season, cover and simmer for 1–1¼ hours.
2 Meanwhile, skin and core the kidneys and cut into bite-size pieces. Trim and slice the leeks, rinse and drain.
3 Stir the kidneys and leeks into the saucepan. Cover and simmer for a further 8–10 minutes. Strain off the liquor and reserve. Spoon into a 10½-inch pie plate.
4 To make the sauce, melt the butter in a saucepan, stir in the flour and cook for 1–2 minutes. Remove from the heat and stir in 2½ cups of the reserved stock. Cook, stirring, until thick. Remove from the heat and stir in 1 tablespoon lemon juice, ¼ teaspoon tarragon and the cream. Season, pour over the veal and cool.
5 To make the dough, mix the flours and cut in the butter. Gradually add about ⅓ cup water. Chill.
6 Roll out the dough and use to cover the pie. Brush with beaten egg. Bake in a preheated oven at 375°F for about 40 minutes or until well browned.

VEAL AND HAM PIE

SERVES 8–10

1 pound lean ground veal	2 medium onions, minced
¼ pound boiled ham, ground	salt and pepper
2 tablespoons chopped parsley	½ cup shortening
	3 cups wholewheat flour
½ teaspoon ground mace	1 egg yolk
¼ teaspoon ground bay leaves	3 eggs, hard-cooked and shelled
finely grated rind of 1 lemon	2 teaspoons powdered aspic jelly

1 Grease a 6-cup loaf pan and line the base with greased baker's parchment.
2 Put the first seven ingredients in a bowl and add 1 teaspoon salt and ¼ teaspoon pepper. Mix well.
3 Put the shortening and 7 fluid ounces water in a saucepan and heat gently to melt. Bring to a boil, remove from the heat and tip in the flour with ½ teaspoon salt. Beat well to form a soft dough. Beat the egg yolk into the dough. Cover with a damp tea towel and rest in a warm place for 20 minutes. Do not allow to cool.
4 Use two thirds of the dough to line the prepared pan. Press in half the meat and place the eggs down the center. Fill with the remaining meat.
5 Roll out the remaining dough and use to cover the pie. Make a hole in the center of the pie. Bake at 350°F for 1½ hours. Leave to cool for 3–4 hours.
6 Make up the aspic jelly with 1¼ cups water and leave to cool for about 10 minutes. Pour the aspic through the hole in the top of the pie. Chill for about 1 hour. Leave at room temperature for 1 hour before serving.

VEAL WITH TUNA MAYONNAISE

SERVES 4–6

2 pound boned, rolled and tied leg or loin of veal	1 small onion
1¼ cups dry white wine	7-ounce can tuna in oil, drained
1 carrot, sliced	4 canned anchovy fillets, soaked in milk for 20 minutes and drained
1 celery stalk, sliced	
a few parsley sprigs	1¼ cups thick mayonnaise
2 bay leaves	1 tablespoons capers, roughly chopped
a few black peppercorns	
salt and pepper	lemon slices, ripe olives and corn salad, for garnish
2 cloves	

1 Put the veal in a large saucepan and add the wine, carrot, celery, parsley, bay leaves, peppercorns and 1 teaspoon salt. Push the cloves into the onion and add to the pan. Add enough water to cover, then bring to a boil.

2 Lower the heat, cover the pan and simmer gently for 1–1¼ hours or until the veal is tender. Remove the pan from the heat and leave the veal to cool in the liquid.

3 When the meat is cold, remove from the pan, reserving the liquid, and dry with kitchen paper towels. Untie the meat, slice and arrange on a platter. Cover.

4 Pound the tuna and anchovies together, then stir into the mayonnaise with the capers and pepper to taste. Thin to a coating consistency with a few spoonfuls of the reserved cooking liquid, taste and adjust the seasoning.

5 Spoon the mayonnaise over the veal, then cover loosely with foil. Chill for 24–48 hours. To serve, leave the veal to stand at room temperature for 1 hour. Uncover and garnish with lemon, olives and corn salad.

PORTMANTEAU LAMB CHOPS

SERVES 4

4 thick lamb loin chops	salt and pepper
3 tablespoons butter	1 egg, beaten
¼ pound chicken livers, thawed if frozen and finely chopped	⅔ cup fresh wholewheat breadcrumbs
	parsley sprigs, for garnish
1 cup finely chopped mushrooms	

1 Using a sharp, pointed knife, make a horizontal cut in each chop, working from the outside fat edge to the bone, to form a pocket.

2 To make the stuffing, melt 1 tablespoon of the butter in a skillet, add the chicken livers and mushrooms and fry for 4–5 minutes or until soft but not brown. Season to taste.

3 Leave the stuffing to cool slightly, then spoon into the cavity in each chop and secure the open edges with wooden toothpicks.

4 Dip the chops in the beaten egg, then in the breadcrumbs to coat thoroughly.

5 Put the chops in a roasting pan. Melt the remaining butter and pour over the chops. Bake in a preheated oven at 400°F for 15 minutes, then turn and bake for a further 15 minutes or until golden brown. Serve hot, garnished with parsley sprigs.

TANGY CHOPS

SERVES 4

2 tablespoons vegetable oil	1 tablespoon chopped fresh mint or 1 teaspoon dried
4 lamb sirloin chops	
salt and pepper	1 teaspoon sugar
juice and finely grated rind of 1 lemon	⅔ cup beef or chicken bouillon
2 tablespoons chopped fresh parsley or 2 teaspoons dried	

1 Heat the oil in a skillet, add the chops and fry over a brisk heat until browned on both sides. Lower the heat and season to taste.
2 Mix the lemon juice and rind with the herbs and sugar, then spoon this mixture over the chops and pour in the bouillon. Cover the pan tightly and simmer gently for 30 minutes or until the meat is tender. Serve hot with the juices poured over.

─────────── **VARIATION** ───────────
You can vary the herbs used in this dish, depending on what is available. Fresh rosemary is, of course, the classic herb to use with lamb.

LAMB STEAKS WITH CAPER SAUCE

SERVES 4

salt and pepper	1¼ cups lamb or beef bouillon
four 6-ounce lamb leg steaks	
	2 tablespoons drained capers
2 tablespoons butter	
1 teaspoon all-purpose flour	1 tablespoon vinegar from the capers

1 Season the lamb steaks to taste. Heat the butter in a skillet and fry the steaks gently for 10–15 minutes or until browned on both sides, turning occasionally. Remove from the pan with a slotted spoon.
2 Stir to loosen any sediment at the bottom of the pan, then stir in the flour and cook for 1–2 minutes. Gradually add the bouillon, stirring all the time, then cook until the sauce thickens, boils and is smooth. Add the capers and vinegar and simmer for 1–2 minutes.
3 Return the lamb steaks to the pan and simmer for 5 minutes or until cooked to your liking. Serve hot.

SHEPHERD'S PIE

SERVES 4

1½ pounds potatoes, peeled	1 tablespoon Worcestershire sauce
salt and pepper	6 tablespoons chopped parsley
1 pound cooked lamb	1 teaspoon dried marjoram
2 tablespoons vegetable oil	½ cup shredded Cheddar cheese
1 medium onion, chopped	chopped parsley, for garnish
2 tablespoons all-purpose flour	
1¼ cups lamb or beef bouillon	

1 Cook the potatoes in boiling salted water for 20 minutes or until tender.
2 Meanwhile, trim the excess fat from the lamb and discard. Chop the meat finely or grind coarsely.
3 Heat the oil in a skillet, add the onion and sauté for 5 minutes or until lightly browned. Stir in the flour and fry for 2–3 minutes. Add the bouillon and simmer, stirring, until thickened.
4 Stir in the lamb, Worcestershire, parsley, marjoram and salt and pepper. Spoon into a 5-cup shallow pie dish.
5 Drain the potatoes. Mash well, then beat in the cheese and salt and pepper. Spoon or pipe over the lamb.
6 Bake in a preheated oven at 400°F for 30 minutes or until well browned. Serve hot, sprinkled with parsley.

––––––––––– **VARIATION** –––––––––––
Cottage Pie
Replace the ground lamb with ground beef and omit the marjoram and cheese for a traditional 'Cottage' pie.

BREADED LAMB CUTLETS

SERVES 4

1 tablespoon butter	2 blades of mace
1 small onion, minced	1 bay leaf
1 medium carrot, finely chopped	4 juniper berries, crushed
2 slices lean ham, cut into thin strips	pinch of dried thyme
¼ cup red wine vinegar	eight 3-ounce lamb rib chops
3 tablespoons port	½ cup ground ham
2½ cups lamb or chicken bouillon	1 cup fresh breadcrumbs
2 cloves	1 egg, beaten
	1 tablespoon cornstarch

1 To make the sauce, melt the butter in a saucepan, add the onion, carrot and ham strips and cook until just turning brown. Add the vinegar and port and boil until almost all the liquid has evaporated.
2 Remove the pan from the heat and add the bouillon, cloves, mace, bay leaf, juniper berries and thyme. Stir well and bring to a boil. Simmer for 30 minutes.
3 Meanwhile, trim the chops to remove most of the surrounding fat. Scrape the bone of each chop absolutely clean to within 1 inch of the 'eye' of the meat.
4 Mix the ground ham and breadcrumbs together. Brush each chop with beaten egg and coat with the ham and breadcrumb mixture. Cover and chill until required.
5 Blend the cornstarch with about 2 tablespoons water and add to the sauce. Stir well and bring the sauce to a boil, stirring continuously. Simmer until thickened.
6 Cook the chops under a preheated broiler for 4 minutes on each side. Reheat the sauce and serve separately.

LAMB FILLET WITH RED CURRANT SAUCE

SERVES 3

6 tablespoons dairy sour cream	1 pound lamb fillet
1 garlic clove, crushed	2 tablespoons dry red wine
1 teaspoon wholegrain mustard	1 tablespoon red currant jelly
salt and pepper	

1 Mix 2 tablespoons of the sour cream with the garlic and mustard. Season to taste.

2 Put the lamb fillet in a roasting pan and spoon the garlic mixture all over. Roast in a preheated oven at 350°F for 30 minutes or until tender and cooked to your liking. Transfer the lamb to a warmed serving dish and keep warm.

3 Add the wine to the roasting pan, stirring in any sediment from the bottom of the pan. Stir in the currant jelly. Bring to a boil, then stir in the remaining sour cream and boil for 2–3 minutes or until thickened slightly.

4 Slice the lamb and serve with the sauce spooned over.

TO MICROWAVE

Complete step 1. Put the lamb in a shallow dish and spoon over the garlic mixture. Cook, uncovered, on HIGH for 3 minutes. Cover and cook on MEDIUM for 10–15 minutes, rearranging twice, until cooked to your liking. Transfer the lamb to a warmed serving dish. Stir the remaining sour cream, the wine and currant jelly into the dish. Cook on HIGH for 1–2 minutes, stirring occasionally, until hot. Complete step 4.

HONEYED LAMB NOISETTES

SERVES 6

2 large lemons	2 garlic cloves, crushed
twelve 3–4-ounce lean lamb noisettes	½-inch piece of fresh root ginger, grated (optional)
2 tablespoons chopped fresh thyme or 1 teaspoon dried	8 tablespoons clear honey
2 tablespoons chopped fresh rosemary or 2 teaspoons dried	¼ cup oil
	salt and pepper
1 bay leaf	bay leaves and thyme and rosemary sprigs, for garnish

1 Pare the rind off one lemon and cut into fine strips. Cover and set aside.

2 Place the lamb in a shallow, non-metallic dish. Sprinkle over the herbs and bay leaf.

3 Whisk together the grated rind of the remaining whole lemon, 6 tablespoons lemon juice, the crushed garlic, ginger (if using), the honey and oil. Season to taste. Pour over the lamb, cover and leave to marinate in the refrigerator overnight.

4 Drain the marinade from the lamb and strain into a small saucepan. Place the meat on a rack over the broiler pan. Cook under a preheated hot broiler for 7 minutes on each side. Transfer to an ovenproof serving dish, cover lightly with foil and keep warm.

5 Carefully pour the broiler pan juices into the strained marinade. Stir in the strips of lemon rind. Bring to a boil and simmer for 2–3 minutes or until syrupy, stirring occasionally. Adjust the seasoning and spoon over the noisettes. Garnish with bay leaves and sprigs of fresh thyme and rosemary.

LAMB NOISETTES WITH RED WINE SAUCE

SERVES 6

12 lamb noisettes	½ pound button mushrooms
flour, for coating	1¼ cups red wine
2 tablespoons butter	⅔ cup chicken bouillon
¼ cup oil	1 tablespoon tomato paste
2 large onions, sliced	2 bay leaves
1 garlic clove, finely chopped	salt and pepper

1 Lightly coat the lamb noisettes with flour. Heat the butter and oil in a large Dutch oven. Add the noisettes, a few at a time, and cook over a high heat until browned on both sides. Remove from the pot with a slotted spoon and set aside.
2 Add the onion and garlic to the pot and fry for about 5 minutes or until golden. Add the mushrooms and fry for a further 2–3 minutes. Stir in the red wine, bouillon, tomato paste and bay leaves. Season to taste.
3 Return the noisettes to the pot and bring to a boil, then cover and simmer gently for about 40 minutes or until tender, turning the meat once during this time.
4 Lift the noisettes out of the sauce and remove the twine. Place the noisettes on a warmed serving dish and keep warm. Boil the remaining sauce rapidly for 5–10 minutes to reduce. Taste and adjust the seasoning, remove the bay leaves, then pour over the noisettes. Serve immediately.

MINTED LAMB BURGERS WITH CUCUMBER

SERVES 4

1 pound lean ground lamb	2 tablespoons all-purpose flour
1 small onion, minced	½ cucumber, cut into 2-inch long wedges
2 cups fresh breadcrumbs	
finely grated rind of ½ lemon	6 scallions, cut into ½-inch pieces
3 tablespoons chopped mint	¾–1 cup lamb or chicken bouillon
1 egg, beaten	1 tablespoon dry sherry
salt and pepper	

1 Mix the lamb, onion, breadcrumbs and lemon rind with 1 tablespoon of the chopped mint and the egg. Season to taste.
2 Shape into eight burgers with floured hands, then completely coat in the flour.
3 Dry-fry the burgers in a large heavy-based non-stick skillet for about 6 minutes or until lightly browned, turning once. Add the cucumber and scallions.
4 Pour in the bouillon and sherry, then add the remaining mint and season to taste. Bring to a boil, cover and simmer gently for about 20 minutes or until the meat is tender. Skim off any excess fat and taste and adjust the seasoning before serving.

EASTERN LAMB KABOBS

SERVES 4–6

1 pound lean ground lamb	2 teaspoons ground turmeric
1 large onion, grated	salt and pepper
1 tablespoon chopped fresh dill or 1 teaspoon dried	2 tablespoons golden raisins
2 tablespoons chopped fresh cilantro or 2 teaspoons dried coriander	1 egg, beaten
1 teaspoon ground fenugreek	cilantro sprigs, for garnish

1 Put the lamb and onion in a medium bowl. Add the remaining ingredients, except the garnish, and mix well, using your fingers.
2 Divide the mixture into 30 walnut-size pieces. Using dampened hands, form into even round shapes.
3 Thread about five balls onto each of six metal skewers, leaving about 1 inch of each skewer exposed at both sides. Place the kabobs on a broiler rack as you prepare them.
4 Cook the kabobs under a preheated broiler for 5–8 minutes. Turn them over and continue to cook for a further 5–8 minutes or until the meat is cooked. Garnish with cilantro sprigs.

TO MICROWAVE

Complete steps 1 and 2. Thread the balls onto wooden skewers and arrange on a microwave roasting rack. Microwave on HIGH for 12-15 minutes, re-arranging occasionally. Stand for 2 minutes. Garnish with cilantro.

CROWN ROAST

SERVES 6

12-rib crown roast of lamb, with backbone removed and ribs frenched	juice and grated rind of ½ lemon
1 tablespoon butter	1 egg, beaten
1 medium onion, chopped	salt and pepper
3 celery stalks, chopped	2 tablespoons all-purpose flour
2 dessert apples, chopped	2 cups lamb or beef bouillon
2 cups fresh breadcrumbs	mint sprigs, for garnish
2 tablespoons chopped mint	

1 Cover the exposed rib bones on the crown roast with foil.
2 Melt the butter in a saucepan and cook the onion, celery and apples until brown. Stir in the breadcrumbs, mint, lemon juice and rind and egg. Season to taste and cool, then fill the center of the crown roast with the stuffing and weigh. Roast in a preheated oven at 350°F for 25 minutes per pound plus 25 minutes.
3 Transfer the roast to a warmed serving dish and keep warm. Drain off all but 2 tablespoons of the fat in the roasting pan, then add the flour and blend well. Cook for 2–3 minutes, stirring continuously. Remove from the heat and gradually add the bouillon. Boil for 2–3 minutes. Adjust the seasoning and serve with the roast. Garnish with mint.

VARIATION

For a 'Guard of Honour', have the butcher trim the lamb ribs as above but ask him to interlace the bones, fat sides outwards, to form an arch.

31

BRAISED SHOULDER OF LAMB WITH APRICOT STUFFING

SERVES 6

2 tablespoons butter	salt and pepper
1 tablespoons chopped onion	4½ pound shoulder of lamb, boned
4 tablespoons fine fresh white breadcrumbs	2½ cups beef or lamb bouillon
1 tablespoon chopped parsley	½ pound onions, quartered
1–2 tablespoons milk	2 cups sliced carrots
½ cup no-soak dried apricots, chopped	6 celery stalks, sliced
	¾ pound turnips, quartered

1 Melt the butter in a saucepan, add the chopped onion and sauté for about 5 minutes or until soft and transparent.
2 Remove the pan from the heat and add the breadcrumbs, parsley, milk and apricots. Season to taste.
3 Sprinkle the cut surface of the lamb with seasoning and spread the stuffing over. Roll up and tie with twine. Place the roast in a greased Dutch oven and cook in a preheated oven at 450°F for 15 minutes.
4 Remove the pot from the oven and add half the bouillon. Reduce the oven temperature to 350°F, re-cover and cook the meat for 45 minutes.
5 Arrange the onions, carrots, celery and turnips round the meat and add the remaining bouillon. Re-cover and cook for a further 1¼ hours.
6 Remove the pot from the oven and lift the meat and vegetables onto a warmed serving dish. Skim the fat off the stock in the pot, then boil fast for 3–5 minutes to reduce by half. Serve with the lamb.

ROLLED STUFFED BREASTS OF LAMB

SERVES 4

2 tablespoons butter or margarine	1 tablespoon lemon juice
1 medium onion, chopped	pinch of grated nutmeg
3 bacon slices, chopped	1 egg, beaten
10-ounce packet frozen leaf spinach, thawed	salt and pepper
1½ cups breadcrumbs	2 large breasts of lamb, boned and trimmed (total weight about 2½ pounds)
3 tablespoons chopped parsley	3 tablespoons corn oil
finely grated rind of ½ lemon	watercress, for garnish

1 Melt the butter or margarine in a saucepan, add the onion and bacon and sauté for about 5 minutes or until lightly browned.
2 Drain the spinach and chop roughly. Place in a bowl with the onion and bacon, breadcrumbs, parsley, lemon rind and juice, nutmeg and egg. Mix together well and season to taste.
3 Lay the breasts of lamb, fat side down, on a work surface and spread the stuffing evenly over them with a spatula.
4 Roll up the lamb breasts loosely and tie in several places with strong thread or fine twine to hold their shape.
5 Weigh each roast and calculate the cooking time, allowing 25 minutes per pound plus 25 minutes for each. Heat the oil in a roasting pan and place the stuffed breasts in the pan. Roast in a preheated oven at 350°F for the calculated cooking time, basting occasionally. Serve hot, garnished with watercress.

LAMB IN TOMATO SAUCE WITH HERB BREAD

SERVES 4

2 tablespoons vegetable oil	4 tablespoons red wine (optional)
2¼ pounds boneless lean shoulder of lamb, cubed	salt and pepper
1 medium onion, sliced	lamb or beef bouillon, if necessary
4 teaspoons all-purpose flour	3 tablespoons butter
1-pound can tomatoes	1 tablespoon chopped chives
2 tablespoons tomato paste	eight ½-inch slices of French bread
pinch of sugar	
½ teaspoon dried rosemary	

1 Heat the oil in a Dutch oven, add the lamb and cook over a high heat until browned on all sides. Remove from the pot with a slotted spoon and set aside.

2 Add the onion to the pot and fry for 5 minutes or until soft. Stir in the flour and cook for 1 minute. Add the tomatoes with their juice, the tomato paste, sugar, rosemary and wine, if using. Bring to a boil, stirring.

3 Return the meat to the pot and add salt and pepper to taste. Add a little bouillon, if necessary, to cover the meat. Cover the casserole and cook in the oven at 325°F for about 1¼ hours.

4 Meanwhile, make the herb butter. Beat the butter until soft, then beat in the chives and salt and pepper to taste.

5 Spread the butter on the slices of French bread. Uncover the casserole and place the bread, butter side up, on top. Cook for a further hour, or until tender. Serve hot.

PARSON'S 'VENISON'

SERVES 4–6

	FOR THE MARINADE
2 tablespoons drippings or butter	1 cup red wine
1 small onion, minced	⅓ cup tawny port
1 cup chopped mushrooms	6 juniper berries, crushed
1 cup chopped ham	¼ teaspoon ground allspice
2 tablespoons chopped chives	2 tablespoons vegetable oil
salt and black pepper	3 tablespoons red wine vinegar
4–4½ pound leg of lamb, skinned and boned	1 bay leaf
watercress sprigs, for garnish	¼ teaspoons grated nutmeg

1 Melt half the drippings in a saucepan and cook the onion and mushrooms for 5 minutes or until soft, stirring frequently. Stir in the ham and chives, season and cool.

2 Season the lamb inside and out with black pepper, then spread the onion mixture over the inside. Roll up tightly and tie securely. Place in an ovenproof casserole.

3 Mix the marinade ingredients, pour over the lamb, cover and leave in a cool place for 24 hours, turning occasionally. Remove the meat from the marinade, drain and dry.

4 Melt the remaining drippings in a skillet. Add the meat and cook until browned. Transfer to a casserole.

5 Pour the marinade into the skillet, bring to a boil, then pour over the meat. Cover, then cook at 350°F for 1¾–2 hours, basting occasionally.

6 Transfer the meat to a warmed plate and keep warm. Skim the fat from the surface of the liquid, then boil the liquid rapidly until reduced and slightly thickened. Season to taste. Garnish the meat and serve with the gravy.

LAMB WITH CHERRIES

SERVES 6

½ pound bacon slices, chopped	1 garlic clove, sliced
1 tablespoon butter	2½ cups dry red wine
3 pound boneless leg or shoulder of lamb, cut into 1½-inch cubes	bouquet garni
	pinch of grated nutmeg
1 medium onion, sliced	salt and pepper
1 medium carrot, sliced	1 pound fresh red cherries, pitted
1 celery stalk, sliced	

1 In a large skillet, fry the bacon in its own fat until browned. Add the butter to the pan and fry the lamb, a little at a time, until browned. Remove from the pan with the bacon and put in an ovenproof casserole.
2 Add the onion, carrot, celery and garlic to the fat remaining in the pan and fry for about 5 minutes or until lightly browned. Add the vegetables to the casserole.
3 Pour over the wine and add the bouquet garni and nutmeg. Season to taste, cover and cook in a preheated oven at 300°F for about 2½ hours or until tender.
4 Thirty minutes before the end of the cooking time, stir the cherries into the casserole and continue to cook until the meat is tender and the cherries soft. Remove the bouquet garni and serve hot.

----------------- COOK'S TIP -----------------
Look for red-skinned sour cherries such as Montmorency for this dish. Dark-skinned Morellos are also a good choice.

ORIENTAL LAMB

SERVES 4

3 pound lean shoulder of lamb, boned	1 tablespoon all-purpose flour
2 tablespoons vegetable oil	1 teaspoon ground ginger
2 tablespoons butter or margarine	1¼ cups chicken bouillon
1 pound small new potatoes, scrubbed or scraped	1 tablespoon Worcestershire sauce
	2 tablespoons soy sauce
½ pound small pickling onions, skinned	salt and pepper
	2 canned pimientos, diced

1 Cut the lamb into 1-inch pieces about ¼ inch thick, discarding any excess fat.
2 Heat the oil and butter or margarine in a large skiilet and add the meat, a few pieces at time. Fry until browned on all sides, turning frequently. Remove from the pan with a slotted spoon.
3 Add the potatoes and onions to the fat remaining in the pan and fry until lightly browned, turning frequently.
4 Return the meat to the pan, sprinkle in the flour and ginger and stir well. Cook gently, stirring, for 2 minutes.
5 Add the bouillon, Worcestershire and soy sauce, and season to taste. Bring to a boil, stirring, then cover and simmer for 30 minutes or until the meat is tender.
6 Add the pimientos and stir over a low heat to heat through. Taste and adjust the seasoning, then transfer the lamb to a warmed serving dish. Serve hot.

BROWN RAGOUT OF LAMB

SERVES 6

⅓ cup butter, diced	3 carrots, cut into pieces
2 pounds boneless leg of lamb, cut into 1-inch pieces	12 small onions, skinned
3 cups brown stock, preferably veal	¼ pound button mushrooms
4 cloves	squeeze of lemon juice
1 onion	½ cup cooked hulled fava beans
3 parsley sprigs	FOR THE GARNISH
2 thyme sprigs	flesh of 2 large firm tomatoes, cut into strips
2 bay leaves	2 tablespoons finely chopped parsley
1 rosemary sprig	
salt and pepper	

1 Melt half the butter in a skillet and cook the lamb until brown. Transfer to a Dutch oven.

2 Put the stock in a saucepan. Push the cloves into the unskinned onion and add to the stock with the herbs. Season and bring to a boil. Pour over the lamb, cover and cook at 350°F for 1 hour.

3 Add another 1 tablespoon butter to the skillet and melt. Fry the carrots and small onions until browned. Drain, then stir into the pot and cook for a further 30 minutes. Cook the mushrooms in the remaining butter with the lemon juice. Drain on kitchen paper towels.

4 Remove the onion and cloves from the pot, then stir in the mushrooms and cook, uncovered, for 10 minutes. Lift the meat and vegetables from the pot and keep warm. Boil the liquid until reduced. Arrange the meat on a plate with all the vegetables. Garnish and serve.

LAMB AND ORANGE CASSEROLE WITH CHOUX DUMPLINGS

SERVES 4

3 tablespoons corn oil	⅔ cup chicken bouillon
2 pounds lean boneless leg of lamb, cubed	2 bay leaves
1 medium onion, chopped	salt and pepper
2 turnips, roughly chopped	¼ cup butter
3 carrots, roughly chopped	2 eggs, beaten
¾ cup all-purpose flour	finely grated rind of 2 oranges
1 tablespoon tomato paste	1 tablespoon chopped parsley
1¼ cups unsweetened orange juice	

1 Heat the oil in a Dutch oven and fry the lamb until brown. Remove and set aside. Sauté the onion for 5 minutes. Add the turnips and carrots and sauté for 5 minutes.

2 Stir in 2 tablespoons of the flour, then add the tomato paste. Add the orange juice and bouillon and boil, stirring.

3 Return the meat, add the bay leaves, season and stir well. Cover and cook at 350°F for 1½ hours.

4 To make the dumplings, sift together the remaining flour and a pinch of salt. Put the butter in a medium saucepan, add ⅔ cup water and heat gently until the butter has melted. Bring to a rolling boil and tip in the flour and salt. Immediately take the pan off the heat and beat vigorously until the mixture forms a ball. Turn into a bowl and cool slightly, then beat in the eggs, a little at a time. The paste should be quite stiff.

5 Beat the orange rind and parsley into the choux paste. Remove the bay leaves from the pot, then pipe or spoon eight choux balls on top. Bake, uncovered, at 400°F for 1 hour.

LANCASHIRE HOT POT

SERVES 4

8 lamb blade chops	salt and pepper
2 lamb's kidneys, halved and cored	3 cups finely sliced potatoes
8 shucked oysters (optional)	2 cups lamb or beef bouillon
2 medium onions, sliced	2 tablespoons shortening or drippings
1 cup sliced mushrooms	
1 teaspoon dried thyme	

1 Remove any excess fat from the lamb. Select a large, deep casserole. If it is not deep enough to hold the meat, chop the ends off the bones.

2 Cut each kidney half into three or four pieces.

3 Layer the meat in the casserole with the oysters (if using), the kidneys, onions and mushrooms. Sprinkle each layer with thyme and seasoning to taste. If the casserole has a narrow top, add some of the potatoes at this stage. Pour in the bouillon.

4 Arrange a layer of overlapping potato slices on top. Melt the shortening or drippings and brush over the potatoes. Cover and cook in a preheated oven at 325°F for 2 hours or until both the meat and the potatoes are tender when tested with a skewer.

5 Remove the lid carefully, increase the oven temperature to 425°F and continue cooking for about 20 minutes or until the potatoes are golden brown and crisp.

LAMB AND MAÎTRE D'HÔTEL BUTTER

SERVES 4

4 large lamb loin chops	1 egg, beaten
¼ cup butter	1 tablespoon vegetable oil
½ cup finely chopped button mushrooms	FOR THE BUTTER
½ cup finely chopped ham	½ cup butter, softened
grated rind of 1 small lemon	2 tablespoons finely chopped parsley
½ cup fresh breadcrumbs	squeeze of lemon juice
salt and pepper	salt and cayenne

1 To make the maître d'hôtel butter, beat the butter until very soft, then add the parsley, lemon juice and salt with cayenne to taste. Shape into a roll, wrap in wax paper and chill in the refrigerator until required.

2 Using a sharp knife, slit the lean 'eye' of each chop horizontally through the fat edge.

3 Melt 2 tablespoons of the butter in a small saucepan, add the mushrooms and fry lightly until soft. Add the ham, lemon rind and breadcrumbs, season to taste and bind with a little beaten egg. Let cool, then stuff the mixture into the incisions in the chops. Secure each chop with strong thread or fine twine.

4 Heat the oil and remaining butter in a large skillet, add the chops and sauté over a high heat, until well browned on both sides. Reduce the heat and continue to cook for 20 minutes. Remove the chops from the pan and remove the twine.

5 Cut the maître d'hôtel butter into pats and place several on each of the chops to serve.

BLANQUETTE
D'AGNEAU
SERVES 4

1½ pounds boneless lean shoulder of lamb, diced	1¼ cups bouillon or water
⅔ cup sliced carrots	2 tablespoons butter, softened
1 onion, sliced	3 tablespoons all-purpose flour
2 celery stalks, sliced	
1 small bay leaf	1 egg yolk
1 teaspoon dried thyme	⅔ cup light cream
salt and pepper	chopped parsley, for garnish

1 Put the meat, carrots, onion, celery, bay leaf and thyme in a large saucepan. Season to taste. Cover with bouillon or water, cover and simmer for 1½ hours or until the meat is tender. Remove the bay leaf.

2 Blend together the softened butter and flour and add to the stew in small knobs, stirring after each addition until the stew is thickened. Simmer for 10 minutes, adding more liquid if necessary.

3 Blend together the egg yolk and cream, add to the stew and reheat without boiling. Garnish with parsley.

—————— **VARIATION** ——————

Blanquette de Veau

This classic creamy stew can also be made with 1½ pounds stewing veal. Substitute a bouquet garni for the bay leaf and thyme.

SPICED LAMB
SERVES 4

2 cups all-purpose flour	4 cups thinly sliced onions
salt and pepper	¼ teaspoon ground allspice
¼ cup butter	¼ teaspoon grated nutmeg
¼ cup shortening	⅔ cup lamb or beef bouillon
1½ pounds lamb neck fillets, sliced into 12 pieces	
1 large cooking apple, peeled, cored and sliced	milk, to glaze

1 Put the flour and a pinch of salt in a bowl. Cut in the butter and shortening until the mixture resembles fine breadcrumbs. Add enough cold water to mix to a firm dough. Knead lightly until smooth, then chill until required.

2 Place half the lamb in the base of a 4-cup pie dish. Arrange half the apple slices and half the onion slices over the top. Sprinkle over the allspice and nutmeg and season to taste. Repeat the layers, then pour over the bouillon.

3 Roll out the dough to fit the dish and use to cover the pie, moistening the edges so the crust is well sealed. Use any trimmings to decorate.

4 Brush the crust with milk and bake in a preheated oven at 400°F for 20 minutes. Reduce the temperature to 350°F and cook for a further 1¼ hours. Cover the crust with baker's parchment or foil if it shows signs of becoming too brown. Serve hot.

CHILI LAMB AND COCONUT CURRY

SERVES 4–6

⅔ cup shredded coconut	2 cups apple slices
1 cup milk	½ teaspoon chili powder
¼ cup corn oil	1 teaspoon ground cinnamon
3 pounds boneless shoulder of lamb, cut into 1-inch cubes	¼ cup all-purpose flour
4 celery stalks, cut into 2-inch pieces	2 cups chicken bouillon
	salt and pepper
1 onion, sliced	chopped parsley, for garnish

1 Put the coconut in a saucepan with the milk and ¾ cup water. Bring to a boil, then remove from the heat and leave to infuse for 30 minutes. Strain into a pitcher, pressing the coconut to extract all the juice.
2 Heat the oil in a Dutch oven, add the lamb and cook until browned. Remove the meat with a slotted spoon.
3 Add the celery, onion and apple to the oil in the pan and cook for about 10 minutes or until browned.
4 Stir in the spices and flour, then gradually stir in the bouillon and coconut milk. Season to taste and bring to a boil.
5 Return the meat to the casserole, cover and cook in a preheated oven at 350°F for about 1¼ hours. Garnish with parsley before serving.

LAMB AND EGGPLANT MOUSSAKA

SERVES 4

2 pounds eggplants, sliced	½ teaspoon dried basil
salt and pepper	2 tablespoons all-purpose flour
oil, for frying	
¾ pound lean ground lamb	1½ cups fresh breadcrumbs
2 medium onions, chopped	1 tablespoon butter
3 tablespoons tomato paste	1¼ cups milk
⅔ cup dry white wine	¾ cup shredded Cheddar cheese
8-ounce can tomatoes	
½ teaspoon dried oregano	1 egg yolk

1 Put the eggplant slices in a colander, sprinkling each layer generously with salt. Leave to drain for 30 minutes.
2 Heat 1 tablespoon oil in a saucepan, add the lamb and cook until well browned. Stir in the onion, tomato paste, wine, tomatoes with their juice, herbs and 1 tablespoon flour. Boil, cover and simmer for 30 minutes. Season.
3 Rinse the eggplant slices and pat dry on kitchen paper towels. Heat some oil in a large skillet and fry the eggplant slices, in batches, until browned on both sides. Drain well. Layer the eggplant in a shallow ovenproof dish with the lamb and 1 cup breadcrumbs.
4 To make the sauce, melt the butter in a saucepan, stir in the remaining flour and cook for 1 minute, stirring. Remove from the heat and gradually stir in the milk. Bring to a boil and cook, stirring, until thick. Stir in ½ cup of the cheese and the egg yolk.
5 Spoon the sauce over the moussaka, then sprinkle with the remaining cheese and breadcrumbs. Bake at 350°F for 45 minutes or until golden.

LAMB AND WATERCRESS BAKE

SERVES 4–6

1 pound lean ground lamb	¼ cup dry white wine
2 large onions, minced	salt and pepper
2 bunches of watercress, finely chopped	2 tablespoons butter
2 teaspoons dried oregano	2½ cups milk
7 tablespoons all-purpose flour	1½ cups crumbled Lancashire cheese
1¼ cups lamb or chicken bouillon	½ pound oven-ready lasagne verdi

1 Put the lamb in a large, preferably non-stick saucepan and fry in its own fat until well browned, stirring constantly. Pour off excess fat. Add the onion and cook for 5 minutes, stirring occasionally. Add the watercress, oregano and 2 tablespoons of the flour. Cook for 1–2 minutes, then gradually stir in the bouillon and wine. Season to taste. Bring to a boil, then simmer gently, uncovered, for 45 minutes, stirring occasionally.

2 Put the butter, remaining flour and milk in a saucepan. Heat, whisking continously, until the sauce thickens, boils and is smooth. Simmer for 1–2 minutes. Remove the pan from the heat and add 1 cup of the cheese, stirring until melted. Season to taste.

3 Layer the lamb mixture with the uncooked lasagne in a fairly deep ovenproof serving dish. Spoon over the cheese sauce and sprinkle with the remaining cheese.

4 Bake in a preheated oven at 375°F for about 40 minutes or until browned. Serve hot straight from the dish.

SPICED LENTIL BAKE

SERVES 4

3 tablespoons corn oil	1 teaspoon ground cinnamon
8 middle neck lamb chops (total weight about 2½ pounds)	½ cup red lentils
	salt and pepper
2 medium onions, thinly sliced	3 cups sliced potatoes
1 tablespoon ground turmeric	3 cups sliced rutabagas
1 teaspoon mild paprika	1¼ cups lamb or chicken bouillon

1 Heat the oil in a large skillet, add the chops and fry until well browned on both sides. Remove from the pan with a slotted spoon.

2 Add the onions to the pan with the turmeric, paprika, cinnamon and lentils. Fry for 2–3 minutes, then add plenty of salt and pepper and spoon into a shallow 8-cup ovenproof dish.

3 Place the chops on top of the onion and lentil mixture. Arrange the vegetable slices on top of the chops, then season to taste and pour over the bouillon.

4 Cover the dish tightly and cook in a preheated oven at 350°F for about 1½ hours, or until the chops are tender. Uncover and cook for a further 30 minutes, or until lightly browned on top. Serve hot.

COOK'S TIP

There are many different types of lentil available. The red lentils used in this recipe are the most common kind, sometimes also described as 'split red lentils' or even 'Egyptian lentils'. They do not need soaking and are quick-cooking, but they tend to lose their shape.

LAMB CRUMBLE

SERVES 4

¾ pound leftover roast lamb	salt and pepper
1 medium onion	¼ cup butter
1 cup all-purpose flour	½ cup shredded Cheshire or Cheddar cheese
1 tablespoon tomato paste	½ teaspoon dried mixed herbs
1¼ cups beef bouillon	

I Grind the meat and onion together. Mix in 2 tablespoons flour, the tomato paste and the bouillon. Season to taste. Turn into a shallow ovenproof dish.

2 Put the remaining flour in a bowl, cut in the butter and rub in until the mixture resembles fine breadcrumbs. Stir in the shredded cheese, herbs and seasoning. Spoon the crumble over the meat.

3 Bake in a preheated oven at 375°F for 45 minutes–1 hour. Serve immediately.

─────────── **VARIATION** ───────────
Beef Crumble
Substitute ¾ pound leftover roast beef for the lamb.

LAMB KABOBS IN SPICY YOGURT DRESSING

SERVES 4

1 large corn-on-the-cob	1 tablespoon coriander seeds
salt and pepper	1½ pounds boneless leg of lamb, cut into 1-inch cubes
8 shallots	
⅔ cup plain yogurt	½ pound zucchini, cut into ¼-inch slices
1 garlic clove, crushed	
2 bay leaves, crumbled	4 tomatoes, halved
1 tablespoon lemon juice	lemon wedges, for garnish
1 teaspoon ground allspice	

I Blanch the corn in boiling salted water for 1 minute, drain well, then cut into eight pieces and set aside. Blanch the shallots in boiling salted water for 1 minute, skin and set aside.

2 To make the marinade, pour the yogurt into a shallow dish and stir in the garlic, bay leaves, lemon juice, allspice, coriander seeds and salt and pepper to taste.

3 Thread the lamb cubes onto eight skewers with the zucchini, tomatoes, corn and shallots. Place in the dish, spoon over the marinade, cover and leave for 2–3 hours, turning occasionally to ensure even coating.

4 Cook the kabobs under a preheated broiler for 15–20 minutes, turning and brushing with the marinade occasionally. To serve, spoon the remaining marinade over the kabobs and garnish with lemon wedges.

ROAST PORK WITH APPLES

SERVES 6–8

3½ pound rolled pork loin roast	salt and pepper
3 tablespoons butter	⅔ cup dry white wine (optional)
coarse salt	⅔ cup chicken bouillon
fresh rosemary sprig	fresh watercress sprigs, for garnish
6 Newtown Pippins or other juicy apples, cored	

1 Score the pork rind all over with a sharp knife. Rub with the butter, then sprinkle with coarse salt.
2 Place the rosemary on a rack in a roasting pan, put the pork on top and roast in a preheated oven at 350°F for 2 hours.
3 Season the apples to taste inside and make a shallow cut through the skin around the apples about one third of the way down. Place in a pan or ovenproof dish and baste with some of the fat from the pork. Cook on a lower shelf for the last 30 minutes of the meat roasting time.
4 Transfer the pork, still on the rack, to a plate and keep warm. Drain off most of the fat from the roasting pan, leaving the meat juices. Stir in the wine, if using, loosening the sediment at the bottom of the pan. Boil until almost completely evaporated. Stir in the bouillon and boil for 2–3 minutes. Strain into a sauceboat.
5 Put the pork on a warmed serving plate. Arrange the apples around the pork, garnish with watercress and serve accompanied by the gravy.

DANISH ROAST LOIN OF PORK

SERVES 6

3–3½ pound rolled pork loin roast	18 no-soak prunes, pitted
salt and pepper	2 tablespoons all-purpose flour
2 tart apples, peeled, cored and cut into eighths	¼ cup heavy cream

1 Score the rind of the pork with a very sharp knife, if the butcher has not already done so. Weigh the roast and calculate the cooking time, allowing 40 minutes per pound.
2 Dry the rind thoroughly with kitchen paper towels, then rub with 2 teaspoons salt. Place the meat, rind side uppermost, on a rack in a roasting pan.
3 Roast the pork in a preheated oven at 425°F for 40 minutes, then remove from the oven and pour 1¼ cups water into the roasting pan, underneath the rack. Return the pork to the oven, lower the temperature to 350°F, and roast for the remaining cooking time, adding the apples and prunes to the water for the last 45 minutes. Do not baste.
4 Transfer the pork to a warmed carving dish and leave to settle for about 15 minutes before carving. Remove the fruit from the water with a slotted spoon and keep hot.
5 Make a gravy from the pan juices. In a liquid measure, mix the flour to a paste with a little cold water. Stir in more cold water up to the 1¼ cup mark.
6 Remove the rack from the roasting pan and transfer the pan to the hob. Stir the flour mixture into the liquid in the pan, a little at a time, then bring to a boil. Simmer, stirring, until thickened, then stir in the cream and season to taste. Heat through, then pour into a gravyboat. Serve the pork with the fruit and the gravy.

POT ROAST OF PORK AND RED CABBAGE

SERVES 4

3 tablespoons red wine vinegar	1 tablespoon all-purpose flour
1 pound red cabbage	salt and pepper
1 large cooking apple	1½–2 pound cushion-style picnic shoulder of pork, rinded
1 tablespoon demerara sugar	cilantro sprigs, for garnish

1 Bring a large saucepan of water, to which 1 tablespoon of the vinegar has been added, to a boil.
2 Meanwhile, shred the red cabbage. When the water is boiling, add the cabbage, bring back to a boil, then drain well.
3 Peel, core and slice the apple and place with the cabbage in a casserole just wide enough to take the pork roast.
4 Add the sugar, the remaining vinegar and the flour. Season to taste and stir well together.
5 Slash the fat side of the roast several times and sprinkle with plenty of salt and pepper. Place on top of the cabbage and cover the casserole.
6 Cook in a preheated oven at 375°F for about 1¾ hours or until the pork is tender. Slice the pork and serve on a warmed platter surrounded by cabbage. Garnish with cilantro and serve the remaining cabbage in a separate serving dish.

CHILI PORK AND BEANS

SERVES 4–6

2 tablespoons vegetable oil	¾ cup red kidney beans, soaked in cold water overnight
2 pounds boneless pork shoulder, cubed	1 tablespoon molasses
1 large onion, roughly chopped	1 tablespoon Dijon mustard
2 celery stalks, sliced	1 teaspoon chili powder
1–2 garlic cloves, crushed	salt and pepper

1 Heat 1 tablespoon of the oil in a Dutch oven, add the pork in batches and fry over a high heat until colored on all sides. Remove with a slotted spoon and drain on kitchen paper towels.
2 Lower the heat, then add the remaining oil to the pan with the onion, celery and garlic. Fry gently for 10 minutes or until softened.
3 Drain the kidney beans and add to the pan with 5 cups fresh water. Bring to a boil, stirring, then boil rapidly for 10 minutes.
4 Lower the heat, return the pork to the pan and add the molasses, mustard, chili powder and pepper to taste. Stir well to mix.
5 Cover the casserole and cook in a preheated oven at 300°F for 3 hours. Stir the pork and beans occasionally during the cooking time and add more water if dry. Add 1 teaspoon salt halfway through, then taste and adjust the seasoning before serving, adding more chili powder if a hotter flavor is preferred.

PORK IN PLUM SAUCE

SERVES 4

1 pound plums	2 tablespoons butter
1¼ cups rosé wine	1 large onion, chopped
salt and pepper	2¼–2½ cups shredded white cabbage
¼ cup wholewheat flour	2 tablespoons plain yogurt
1½ pounds pork tenderloin, cubed	

1 Put the plums and wine in a saucepan and simmer for 5 minutes or until tender. Strain, reserving the juice. Remove the stones from the plums and purée half the flesh in a blender or food processor.

2 Season the flour, add the pork and toss until coated.

3 Melt the butter in a large saucepan or Dutch oven and lightly fry the onion and cabbage for 3–4 minutes. Add the meat and fry until brown on all sides.

4 Pour in the reserved plum juice and puréed plums, then simmer, uncovered, for 10–15 minutes or until tender. Add the remaining plums and yogurt and reheat gently.

TO MICROWAVE

Put the plums and wine in a large bowl and cook on HIGH for 3–4 minutes. Complete the remainder of step 1 and step 2. Melt the butter in a large bowl on HIGH for 45 seconds. Add the onion and cabbage and cook on HIGH for 7 minutes, stirring occasionally. Add the pork and cook on HIGH for 3 minutes. Pour in ¾–1 cup plum juice and the puréed plums and cook on HIGH for 3–4 minutes or until boiling, stirring occasionally. Cook on LOW for 7–8 minutes or until the pork is tender. Stir in the remaining plums and yogurt. Stand, covered, for 5 minutes.

PORK SCALLOPS WITH JUNIPER

SERVES 4

1 pound pork tenderloin	4 juniper berries, lightly crushed
salt and pepper	⅔ cup heavy cream
6 tablespoons all-purpose flour	chopped fresh parsley, for garnish
2 tablespoons butter	
⅓ cup dry white wine	

1 Trim any fat from the pork tenderloin and cut the meat into ¼-inch slices. Place the slices between two sheets of dampened baker's parchment and beat out into even thinner slices, using rolling pin or meat mallet.

2 Season the flour, then dip each pork scallop in the flour, turning to coat and shaking off any excess.

3 Melt the butter in a large skillet and sauté the scallops over a high heat for 2 minutes on each side. Remove and keep warm while making the sauce.

4 Add the wine and juniper berries to the pan and boil rapidly, scraping the bottom of the pan to loosen any sediment, until reduced by half. Pour in the cream, season to taste and bring to a boil. Boil rapidly for 1 minute, stirring. Pour over the scallops and serve immediately, garnished with chopped parsley.

COOK'S TIP

Juniper berries are small purple-black berries with an aromatic scent and pine-like tang. They should be crushed before being added to a dish to release maximum flavor. They are readily available in delicatessens.

PORK CHOPS WITH PEPPERS

SERVES 4

1 tablespoon vegetable oil	1 sweet red pepper, thinly sliced
1 tablespoon butter	1 sweet green pepper, thinly sliced
1 medium onion, chopped	3 tablespoons dry sherry
1-inch piece of fresh root ginger, finely grated	2 tablespoons soy sauce
1 garlic clove, crushed	⅔ cup unsweetened pineapple juice
four 5-ounce boneless pork loin chops	salt and pepper

1 Heat the oil and butter in a large skillet, add the onion, ginger and garlic and sauté gently for 5 minutes or until soft. Push to one side of the pan.

2 Add the chops to the pan and cook until brown on both sides, then add the remaining ingredients and stir to mix thoroughly together.

3 Cover tightly and simmer gently for 8–10 minutes or until the chops are tender and the peppers are soft. Transfer the chops and peppers to warmed serving plates. Bring the remaining liquid in the pan to a boil and boil for 2–3 minutes or until reduced slightly. Spoon over the chops and serve immediately.

FRUITY STUFFED PORK CHOPS

SERVES 4

4 thick pork loin chops	juice and finely grated rind of 1 large orange
4 tablespoons vegetable oil	⅓ cup no-soak prunes
1 small onion, minced	⅓ cup no-soak dried apricots
2 celery stalks, finely chopped	½ cup blanched almonds
3 tablespoons Italian risotto rice	1 teaspoon ground cinnamon
2 cups chicken bouillon	salt and pepper

1 Using a sharp knife, make a horizontal cut in each pork chop, working from the outside edge to the bone.

2 To make the stuffing, heat 2 tablespoons of the oil in a heavy-based saucepan, add the onion and celery and sauté gently for 5 minutes or until soft and lightly colored.

3 Add the rice and stir well, then add ⅔ cup of the bouillon and half of the orange juice. Bring to a boil, stirring all the time. Lower the heat and simmer for 15–20 minutes, stirring frequently and adding more bouillon if necessary. When cooked, turn into a bowl and cool.

4 Meanwhile, pit the prunes and chop finely with the apricots and almonds. Add to the rice mixture with the cinnamon. Season to taste. Spoon the stuffing into the cavities in the chops, then secure the open edges with wooden toothpicks. Reserve any remaining stuffing.

5 Heat the remaining oil in a flameproof casserole, add the chops and fry until browned on both sides. Pour in the remaining bouillon and orange juice, add any reserved stuffing, season and bring to a boil. Cover and simmer for 40 minutes or until the chops are tender, basting frequently.

6 Transfer the chops to a warmed serving dish, pour over the pan juices and sprinkle with the grated orange rind.

CRUMB-TOPPED PORK CHOPS

SERVES 4

4 lean pork loin chops	pinch of dried thyme
1 cup fresh white breadcrumbs	finely grated rind of 1 lemon
1 teaspoon chopped fresh parsley or 1 teaspoon dried	½ teaspoon coriander seeds, crushed
1 teaspoon chopped fresh mint or ½ teaspoon dried	1 egg, beaten
	salt and pepper

1 Cut the rind off the chops and put them in one layer in a baking pan.
2 Mix the remaining ingredients together and season to taste. Spread this mixture evenly over the chops with a spatula.
3 Bake in a preheated oven at 400°F for 45–50 minutes or until golden. Serve hot.

VARIATION
Crumb-topped Lamb Chops
Substitute four lamb loin chops for the pork and use rosemary instead of thyme in the crumb topping. Omit the coriander, if preferred.

PARCELED PORK

SERVES 4

4 medium pork chops	6 tablespoons hard cider
2 tablespoons butter	2 tablespoons lemon juice
1 medium onion, finely chopped	⅔ cup dairy sour cream
2 cups sliced mushrooms	salt and pepper

1 Trim the chops of any rind and excess fat. Melt the butter in a large skillet, add the chops and cook until well browned. Remove the chops from the pan and place each one on a piece of foil about 8 inches square.
2 Add the onion and mushrooms to the butter remaining in the pan and cook for 5 minutes.
3 Stir in the cider and lemon juice and bring to a boil. Boil the liquid over a high heat until reduced by half, then remove from the heat and stir in the sour cream. Season well.
4 Place a quarter of the mushroom mixture on top of each chop, then shape the foil into neat parcels and seal well.
5 Place the parcels in a small ovenproof dish and bake in a preheated oven at 350°F for about 50 minutes or until the chops are tender.
6 To serve, place each parcel on a warmed plate and open carefully so that no juices escape.

PORK TENDERLOIN WITH WHITE WINE AND MUSHROOMS

SERVES 6

2½ pounds pork tenderloin	⅔ cup beef bouillon
vegetable oil, for frying	⅔ cup dry white wine
5 tablespoons butter or margarine	salt and pepper
2 medium onions, chopped	twelve ½-inch slices of French bread
½ pound button mushrooms	chopped fresh parsley, for garnish
3 tablespoons all-purpose flour	

1 Cut the pork tenderloin into slices, place between two sheets of dampened baker's parchment and beat out with a rolling pin or meat mallet. Heat 2 tablespoons of the oil in a skillet, add the pork and cook over a high heat until browned. Remove from the pan and set aside.

2 Melt 2 tablespoons of the butter or margarine in the skillet, add the onions and sauté for 5 minutes. Add the mushrooms to the pan, increase the heat and sauté for 1–2 minutes, tossing constantly.

3 Blend the flour into the juices in the pan, with the remaining butter or margarine. Cook, stirring, for 1–2 minutes, then gradually blend in the bouillon and wine. Season to taste and simmer for 2–3 minutes.

4 Return the meat to the pan, cover and cook for 20–25 minutes or until the pork is tender.

5 Meanwhile, heat some oil in a skillet, add the French bread slices and fry until golden brown on both sides. Drain well on kitchen paper towels.

6 Serve the pork hot with the French bread and sprinkled liberally with chopped parsley.

PORK WITH CIDER AND CORIANDER

SERVES 4

1 pound pork tenderloin	1 tablespoon ground coriander
2 tablespoons oil	1 tablespoon all-purpose flour
¼ cup butter	
1 sweet green pepper, cut into rings	⅔ cup hard cider
2 cups sliced celery	⅔ cup chicken or vegetable bouillon
1 cup chopped onion	salt and pepper

1 Trim excess fat from the pork tenderloin and slice into ¼-inch thick pieces. Place between two sheets of dampened baker's parchment and beat out until thin with a rolling pin or meat mallet.

2 Heat the oil with half the butter in a large skillet. Add the green pepper and celery and fry gently for 2–3 minutes. Lift out with a slotted spoon and keep the mixture warm on a serving plate.

3 Add the remaining butter to the pan, increase the heat to high, then add the pork, a few pieces at a time. Cook the pork until browned on all sides, then remove from the pan with a slotted spoon.

4 Add the onion to the fat remaining in the pan and fry until golden brown. Stir in the coriander and flour and cook for 1 minute. Gradually add the cider and bouillon and bring quickly to a boil, stirring constantly. Return the pork to the pan, season to taste and simmer for about 5 minutes. Serve hot, with the green pepper and celery.

SWEET AND SOUR PORK

SERVES 2–3

¾ pound lean boneless pork	1 sweet green pepper, chopped
2 tablespoons all-purpose flour	FOR THE SAUCE
8-ounce can pineapple pieces	1 tablespoon cornstarch
	2 teaspoons soy sauce
1 tablespoon vegetable oil	3 tablespoons vinegar
1 dessert apple, cored and sliced	2 tablespoons sugar
	⅔ cup chicken bouillon

1 Cut the pork into 1-inch cubes, add to the flour and toss until coated.
2 Drain the pineapple, reserving ¼ cup juice.
3 Heat the oil in a pan, add the pork and fry until lightly browned. Lower the heat and add the apple, green pepper and pineapple pieces.
4 To make the sauce, put all the ingredients in a small bowl and mix thoroughly, adding the reserved pineapple juice.
5 Add the sauce to the pork, bring to a boil, cover and simmer for 25–35 minutes or until the pork is tender. Serve immediately.

BARBECUED SPARERIBS

SERVES 4–6

2 tablespoons vegetable oil	½ teaspoon black pepper
1 large onion, minced	½ teaspoon dried sage or rosemary
1 garlic clove, crushed	
⅔ cup tomato paste	2 teaspoons dry mustard
3 tablespoons lemon juice	4 tablespoons soft light brown sugar
4 tablespoons Worcestershire sauce	½ cup beef bouillon
½ teaspoon salt	3 pounds pork spareribs, cut into serving pieces

1 Heat the oil in a large saucepan, add the onion and garlic and cook for 5–10 minutes or until transparent.
2 Add the tomato paste, lemon juice, Worcestershire, salt, pepper, sage or rosemary, mustard and sugar. Pour in the bouillon and simmer for 10 minutes, stirring.
3 Put the spareribs on a rack in a roasting pan and pour the sauce over them. Roast in a preheated oven at 400°F for 1 hour or until crisp, basting every 15 minutes with sauce from the bottom of the pan.

VARIATION
Honeyed Spareribs
For an alternative sauce, mix together ⅓ cup clear honey, 4 tablespoons soft dark brown sugar, 4 tablespoons tomato ketchup, 2 tablespoons Worcestershire, 2 tablespoons prepared English mustard and 2 tablespoons red wine vinegar. Roast the ribs for 30 minutes, then pour over the sauce and continue roasting until the ribs are tender and the sauce syrupy.

GOURMET PORK ROLLS

SERVES 4

¾ pound pork tenderloin	4 slices Gruyère cheese
4 thin slices of lean cooked ham	salt and pepper
1 garlic clove, crushed	3 tablespoons all-purpose flour
2 tablespoons pignoli (pine nuts)	1 tablespoon vegetable oil
1⅓ cup fresh wholewheat breadcrumbs	1 cup dry white wine
⅓ cup no-soak dried apricots, chopped	¾ cup unsweetened apple juice
3 tablespoons chopped fresh parsley or 1 tablespoon dried	1 tablespoon butter
	apple slices and parsley sprigs, for garnish

1 Cut the pork into four equal pieces. Place between two sheets of dampened baker's parchment and beat with a rolling pin or meat mallet to flatten to about ¼-inch thick. Lay a slice of ham on each scallop.

2 Mix the garlic, pignoli, breadcrumbs, apricots and 2 tablespoons fresh parsley or 2 teaspoons dried. Spread over each scallop and lay a slice of Gruyère cheese on top.

3 Roll up each scallop and secure with a wooden toothpick. Season 2 tablespoons of the flour and use to dust the pork rolls. Heat the oil in a skillet and cook the rolls for 5–7 minutes, turning frequently.

4 Pour in the wine and apple juice. Bring to a boil and simmer for 20–25 minutes or until the meat is tender.

5 Using a slotted spoon, transfer the rolls to a warmed dish. Remove the toothpicks and keep the rolls warm.

6 Increase the heat and reduce the liquor in the pan to about ⅔ cup. Mix the butter with the remaining flour and gradually whisk in until thickened. Stir in the remaining parsley, pour the sauce over the rolls and garnish.

STUFFED CABBAGE PARCELS

SERVES 4

¾ pound lean ground pork	3 tablespoons butter
1 medium onion, minced	6 tablespoons all-purpose flour
8-ounce can tomatoes	2 cups milk
salt and pepper	½ cup shredded Cheddar cheese
10-ounce can red kidney beans, drained and rinsed	pinch of cayenne
16 large Savoy cabbage leaves	

1 Put the pork in a saucepan and cook in its own fat until beginning to brown, stirring from time to time. Drain off excess fat.

2 Add the onion and sauté until softened and lightly colored. Add the tomatoes with their juice and bring to a boil, stirring. Season to taste, then simmer over a moderate heat for 20 minutes or until the pork is cooked and the sauce thick and well reduced, stirring occasionally. Stir in the kidney beans and remove the pan from the heat.

3 Blanch the cabbage for 3 minutes, in batches of four leaves at a time, in a large pan of boiling salted water. Drain the leaves, rinse and pat dry, then cut out and discard the thick central stalks.

4 Put 1–1½ tablespoons filling mixture at the stalk end of each cabbage leaf. Fold the two sides inward to cover the filling, then roll into neat parcels. Arrange, seam sides down, in a single layer in a well-buttered heatproof serving dish.

5 Heat the butter, flour and milk, whisking continuously, until the sauce thickens, boils and is smooth. Simmer for 1–2 minutes, then season. Pour over the cabbage parcels.

6 Sprinkle the parcels with cheese and cayenne and place under a preheated broiler until golden brown and bubbling.

CANADIAN PORK AND VEAL PIE

SERVES 6

¼ cup butter	about ½ cup fresh breadcrumbs
2 large onions, minced	4–6 tablespoons chopped fresh parsley and thyme, mixed
1 pound lean boneless pork	
1 pound stewing veal	5 ounces frozen pie dough, thawed
⅔ cup dry white wine or chicken bouillon	½ pound frozen puff pastry, thawed
1 teaspoon ground allspice	
salt and pepper	beaten egg, to glaze

1 Melt the butter in a large skillet and sauté the onions very gently for 10–15 minutes or until soft.
2 Meanwhile, cut the pork and veal into fine dice. Add to the onions and sauté for 10 minutes.
3 Stir in the wine or bouillon, then add the allspice. Season, cover and cook for 30 minutes, stirring occasionally.
4 Remove the meat and onions from the cooking liquid and set aside. Boil the liquid in the pan to reduce slightly, then pour over the meat. Add enough breadcrumbs to absorb the liquid, then stir in the herbs. Leave to cool.
5 Meanwhile, roll out the pie dough on a floured surface and use to line a 9-inch pie plate. Pile the cooled meat mixture on top, doming it in the center.
6 Roll out the puff pastry to a circle slightly larger than the first. Moisten the rim of pie dough with water, then place the puff pastry lid on top. Press to seal.
7 Decorate the top of the pie with pastry trimmings and make a hole in the center. Brush with egg.
8 Bake in a preheated oven at 400°F for 30 minutes or until the crust is golden brown. Serve hot.

BAKED HAM

SERVES 8–10

4 pound boneless cook-before-eating cured ham	1 bay leaf
2 medium onions, quartered	5 black peppercorns
	cloves
2 medium carrots, thickly sliced	demerara sugar, to glaze

1 Weigh the ham and calculate the cooking time, allowing 20 minutes per pound plus 20 minutes. Place the ham in a large saucepan and cover with cold water. Bring slowly to a boil, then drain.
2 Return the ham to the saucepan. Add the vegetables, bay leaf and peppercorns, cover with cold water and bring slowly to a boil. Skim the surface with a slotted spoon. Cover and boil for half the calculated cooking time.
3 Drain the ham and wrap in foil. Place in a roasting pan and bake in a preheated oven at 350°F until 30 minutes before the cooking time is completed.
4 Remove the foil and rind from the ham. Score the fat in diamonds and stud with cloves. Sprinkle the surface with demerara sugar and pat in.
5 Bake at 425°F for 30 minutes or until crisp and golden. Serve hot or cold.

GLAZED HAM STEAKS

SERVES 4

1 tablespoon soy sauce	garlic salt
½ teaspoon dry mustard	black pepper
1 tablespoon light corn syrup	1 tablespoon cornstarch
¼ teaspoon ground ginger	1 tablespoon lemon juice
6 tablespoon orange juice	4 uncooked smoked ham steaks

1 In a small saucepan, combine the first five ingredients and add garlic salt and pepper to taste.
2 Blend the cornstarch with the lemon juice, stir in a little of the mixture from the pan and then return it all to the pan. Bring to a boil, stirring all the time, until the mixture has thickened to a glaze. Remove from the heat.
3 Cut most of the fat from the steaks and then brush half of the glaze on one side.
4 Cook under a preheated moderate broiler for 15 minutes or until the meat is cooked right through, brown and bubbling. Turn several times and brush with the remaining glaze during cooking. Serve hot.

SMOKED LOIN CHOPS IN CIDER

SERVES 4

four 6-ounce uncooked smoked pork loin chops	1 tablespoon butter
1 tablespoon prepared English mustard	5 teaspoons all-purpose flour
2 tablespoons demerara sugar	salt and pepper
1¼ cups hard cider	chopped fresh parsley, for garnish

1 Put the chops side by side in a large ovenproof dish. Mix the mustard and sugar with enough cider to make a smooth paste. Spread over the chops and leave for 30 minutes.
2 Bake the chops in a preheated oven at 400°F for 15 minutes.
3 Meanwhile, put the butter, flour and remaining cider in a saucepan. Heat, whisking continuously, until the sauce thickens, boils and is smooth. Simmer for 1–2 minutes. Season to taste.
4 Pour the sauce over the chops. Bake for a further 15 minutes or until cooked. Serve garnished with parsley.

— COOK'S TIP —

For a stronger cider flavor, use one third to one half more cider than the recipe states and reduce it by boiling to concentrate the flavor before using.

BACON AND LIVER ROULADES

SERVES 3–4

12 bacon slices	1 tablespoon chopped fresh marjoram or oregano or 1 teaspoon dried
½ pound lamb's liver	
¼ cup orange juice	salt and pepper
2 tablespoons brandy	

1 Stretch the bacon slices with a blunt-edged knife.

2 Divide the liver into 12 even-size pieces, removing any skin and ducts.

3 Roll a slice of bacon around each piece of liver and secure with a toothpick. Place in the base of a foil-lined broiler pan.

4 Mix the orange juice, brandy, herbs and seasoning together and spoon over the bacon rolls. Leave to marinate in a cool place for at least 1 hour.

5 Cook under a moderate broiler for 12–15 minutes, turning and basting occasionally. Remove the toothpicks before serving, replacing them with fresh ones if liked. Serve hot.

SMOKED PORK CHOPS WITH GOOSEBERRY SAUCE

SERVES 4

1 tablespoon dark soft brown sugar	1 tablespoon butter
1 teaspoon dry mustard	1 large onion, chopped
pepper	⅔ cup vegetable stock
four 6-ounce uncooked smoked pork loin chops	⅔ cup trimmed gooseberries

1 Mix together the brown sugar, mustard and pepper to taste and rub into both sides of the chops.

2 Melt the butter in a large skillet or flameproof casserole, add the onion and cook for 2 minutes, then add the chops, half the stock and the gooseberries. Simmer gently for 15 minutes.

3 Remove the chops from the pan. Purée the onions and gooseberries in a blender or food processor until smooth.

4 Return the chops and purée to the pan with the remaining stock. Simmer gently for 10 minutes or until the chops are cooked through and tender. Serve at once.

SAUSAGE POPOVERS WITH ONION SAUCE

SERVES 4

¾ pound bulk pork sausage	2 eggs
1 large cooking apple, peeled and cored	2½ cups milk
1 teaspoon chopped parsley	lard
salt and pepper	1½ cups sliced onions
1 cup plus 1 tablespoon all-purpose flour	1 tablespoon butter

1 Place the sausage in a bowl and grate in the apple. Stir in the parsley and season to taste. Work the ingredients together and form into 16 small balls.
2 Make a batter from the cup of flour, the eggs, and 1¼ cups milk.
3 Put a little lard in the base of each of four 1¼-cup individual ramekin dishes and heat in a preheated oven at 425°F until sizzling hot. Divide the sausage balls among the dishes and cook in the oven for 10 minutes.
4 Pour the batter over the sausage balls and return to the oven for 35–40 minutes or until risen and golden.
5 Meanwhile, put the onion in a saucepan with the remaining milk, bring to a boil and cook until the onion is soft. To make the sauce, melt the butter in a pan, stir in the remaining flour and cook gently for 1 minute, stirring. Remove the pan from the heat and gradually stir in the onions and milk. Bring to a boil and continue to cook, stirring, until the sauce thickens, then season to taste.
6 When the popovers are baked, turn them out onto warmed serving plates and pour a little onion sauce into the center of each. Serve immediately.

BACON AND APPLE PIE

SERVES 4

2¼ cups all-purpose flour	½ pound cooking apples, peeled, cored and roughly chopped
salt and pepper	
½ cup butter, diced	1 tablespoon chopped parsley
½ pound Canadian bacon, roughly chopped	⅔ cup hard cider
1 medium onion, coarsely chopped	1 egg, beaten, to glaze

1 To make the pie dough, sift 2 cups of the flour and a pinch of salt into a bowl. Cut in the butter until the mixture resembles breadcrumbs. Add just enough water to mix to a firm dough.
2 Gather the dough into a ball and knead lightly. Wrap in foil and chill in the refrigerator for 30 minutes.
3 Meanwhile, combine the bacon, onion and apples in a 3-cup pie dish. Add the parsley and season to taste.
4 Mix the remaining flour with the cider, a little at a time, then pour into the pie dish.
5 Roll out the dough on a lightly floured surface to 2-inches wider than the dish. Cut a 1-inch strip from the outer edge and use to line the dampened rim of the pie dish.
6 Moisten the strip of dough, then place the lid on top and press to seal. Flute the edge.
7 Make a diagonal cross in the center almost to the edges of the dish, then fold the crust back to reveal the filling.
8 Brush the crust with the egg. Bake in a preheated oven at 375°F for about 45 minutes or until the crust is golden and the filling is cooked through. Serve the pie hot or cold.

HAM IN CIDER WITH SAGE AND ONION DUMPLINGS

SERVES 6

2½ pound boneless cook-before-eating cured ham	½ cup shredded suet
4 cloves	1 teaspoon fresh sage
1¼ cups hard cider	2 tablespoons butter or margarine
1 bay leaf	2 medium onions, skinned
2 cups fresh white breadcrumbs	salt and pepper
1½ cups self-rising flour	parsley sprigs, for garnish

1 Place the ham in a saucepan and cover with cold water. Bring slowly to a boil. Drain off the water. Pat the ham dry.
2 Slice or peel off the ham rind. Stud the fat with cloves.
3 Put the ham in a shallow casserole with the cider and bay leaf. Cover tightly and cook in a preheated oven at 350°F for 2¼ hours.
4 Meanwhile, mix the breadcrumbs, flour, suet and sage together in a bowl. Cut in the butter. Coarsely grate in the onions. Bind to a soft dough with water, then add a little salt and pepper.
5 Shape the dough into 12 dumplings. Forty-five minutes before the end of the cooking time, add the dumplings to the juices surrounding the ham. Cover again and finish cooking. Serve the ham sliced, with a little of the cooking liquid spooned over, surrounded by the dumplings. Garnish with parsley sprigs.

LIKKY PIE

SERVES 4

2 cups sliced leeks	⅓ cup light cream
salt and pepper	2 eggs, lightly beaten
1 pound lean boneless pork, cut into 1-inch cubes	7½-ounce packet frozen puff pastry, thawed
⅔ cup milk	

1 Parboil the leeks in salted water for about 5 minutes. Drain well. Fill a 5-cup pie dish with the leeks and pork. Season to taste and pour in the milk.
2 Cover with foil and bake in a preheated oven at 400°F for about 1 hour. (Don't worry if it looks curdled.)
3 Stir the cream into the eggs, then pour into the dish. Allow the mixture to cool.
4 Roll out the puff pastry on a lightly floured surface to 2-inches wider than the dish. Cut a 1-inch strip from the outer edge and use to line the dampened rim of the pie dish. Dampen the pastry rim with water, cover with the pastry lid and seal the edges well, then flute. Make a hole in the center of the pie and use pastry trimmings to decorate.
5 Bake in a preheated oven at 425°F for about 25–30 minutes or until risen and golden brown.

SAUSAGE AND EGG PIE

SERVES 4–6

10-ounce frozen pie dough, thawed	2 eggs, beaten
3 eggs, hard-cooked	⅔ cup light cream or milk
2 teaspoons horseradish sauce	1 teaspoon chopped fresh sage or ½ teaspoon dried
½ pound bulk pork sausage	salt and pepper

1 Roll out two thirds of the dough on a lightly floured surface and use to line an 8-inch flan ring placed on a baking sheet.
2 Shell the hard-cooked eggs and halve lengthwise. Mix the horseradish sauce with the sausage, divide into six and mold over the white of each egg half. Place yolk sides down in the flan case.
3 Reserve 2 teaspoons of the beaten eggs for glazing, then mix the remainder with the cream or milk and sage. Season to taste and pour into the flan case.
4 Roll out the remaining dough and use to cover the pie, sealing the edges well. Decorate with dough trimmings.
5 Brush the pie with the remaining beaten egg and bake in a preheated oven at 325°F for about 1 hour. Serve hot or cold.

SAUSAGES AND BEANS

SERVES 4

2 tablespoons vegetable oil	1-pound can red kidney beans, drained and rinsed
1 pound small pork sausage links	⅔ cup beef bouillon
1 large onion, sliced	salt and pepper
4 bacon slices, chopped	chopped fresh parsley, for garnish

1 Heat the oil in a flameproof casserole, add the sausages and fry until browned on all sides. Remove the sausages from the pan with a slotted spoon and set aside.
2 Add the onion and bacon to the pan and sauté for about 5 minutes or until they begin to turn brown, stirring occasionally.
3 Cut each sausage into four and return to the pan with the kidney beans and beef bouillon. Season to taste, cover and cook gently for about 15 minutes or until the sausages are tender. Serve hot, garnished with parsley.

TOAD IN THE HOLE

SERVES 3–4

1 pound pork sausage links	1 cup all-purpose flour
2 tablespoons lard or drippings	pinch of salt
1 cup milk	1 egg

1 Prick the sausages all over with a fork. Put the lard or drippings in a small roasting pan and add the sausages.
2 Bake in the oven at 425°F for 10 minutes or until the fat is hot.
3 Meanwhile, make the batter. Mix the milk and ¼ cup water together in a pitcher. Put the flour and salt in a bowl. Make a well in the center and break in the egg.
4 Mix the flour and egg together gradually, then add the milk and water, a little at a time, and beat until the mixture is smooth.
5 Pour the batter over the sausages in the pan. Bake for about 30 minutes or until the batter is golden brown and well risen. Do not open the oven door during baking or the batter might sink. Serve at once.

--------------- **VARIATION** ---------------
Kidney Toad in the Hole
Skin, core and slice three lambs' kidneys and cook with the sausages before pouring in the batter.

ITALIAN LIVER

SERVES 4

¾ pound lamb's liver	2 tablespoons tomato paste
salt and pepper	1 garlic clove, finely chopped
¼ cup all-purpose flour	
3 tablespoons butter or margarine	¼ teaspoon dried mixed herbs
4 cups sliced onions	2 tablespoon heavy cream
⅔ cup beef bouillon	chopped parsley
1¼ cups milk	

1 Cut the liver into small pieces. Season the flour, add the liver and toss until coated.
2 Melt the butter or margarine in a skillet and add the liver. Fry until browned on all sides, then remove from the pan and set aside.
3 Add the onions to the butter remaining in the pan and fry slowly for about 5 minutes or until soft. Gradually stir in the bouillon, milk, tomato paste, garlic and herbs. Bring the sauce to a boil, stirring continuously.
4 Add the liver to the sauce. Cover the pan and cook gently for 10–15 minutes or until the liver is tender. Adjust the seasoning to taste.
5 Transfer the liver and sauce to a hot serving dish. Trickle the cream over the sauce, sprinkle with chopped parsley and serve immediately.

LIVER GOUJONS WITH ORANGE SAUCE

SERVES 4

¾ pound sliced lamb's liver	1¼ cups lamb or beef bouillon
5 tablespoons all-purpose flour	juice and finely grated rind of 1 medium orange
salt and pepper	1 teaspoon dried sage
1 egg, beaten	a few drops of gravy coloring
⅔ cup medium oatmeal	¼ cup vegetable oil
¼ cup butter	
1 medium onion, sliced	

I Cut the liver into 2-inch pencil-thin strips. Put 3 tablespoons of the flour in a bowl, season with salt and pepper, add the liver and toss until coated.
2 Dip the liver in the beaten egg, then roll in the oatmeal to coat. Chill in the refrigerator while preparing the sauce.
3 Melt half the butter in a saucepan, add the onion and fry gently for about 10 minutes or until golden brown. Add the remaining flour and cook gently, stirring, for 1–2 minutes.
4 Gradually stir in the bouillon, orange rind and juice and sage. Season to taste. Bring to a boil, then simmer for 10–15 minutes, stirring constantly. Add the gravy coloring and taste and adjust the seasoning.
5 Heat the remaining butter and the oil in a skillet, add the liver goujons and fry gently for 1–2 minutes or until tender.
6 Arrange the goujons on a warmed serving platter and pour over a little of the sauce. Serve the remaining sauce separately in a warmed sauceboat or pitcher.

LIVER IN STROGANOFF SAUCE

SERVES 4

1 pound sliced lamb's liver	1 pound tomatoes, peeled and quartered, or 1-pound can tomatoes, drained
salt and pepper	2 teaspoons dried sage
2 tablespoons all-purpose flour	⅔ cup dairy sour cream, beaten
⅓ cup butter or margarine	
2 cups thinly sliced onions	

I Slice the lamb's liver into thin strips. Season the flour with salt and pepper, add the liver and toss until coated.
2 Melt the butter or margarine in a skillet, add the onions and sauté for 5–10 minutes or until lightly browned. Add the tomatoes, push to the side of the pan, then add the liver and cook over a high heat for about 5 minutes.
3 Sprinkle over the sage. Reduce the heat and stir in the sour cream.
4 Combine all the ingredients in the pan, taste and adjust the seasoning. Heat gently, but do not boil, and serve hot.

LIVER SAUTÉ

SERVES 5

salt and pepper	1 onion, thinly sliced
3 tablespoons all-purpose flour	1¼ cups beef bouillon
¾ pound thinly sliced lamb's liver	1 tablespoon tomato paste
2 tablespoons vegetable oil	¾ cup frozen peas

1 Season the flour with salt and pepper, add the liver and toss until coated. Shake off and reserve any excess flour. Heat the oil in a skillet and lightly fry the liver for 1 minute on each side. Remove the liver from the pan with a slotted spoon and keep hot.

2 Add the onion to the oil remaining in the pan and fry for about 5 minutes or until soft. Stir in any remaining flour and cook for 1 minute, then gradually add the bouillon. Bring to a boil, stirring constantly, and cook for 5 minutes.

3 Stir in the tomato paste, taste and adjust the seasoning. Return the liver to the pan with the frozen peas and cook for a further 5 minutes or until the peas are tender. Serve hot.

─────────── **VARIATION** ───────────

Kidney Sauté

Substitute ¾ pound lambs' kidneys for the liver. Skin, core and slice before tossing in the seasoned flour.

LAMB'S LIVER AND MUSHROOMS

SERVES 3

1 tablespoon butter	⅔ cup beef bouillon
1 medium onion, sliced	4 tomatoes, peeled and roughly chopped
1 pound sliced lamb's liver	2 tablespoons Worcestershire sauce
1 tablespoon all-purpose flour	salt and pepper
¼ pound button mushrooms	⅔ cup dairy sour cream

1 Melt the butter in a large skillet and gently fry the onion for 5 minutes or until soft.

2 Cut the liver into thin strips, add to the flour and toss until coated. Add to the pan with the mushrooms. Sauté for 5 minutes, stirring well, then add the bouillon and bring to a boil.

3 Stir in the tomatoes and Worcestershire. Season to taste, then simmer for 3–4 minutes. Stir in the sour cream and reheat without boiling. Serve hot.

─────────── **TO MICROWAVE** ───────────

Cut the butter into small pieces and melt in a large bowl on HIGH for 30 seconds. Add the onion, cover and cook on HIGH for 5–7 minutes or until softened. Coat the liver in the flour and add to the bowl with the mushrooms. Cover and cook on HIGH for 2–3 minutes or until the liver just changes color, stirring once. Add the stock, tomatoes, Worcestershire and salt and pepper, re-cover and cook on HIGH for 2–3 minutes or until boiling, stirring once. Stir in the sour cream and serve immediately.

CHICKEN LIVERS IN SHERRY CREAM SAUCE

SERVES 2

salt and pepper	⅓ cup sherry
¼ cup all-purpose flour	¼ cup chicken bouillon
½ pound chicken livers, thawed if frozen	⅓ cup purple or green seedless grapes, halved
2 tablespoons butter	⅔ cup dairy sour cream

1 Season the flour with salt and pepper, add the chicken livers and toss until coated. Shake off and reserve any excess flour.

2 Melt the butter in a medium skillet and sauté the livers with any remaining flour for about 4 minutes, stirring once or twice. Gradually stir in the sherry and bouillon and simmer for 1–2 minutes.

3 Add the grapes and sour cream. Heat through without boiling and serve hot.

--------- TO MICROWAVE ---------

Complete step 1. Melt the butter in a large shallow dish on HIGH for 45 seconds. Add the livers with any remaining flour and cook on HIGH for 2 minutes, stirring occasionally. Gradually add the sherry and bouillon and cook on HIGH for 3 minutes, stirring occasionally. Add the grapes and cream and cook on HIGH for 1 minute before serving hot.

--------- VARIATION ---------

If grapes are not available, substitute 2 tablespoons golden raisins for the fresh grapes.

KIDNEYS IN BATTER

SERVES 4

2 cups all-purpose flour	1 large onion, minced
pinch of salt	3 cups finely chopped mushrooms
2 eggs	
2½ cups milk	1 garlic clove, crushed
⅓ cup butter	1½ cups dry sherry
8 lambs' kidneys, skinned, cored and chopped	⅔ cup heavy double cream
	salt and pepper

1 Sift the flour and salt into a bowl. Make a well in the center, add the eggs and gradually blend in the flour. Gradually add the milk and whisk the batter until smooth.

2 Melt ¼ cup of the butter in a skillet, add the kidneys and onion and sauté for about 5 minutes or until the onion is transparent. Add the mushrooms, garlic and sherry. Cook gently for a few minutes, then add the cream.

3 Simmer gently until the sauce is reduced and thick, then season to taste.

4 Heat the remaining butter in an ovenproof dish in a preheated oven at 400°F. Add the batter and pour the kidney mixture in the center. Bake in the oven for 35 minutes or until the batter is crisp, golden and well risen. Serve at once.

KIDNEYS À LA CRÈME

SERVES 4

2 tablespoons butter	2 tablespoons all-purpose flour
8 lambs' kidneys, skinned, cored and halved	⅔ cup beef bouillon
1 small onion, chopped	⅔ cup heavy cream
1 garlic clove, crushed	salt and pepper

1 Melt the butter in a skillet, add the kidneys, onion and garlic and cook for 3–4 minutes or until the kidneys are evenly browned.
2 Push the kidneys to one side of the pan, stir in the flour and cook for 2 minutes, gradually adding the bouillon and cream. Stir gently and reheat without boiling.
3 Season to taste and serve immediately.

CREAMED KIDNEYS IN WINE

SERVES 4

2 tablespoons butter	¼ cup all-purpose flour
12 lambs' kidneys, skinned, halved and cored	1¼ cups dry red wine
2 cups sliced mushrooms	1 teaspoon dry mustard
3 celery stalks, diced	salt and pepper
1 medium onion, minced	⅔ cup heavy cream

1 Melt the butter in a medium saucepan. Add the kidneys, mushrooms, celery and onion and fry gently for 10 minutes or until tender.
2 Stir in the flour and cook for 1–2 minutes. Gradually stir in the wine and mustard, then season to taste. Cook for a further 5 minutes. Stir in the cream and reheat gently without boiling.

TO MICROWAVE

Melt the butter in a large bowl on HIGH for 45 seconds. Add the kidneys, mushrooms, celery and onion. Cook, covered, on HIGH for 10 minutes. Stir in the flour and cook on HIGH for 1 minute. Gradually stir in the wine, mustard and salt and pepper. Cook on HIGH for 3 minutes or until boiling and thickened, stirring occasionally. Stir in the cream and cook on HIGH for 30 seconds.

KIDNEY AND MUSHROOM SAUTÉ

SERVES 3–4

1 pound lambs' kidneys, skinned, halved and cored	2 teaspoons whole grain mustard
1 tablespoon vegetable oil	1 garlic clove, crushed
2 tablespoons butter	salt and pepper
½ pound large flat mushrooms, sliced	chopped parsley, for garnish
2 tablespoons light cream	

1 Cut the kidney halves in half again.
2 Heat the oil and butter in a skillet, add the kidney pieces and sauté quickly until browned on all sides, turning frequently.
3 Stir in the mushrooms and cook for 1 minute, shaking the pan from time to time. Lower the heat and add the cream, mustard and garlic. Season to taste and heat through gently. Serve immediately, garnished with parsley.

CREAMED SWEETBREADS

SERVES 4

1 pound lamb's sweetbreads, thawed if frozen	3 tablespoons butter or margarine
1 small onion, chopped	¼ cup all-purpose flour
1 medium carrot, chopped	1¼ cups milk
a few fresh parsley stalks	a squeeze of lemon juice
1 bay leaf	chopped parsley, for garnish
salt and pepper	

1 Rinse and soak the sweetbreads in cold water for 2 hours. Drain and remove any fat.
2 Put the sweetbreads, vegetables and herbs in a saucepan with water to cover, season to taste, then simmer gently for about 15 minutes or until the sweetbreads are tender. Drain, reserving 1¼ cups of the cooking liquid, and keep hot.
3 Put the butter or margarine, flour, milk and reserved stock in a saucepan. Heat, whisking continuously, until the sauce thickens, boils and is smooth. Simmer for 1–2 minutes. Season to taste and add the lemon juice.
4 Add the sweetbreads to the sauce and simmer gently for 5–10 minutes. Garnish with parsley and serve at once.

—————————— COOK'S TIP ——————————

Sweetbreads, although considered a great delicacy, are not always readily available, so you may have to order them from your butcher. Soaking sweetbreads before use helps to keep them white. Frozen sweetbreads are now available.

CALF'S LIVER WITH GREEN GRAPES AND MADEIRA

SERVES 4

¼ cup butter	24 large green grapes, peeled, halved and seeded
½ cup minced onion or shallot	4 slices of calf's liver – each weighing about 3–4 ounces, trimmed
¾ cup chicken bouillon	
½ cup Madeira	4 sage leaves, thinly sliced
salt and freshly ground pepper	4 sage sprigs for garnish

1 Melt half the butter in a skillet and sauté the onion until golden. Add the bouillon and Madeira, season and bring to a boil. Boil rapidly for 4–5 minutes or until reduced and of a slightly syrupy consistency. Add the grape halves and warm through gently. Taste and adjust the seasoning.
2 Melt the remaining butter in a large skillet. Season the liver, and fry with the sliced sage leaves for 3–5 minutes, turning once.
3 Remove the liver from the pan and serve at once with the Madeira sauce. Garnish with sprigs of fresh sage.

SWEETBREADS WITH MUSHROOMS AND WHITE WINE

SERVES 4

1½ pounds lambs' sweetbreads, thawed if frozen	2 tablespoons butter
	1 tablespoon olive oil
salt and pepper	½ pound button mushrooms, halved or sliced if large
1 onion, chopped	
1 carrot, sliced	⅔ cup heavy cream
1 celery stalk, sliced	4 teaspoons chopped fresh basil or 1 teaspoon dried
1 bouquet garni	
1¼ cups dry white wine	basil sprigs, for garnish

1 Soak the sweetbreads in salted water for about 4 hours to remove traces of blood. Change the water frequently until the sweetbreads turn white. Drain and rinse.
2 Plunge the sweetbreads into a pan of boiling salted water and blanch for 2–3 minutes. Drain and cool.
3 Peel off the skin from the sweetbreads, then cut away all gristle and stringy tissue. Slice thinly and put in a saucepan with the onion, carrot, celery and bouquet garni. Pour in the wine and season.
4 Bring to a boil, then lower the heat, cover and simmer for 10 minutes or until the sweetbreads feel tender. Remove the sweetbreads from the pan, discard the vegetables and bouquet garni, then boil the liquid to reduce to ⅔ cup.
5 Heat the butter and oil in a heavy-based skillet and sauté the mushrooms for 2 minutes.
6 Add the sweetbreads to the pan and toss to mix with the mushrooms. Pour in the cooking liquid and bring to a boil, stirring. Lower the heat and slowly stir in the cream. Heat through gently, then stir in the basil and season. Transfer to a warmed serving dish, garnish and serve.

BRAISED OXTAIL

SERVES 4

salt and pepper	1 tablespoon tomato paste
2 tablespoons all-purpose flour	finely grated rind of ½ lemon
2 small oxtails (total weight about 3 pounds)	2 bay leaves
1 tablespoon butter	1¼ cups thickly sliced carrots
1 tablespoon vegetable oil	2½ cups cubed parsnips
2 large onions, sliced	chopped parsley, for garnish
4 cups beef bouillon	
⅔ cup dry red wine	

1 Season the flour with salt and pepper, add the oxtail pieces and toss until coated. Shake off and reserve any excess flour. Heat the butter and oil in a large Dutch oven, add the oxtail pieces, a few at a time and fry until browned. Remove with a slotted spoon.

2 Add the onions to the fat remaining in the pot and fry for 5 minutes or until lightly browned. Stir in any remaining flour, the bouillon, wine, tomato paste, lemon rind and bay leaves and season well. Bring to a boil and replace the meat. Cover and simmer for 3 hours, then skim well.

3 Stir the carrots and parsnips into the pot. Re-cover the pot and simmer for a further 30 minutes or until the meat is quite tender.

4 Skim all the fat from the surface of the pot, remove the bay leaves, adjust the seasoning and garnish with chopped parsley. Serve at once.

ORANGE OXTAIL STEW

SERVES 4

2 oranges	2 tablespoons vegetable oil
2 tablespoons all-purpose flour	1 onion, roughly chopped
2 teaspoons dried mixed herbs	2 celery stalks, sliced
salt and pepper	3 medium carrots, sliced
3 pounds oxtail, cut into pieces	1¼ cups hard cider
	2 bay leaves

1 Cut the rind of one orange into thin matchstick strips with a cannelle knife. Blanch in boiling water for 2 minutes, then drain and reserve. Finely grate the rind of the remaining orange. Squeeze the juice from both oranges.

2 Put the flour in a large plastic bag with the herbs and salt and pepper to taste. Shake well to mix. Add the oxtail, a few pieces at a time, and shake until evenly coated.

3 Heat the oil in a large Dutch oven, add as many pieces of oxtail as will fit on the base of the pot and fry over moderate heat until well browned. Remove with a slotted spoon and drain. Repeat with the remaining oxtail.

4 Add the onion, celery and carrots to the oil remaining in the pot and fry gently for about 10 minutes or until softened, stirring frequently. Pour in the cider, add the grated orange rind and orange juice and bring to a boil.

5 Return the oxtail pieces to the pot and pour in enough water to cover. Add the bay leaves, bring to a boil, then cover and cook in a preheated oven at 300°F for 3 hours. Cool, then chill overnight.

6 Next day, skim the fat from the pot and remove the bay leaves. Simmer on the hob until heated through, taste and season. Garnish with the reserved orange rind.

POULTRY AND GAME

Chicken is always popular, whether cooked as a roast or as tender breast fillets in a flavorsome sauce; turkey is almost as versatile and the ideal choice for entertaining, at any time of year. Game, such as pheasant, rabbit and venison, makes a welcome change.

GOLDEN BAKED CHICKEN

SERVES 4

4 chicken portions	1 tablespoon chopped fresh parsley and thyme or 1 teaspoon dried mixed herbs
salt and pepper	
1 cup fresh white breadcrumbs	¼ cup butter or margarine, melted
1 small onion, finely chopped	

1 Wipe the chicken pieces and season well with salt and pepper.
2 Mix the breadcrumbs with the onion and herbs.
3 Brush the chicken pieces all over with the butter or margarine, add them to the herbed breadcrumbs and turn until coated. Place in a buttered ovenproof dish.
4 Bake in a preheated oven at 375°F for about 1 hour or until golden. Baste occasionally during cooking. Serve hot, straight from the dish.

STIR-FRIED CHICKEN WITH ZUCCHINI

SERVES 4

2 tablespoons vegetable oil	1 sweet red pepper, cut into thin strips
1 garlic clove, crushed	
1 pound chicken breast fillets, skinned and cut into thin strips	3 tablespoons dry sherry
	1 tablespoon soy sauce
1 pound zucchini, cut into thin strips	¼ cup plain yogurt
	pepper

1 Heat the oil in a large skillet or wok, add the garlic and fry over gentle heat for 1 minute. Add the chicken and cook for 3–4 minutes, stirring continuously.
2 Add the zucchini and pepper and continue frying for 1–2 minutes or until the chicken is cooked and the vegetables are tender but still crisp.
3 Stir in the sherry and soy sauce and cook for 1 minute or until hot. Off the heat, stir in the yogurt and season to taste with pepper. Serve immediately.

CORNISH CAUDLE CHICKEN PIE

SERVES 4

¼ cup butter	⅔ cup milk
1 onion, finely chopped	⅔ cup dairy sour cream
four 4-ounce chicken legs, boned	4 ounces puff pastry, thawed if frozen
1 cup chopped parsley	beaten egg, to glaze
4 scallions, chopped	⅔ cup heavy cream
salt and pepper	1 egg, beaten

1 Melt half the butter and cook the onion until soft. Transfer to a 5-cup pie dish.

2 Add the remaining butter to the pan, add the chicken and cook until browned. Arrange on top of the onion.

3 Stir the parsley, scallions, salt and pepper to taste, milk and sour cream into the pan and bring to a boil. Simmer for 2–3 minutes, then pour over the chicken.

4 Cover the pie dish with foil and cook at 350°F for about 30 minutes. Let cool.

5 Roll out the pastry and use to cover the pie dish. Crimp the edges, make a small hole in the top and insert a funnel of aluminum foil.

6 Brush the top of the pie with beaten egg and bake at 425°F for 15–20 minutes or until brown. Reduce the temperature to 350°F.

7 Beat the cream into the egg, then strain into a pitcher and pour into the pie through the foil funnel. Remove the funnel, shake the dish to distribute the cream and return the pie to the oven for about 5 minutes.

8 Leave the pie to stand in a warm place for 5–10 minutes before serving warm, or let cool and serve cold.

SPICED ROAST CHICKEN

SERVES 4

4 pound oven-ready roasting chicken	4 garlic cloves, crushed
juice of 1 lemon	1 teaspoon mild paprika
2 teaspoons coriander seeds, finely crushed	1 teaspoon ground turmeric
½ teaspoon chili powder	1 teaspoon salt
1¼ cups plain yogurt	¼ cup ghee or melted butter
4 tablespoon chopped cilantro	cilantro and mint sprigs and lemon wedges, for garnish
4 tablepoons chopped mint	
2-inch piece of fresh root ginger, crushed	

1 Prick the skin of the chicken all over with a fine skewer. Mix together the lemon juice, coriander seeds and chili powder and brush over the chicken. Leave for 30 minutes.

2 Meanwhile, mix together the remaining ingredients, except the ghee or butter and the garnish.

3 Stand the chicken, breast side up, in a roasting pan. Brush with one quarter of the yogurt mixture. Roast in a preheated oven at 400°F for about 30 minutes or until the yogurt dries.

4 Turn the chicken over on its side and brush with another quarter of the yogurt mixture. Return to the oven for a further 30 minutes or until the yogurt dries again. Continue turning the chicken and brushing with yogurt twice more, until the chicken has been cooking for 2 hours.

5 Stand the chicken breast side up again, and brush with the ghee or butter. Increase the oven temperature to 425°F and roast the chicken for a further 15 minutes or until the juices run clear. Transfer to a warmed dish, garnish and serve.

STOVED CHICKEN

SERVES 4

2 tablespoons butter	2 large onions, sliced
1 tablespoon vegetable oil	salt and pepper
4 chicken quarters, halved	2 teaspoons chopped fresh thyme or ½ teaspoon dried
¼ pound Canadian bacon, chopped	2½ cups chicken bouillon
2½ pounds mealy potatoes, such as Idahos, peeled and cut into ¼-inch slices	chopped chives, for garnish

1 Heat half the butter and the oil in a large skilllet and sauté the chicken and bacon for 5 minutes or until lightly browned.

2 Place a thick layer of potato slices in the base of a large ovenproof casserole and cover with a layer of onion slices. Season well, add the thyme and dot with half the remaining butter.

3 Add the chicken and bacon, season to taste and dot with the remaining butter. Cover with the remaining onions and finally another layer of potatoes. Season and dot with butter. Pour over the bouillon.

4 Cover the casserole and bake in a preheated oven at 300°F for about 2 hours or until the chicken is tender and the potatoes are cooked, adding a little more hot bouillon if necessary.

5 Just before serving, sprinkle with chopped chives.

CHICKEN THIGHS WITH SPICY TOMATO SAUCE

SERVES 4

1 tablespoon butter	large pinch of chili powder
1 tablespoon vegetable oil	8 chicken thighs
1 medium onion, chopped	1-pound can tomatoes
1 garlic clove, crushed	1 tablespoon tomato paste
1 teaspoon ground cumin	salt and pepper
1 teaspoon ground coriander	2 tablespoons chopped fresh parsley

1 Heat the butter and oil in a large skillet, add the onion and garlic, cover and cook for 4–5 minutes or until the onion is softened. Add the cumin, coriander and chili powder and cook for 1 minute, stirring continously.

2 Push the onions to one side of the pan, then add the chicken and brown on both sides. Stir in the tomatoes and the tomato paste and season to taste.

3 Bring to a boil, stirring continuously. Cover and simmer gently for about 30 minutes or until the chicken is tender. Stir in the parsley and serve immediately.

———— TO MICROWAVE ————

Put all the ingredients, except the butter, oil, chicken and parsley, in a large bowl. Cover and cook on HIGH for 10 minutes. Meanwhile, melt the butter and oil in a skillet and brown the chicken on both sides. Add the chicken to the sauce, re-cover and cook on HIGH for 15 minutes or until the chicken is tender, stirring occasionally. Stir in the parsley and serve immediately.

SHREDDED CHICKEN WITH MUSHROOMS AND WALNUTS

SERVES 4

four 4-ounce chicken breast fillets, skinned and cut into thin strips	3 tablespoons vegetable oil
2-inch piece of fresh root ginger, thinly sliced	1 cup halved mushrooms
3 tablespoons soy sauce	¼ cucumber, cut into chunks
4 tablespoons dry sherry	¾ cup chopped walnut pieces
1 teaspoon five-spice powder	pepper

1 Put the chicken in a bowl with the ginger, soy sauce, sherry and five-spice powder. Stir well to mix, then cover and leave to marinate for at least 1 hour.

2 Remove the chicken from the marinade with a slotted spoon, reserving the marinade.

3 Heat the oil in a large skillet or wok. Add the chicken and cook for 3–4 minutes, stirring continuously.

4 Add the mushrooms, cucumber and walnuts and continue to cook for 1–2 minutes or until the chicken is cooked and the vegetables are tender but still crisp.

5 Stir in the reserved marinade and cook for 1 minute or until hot. Season to taste with pepper. Serve immediately.

────── **TO MICROWAVE** ──────

Complete steps 1 and 2. Put the chicken, oil, mushrooms, cucumber and walnuts in a large bowl. Cook on HIGH for 5–6 minutes, stirring frequently. Stir in the reserved marinade and cook on HIGH for 1 minute or until hot. Season to taste with pepper. Serve immediately.

GINGERED JAPANESE CHICKEN

SERVES 4

3 pound oven-ready broiler/fryer chicken	1 sweet red pepper, sliced
1 tablespoon all-purpose flour	⅔ cup chicken bouillon
1 tablespoon ground ginger	3 tablespoons soy sauce
¼ cup vegetable oil	3 tablespoons medium dry sherry
1 onion, sliced	salt and pepper
10-ounce can bamboo shoots, drained	1 cup sliced mushrooms

1 Cut all the flesh off the chicken and slice into chunky 'fingers', discarding the skin.

2 Mix the flour and ginger together in a plastic bag, add the chicken and toss to coat.

3 Heat the oil in a very large sauté pan or deep skillet and fry the chicken and sliced onion together for 10–15 minutes or until golden.

4 Cut the canned bamboo shoots into ½-inch strips. Add to the pan, together with the sliced pepper, then stir in the bouillon, soy sauce and sherry. Season to taste. Bring to a boil, cover and simmer for 15 minutes.

5 Add the sliced mushrooms, cover again and cook for a further 5–10 minutes or until the chicken is tender.

────── **COOK'S TIP** ──────

Bamboo shoots are used extensively in oriental cooking, although the Chinese and Japanese use fresh shoots rather than the canned version specified above. Canned bamboo shoots are available from specialist oriental food stores, large supermarkets and delicatessens. Look for those canned in water rather than vinegar as they have a milder flavor.

CHICKEN JULIENNE

SERVES 4

1 cup long grain rice	1 cup cooked green beans
3 tablespoons butter or margarine	pinch of dried thyme
	salt and pepper
6 tablespoons all-purpose flour	1 tablespoon chopped parsley
1¼ cups chicken bouillon	1 large carrot, cut into julienne strips, blanched and drained
1¼ cups milk	
¾ pound cooked chicken, cut into long narrow strips	¼ cup slivered almonds, toasted
2 tablespoons lemon juice	

1 Cook the rice in boiling salted water for about 10 minutes or until tender but not soft. Drain, set aside and keep hot.

2 Melt the butter or margarine in a pan, stir in the flour and cook gently for 1 minute, stirring. Remove from the heat and gradually stir in the bouillon and milk. Bring to a boil and continue to cook, stirring, until the sauce thickens.

3 Gently stir in the chicken, lemon juice, green beans and thyme. Season to taste and cook for 5–10 minutes or until heated through.

4 Add the parsley to the cooked rice and toss lightly. Make a border of rice on a serving dish and spoon the chicken into the center. Sprinkle with carrots and almonds.

VARIATION
Turkey Julienne
This is a good recipe for using up leftover cooked turkey. Substitute the same amount of turkey for the chicken in the above recipe.

CHICKEN VÉRONIQUE

SERVES 4

¼ cup butter	3 pound oven-ready roasting chicken
1 tablespoon chopped fresh tarragon or 2 teaspoons dried	1¼ pints chicken bouillon
	⅔ cup dry white wine
finely grated rind of 1 lemon	⅔ cup heavy cream
1 garlic clove, crushed	1½ cups seedless green grapes halved
salt and pepper	

1 Beat the butter in a bowl until soft, then mix in the tarragon, lemon rind and garlic. Season to taste. Put half the mixture in the cavity of the bird.

2 Truss the chicken. Spread the remaining butter mixture over the outside of the bird, then stand the bird on a rack in a roasting pan. Pour the chicken bouillon under the rack.

3 Roast the chicken in a preheated oven at 400°F for about 1¼ hours or until the juices run clear when the thickest part of a thigh is pierced with a skewer. Turn the bird and baste every 15 minutes.

4 Carve the chicken into neat portions, then arrange on a warmed serving platter, cover and keep warm.

5 To make the sauce, blot off any excess fat from the roasting pan with kitchen paper towels, then place the pan on the hob. Pour in the wine, then boil to reduce to about half, stirring to dislodge sediment.

6 Stir in the cream and continue simmering and stirring until thick, smooth and glossy. Add the grapes and heat through, then taste and adjust the seasoning.

7 Pour a little of the sauce over the chicken. Serve immediately, with the remaining sauce and grapes served in a warmed sauceboat.

CHICKEN WITH LEMON AND ALMONDS

SERVES 4

3 pound oven-ready roasting chicken	2 cups chicken bouillon
½ cup blanched almonds	1 cup sliced button mushrooms
1 lemon, thinly sliced	1 tablespoon cornstarch
1 garlic clove	¼ cup light cream
2 tablespoons butter, softened	watercress, for garnish
salt and pepper	

1 Wipe the chicken and loosen the skin all over the breast with your fingertips. Slip the almonds under the skin.
2 Stuff the lemon into the chicken cavity with the garlic. Truss or tie the bird securely.
3 Place the chicken in a roasting pan and spread the butter all over its surface. Season to taste. Pour the bouillon around the bird and roast in a preheated oven at 400°F for 1 hour, basting frequently.
4 Add the mushrooms to the roasting pan. Lay a piece of foil over the bird and continue cooking for a further 20 minutes or until the bird is tender.
5 Drain the bird and discard the lemon and garlic. Joint the chicken neatly so that each person has a breast and leg or thigh portion. Arrange on a platter.
6 Blend the cornstarch to a smooth paste with a little water and pour into the pan juices. Heat, stirring, until thickened. Add the cream and heat through without re-boiling. Adjust the seasoning and spoon over the chicken portions just before serving. Garnish with watercress.

CHICKEN WITH APRICOTS AND BRANDY

SERVES 4–6

4 or 6 chicken breast fillets, with skin on	1¼ cups chicken bouillon
3 tablespoons all-purpose flour, plus extra for dusting	salt and pepper
8 tablespoons butter	3 juniper berries (optional)
¼ cup dry white wine	⅔ cup no-soak dried apricots
1–2 tablespoons brandy	1 bay leaf
12 bacon slices, chopped	4–6 thick round slices of bread
1 cup sliced mushrooms	⅔ cup light cream
1 cup chopped onion	fresh parsley, for garnish

1 Dust the chicken with flour. Melt 3 tablespoons butter in a skillet, add the chicken and cook gently until browned. Transfer to a casserole. Add the wine and brandy to the pan, boil, then pour over the chicken.
2 Melt a further 3 tablespoons butter in the pan and sauté the bacon, mushrooms and onion for 5–10 minutes. Stir in 3 tablespoons flour, then gradually stir in the bouillon. Season and add the juniper berries, apricots and bay leaf.
3 Pour the sauce over the chicken, cover and cook at 325°F for about 1½ hours or until tender.
4 Melt the remaining butter in the pan and fry the bread until crisp. Drain and keep hot.
5 When the chicken is cooked, remove from the casserole and keep hot. Remove the bay leaf, then purée the sauce. Add the cream, adjust the seasoning and reheat.
6 Arrange a chicken breast on each croûton and place on a warmed serving platter. Spoon over some sauce and garnish.

CHICKEN WITH MUSHROOMS AND BACON

SERVES 4

2 tablespoons vegetable oil	1¼ cups chicken bouillon
12 bacon slices, chopped	1-pound can chopped tomatoes
1 medium onion, chopped	
1 garlic clove, crushed	1 bay leaf
1½ cups sliced button mushrooms	salt and pepper
	2 tablespoons chopped parsley, for garnish
4 chicken quarters, skinned	

1 Heat the oil in a large saucepan, add the bacon and sauté for 5 minutes or until crisp.

2 Add the onion, garlic and mushrooms to the pan and fry gently for 3–5 minutes or until the onion has softened. Add the chicken and fry for 8–10 minutes or until evenly browned, turning once.

3 Pour over the bouillon. Add the tomatoes with their juice and the bay leaf. Season to taste. Gradually bring to a boil, stirring occasionally. Simmer for 35–40 minutes or until tender.

4 Remove the bay leaf, transfer to a warmed serving dish and sprinkle with the chopped parsley.

--------------------- **TO MICROWAVE** ---------------------

Place the oil, bacon, onion and garlic in a large bowl, cover and microwave on HIGH for 5 minutes or until softened, stirring occasionally. Add the mushrooms, chicken, tomatoes, bay leaf and 1¼ cups boiling bouillon. Cover and microwave on HIGH for 20–25 minutes or until the chicken is tender and the juices run clear. Turn and rearrange the chicken portions twice during cooking. Complete step 4.

LEMON AND TURMERIC CHICKEN

SERVES 4

4 chicken breast fillets, skinned	6 tablespoons all-purpose flour
pared rind and juice of 1½ lemons	1 teaspoon ground turmeric, or to taste
1 onion, chopped	salt and pepper
½ teaspoon dried thyme	lemon slices and fresh parsley, for garnish
⅔ cup chicken bouillon	
1¼ cups milk	

1 Place the chicken breasts in a roasting pan. Sprinkle with a few curls of lemon rind, the onion and thyme. Add the lemon juice to the bouillon and pour around the chicken. Cover with foil and bake in a preheated oven at 375°F for about 45 minutes or until tender.

2 Remove the chicken from the pan and keep warm. Strain the stock into a liquid measure and add the milk. Mix the flour and turmeric with a little of the milk and bouillon mixture in a saucepan, then gradually add all the liquid. Bring slowly to a boil, stirring constantly, until the sauce thickens. Season to taste.

3 Place the chicken on a warmed serving dish and pour over the sauce. Garnish with lemon slices and parsley.

CHICKEN WITH TARRAGON SAUCE

SERVES 6

6 tablespoons butter or margarine	1 teaspoon chopped fresh tarragon or ½ teaspoon dried
6 chicken breast fillets, skinned	3 tablespoons grated Parmesan cheese
¼ cup all-purpose flour	salt and pepper
2 cups chicken bouillon	⅔ cup light cream
2 tablespoons tarragon vinegar	tarragon sprigs, for garnish
2 teaspoons Dijon mustard	

1 Melt 4 tablespoons butter or margarine in a skillet, add the chicken, cover and cook gently for about 20 minutes or until tender, turning once. Drain.

2 Meanwhile, melt the remaining butter or margarine in a saucepan, stir in the flour and gradually add the bouillon and vinegar. Stir in the mustard, tarragon and cheese, then bring to a boil. Season to taste and simmer for 3 minutes.

3 Remove from the heat and add the cream. Heat gently without boiling. To serve, place the chicken on a warmed serving dish, spoon over the sauce and garnish.

CHICKEN WITH SAFFRON

SERVES 6

salt and pepper	2 tablespoons dry white wine
2 tablespoons all-purpose flour	large pinch of saffron strands
six 6-ounce chicken breast fillets, skinned	2 egg yolks
3 tablespoons butter	¼ cup light cream
1 cup chicken bouillon	vegetable julienne, for garnish

1 Season the flour, add the chicken and turn until coated. Shake off and reserve any excess flour.

2 Melt the butter in a medium flameproof casserole, add the chicken pieces, half at a time, and fry for 5–10 minutes or until golden brown.

3 Return all the chicken pieces to the pan with any remaining flour and pour in the chicken bouillon and white wine.

4 Sprinkle in the saffron, pushing it down under the liquid. Bring to a boil, cover tightly and cook in a preheated oven at 350°F for about 50 minutes or until cooked

5 Lift the chicken out of the juices and place in a warmed serving dish. Cover and keep warm.

6 Strain the cooking juices into a small saucepan. Mix the egg yolks and cream together and stir into the cooking juices until evenly mixed.

7 Cook gently, stirring all the time, until the juices thicken slightly. Do not boil. To serve, adjust the seasoning of the sauce, spoon over the chicken and garnish with vegetable julienne. Serve immediately.

SPICED CHICKEN

SERVES 4

CHICKEN AND RED CURRANT CURRY

SERVES 4

6 tablespoons wholewheat flour	2 cups milk
1 teaspoon curry powder	4 tablespoons apple chutney
½ teaspoon cayenne	⅔ cup golden raisins
¾ pound boneless chicken, skinned and diced	⅔ cup dairy sour cream
3 tablespoons butter	½ teaspoon mild paprika
1 medium onion, chopped	

1 Mix the flour, curry powder and cayenne, add the chicken and toss until coated. Reserve any excess flour.

2 Melt the butter in a large saucepan, add the chicken and onion and fry for 5–6 minutes or until the chicken is brown and the onion is lightly colored.

3 Stir in the remaining flour, then gradually blend in the milk. Heat gently, stirring continuously, until the sauce thickens, boils and is smooth.

4 Add the chutney and raisins and simmer gently for 30–35 minutes or until the chicken is tender.

5 Remove the pan from the heat and drizzle with the cream. Sprinkle with the paprika and serve at once

——— TO MICROWAVE ———

Complete step 1. Cube the butter and melt in a large bowl on HIGH for 1 minute. Add the onion and cook on HIGH for 5 minutes. Add the chicken and cook on HIGH for 3–4 minutes, stirring occasionally. Stir in the flour. Gradually mix in the milk and cook on HIGH for 7–8 minutes, whisking frequently, until boiling and thickened. Add the chutney and golden raisins and cook on MEDIUM for 12–15 minutes or until the chicken is tender. Drizzle with the cream and sprinkle with paprika. Serve.

4 chicken leg portions	1 teaspoon chili powder
3 cups chopped onions	½ teaspoon ground turmeric
1-inch piece of fresh root ginger, finely chopped	2 tablespoons lemon juice
2 garlic cloves, crushed	⅓ cup currant jelly
2 tablespoons vegetable oil	¾–1 cup chicken bouillon
2 teaspoons ground cumin	salt and pepper
2 teaspoons ground coriander	2 bay leaves
	cilantro sprigs, for garnish

1 Cut the chicken legs into thighs and drumsticks. Remove skin and fat.

2 Put the onions, ginger and garlic in a blender or food processor and process until fairly smooth.

3 Heat the oil in a large heavy-based pan, add the onion paste and fry gently until golden. Add the chicken portions and fry until golden on all sides.

4 Add the cumin, coriander, chili, turmeric and lemon juice. Cook for 5 minutes or until the chicken pieces are evenly coated with spices, then stir in the currant jelly and bouillon. Season to taste, bring to a boil, add the bay leaves, cover and simmer for 45–50 minutes or until the chicken is tender.

5 Taste and adjust the seasoning, remove the bay leaves and garnish with cilantro just before serving.

HONEY BARBECUED CHICKEN

SERVES 4

¼ cup butter	1 tablespoon honey
1 cup finely chopped onions	salt and pepper
1 garlic clove, minced (optional)	⅔ cup long grain rice
1-pound can tomatoes	4 chicken drumsticks
2 tablespoons Worcestershire sauce	broiled mushrooms and tomatoes and parsley sprigs, for garnish

1 To make the barbecue sauce, combine the butter, onions, garlic (if using), tomatoes with their juice, Worcestershire and honey in a saucepan. Season to taste and cook gently for 30 minutes.

2 Meanwhile, cook the rice in boiling salted water for about 10 minutes or until tender but not soft. Drain, set aside and keep hot.

3 Place the chicken drumsticks in the broiler pan and brush liberally with the barbecue sauce. Cook under a preheated broiler for 10 minutes on each side, brushing frequently with more sauce.

4 Serve on a bed of rice garnished with broiled mushrooms and tomatoes and sprigs of parsley. Serve the remaining sauce separately.

CHEESE AND ANCHOVY BROILED CHICKEN BREASTS

SERVES 6

2-ounce can anchovy fillets in oil	6 chicken breast fillets, with skin on
2 tablespoons minced onion	vegetable oil, for brushing
1 teaspoon lemon juice	12–18 slices Mozzarella cheese

1 Drain 1 tablespoon of the oil from the anchovy can into a small saucepan. Chop the anchovies finely.

2 Heat the anchovy oil, add the anchovies and onion and cook for about 5 minutes or until a paste forms. Stir in the lemon juice, then remove from the heat and let cool.

3 Lift the skin from each chicken breast and rub 1 teaspoon of the anchovy mixture on the flesh underneath the skin.

4 Put the chicken pieces, skin side down, on to a rack placed over a broiler pan. Cook under a preheated moderate broiler for 35–40 minutes or until tender, turning once. Brush with oil occasionally during cooking, to moisten.

5 Cover the chicken breasts with slices of cheese and broil for a further 5 minutes, or until the cheese bubbles.

─────────── **COOK'S TIP** ───────────

If you find anchovies rather salty, soak them in milk for about 30 minutes, then drain before use.

CHICKEN SUPREMES IN WINE AND CREAM

SERVES 6

3 tablespoons red wine vinegar	1 tablespoon tomato paste
¼ cup sweet butter	1 large garlic clove, crushed
six 6-ounce French-style chicken supremes (with the wing bone attached), wiped and trimmed of excess skin	⅔ cup dry white wine
	1¼ cups chicken bouillon
	salt and pepper
	⅔ cup heavy cream
1 small onion, roughly chopped	chopped parsley, for garnish
1½ cups chopped tomatoes	

1 Place the vinegar in a small saucepan and boil to reduce by half. Heat the butter in a large sauté pan or deep skillet. Add the chicken pieces and cook until browned well on all sides. Remove from the pan with a slotted spoon.
2 Add the onion, tomatoes, tomato paste and garlic to the butter remaining in the pan, cover and cook gently for about 5 minutes.
3 Add the wine and cook, uncovered, over a high heat for 5–10 minutes or until the wine reduces by half. Add the vinegar and bouillon, season to taste and bring to a boil.
4 Replace the chicken, covering it with the sauce. Simmer gently, covered, for about 25 minutes or until the chicken is quite tender. Lift the chicken out of the pan with a slotted spoon and keep warm.
5 Boil the sauce until it is reduced by half, then stir in the cream. Continue reducing the sauce until a thin pouring consistency is obtained.
6 Adjust the seasoning, pass the sauce through a sieve and spoon over the chicken just before serving. Garnish with chopped parsley.

CHICKEN KIEV

SERVES 4

½ cup butter, softened	4 large chicken breast fillets, skinned
finely grated rind of ½ lemon	¼ cup all-purpose flour
1 tablespoon lemon juice	1 egg, beaten
1 tablespoon chopped parsley	2 cups fresh white breadcrumbs
1 garlic clove, crushed	vegetable oil, for deep-frying
salt and pepper	

1 Beat the butter until soft, then work in the lemon rind and juice, the parsley, garlic and salt and pepper to taste.
2 Place the butter on a sheet of wax paper or baker's parchment and form into a roll. Refrigerate until firm.
3 Meanwhile, place the chicken breasts on a wooden board and pound them to an even thickness with a meat mallet or rolling pin.
4 Cut the butter into four pieces and place one piece on each of the flattened chicken breasts. Roll up the chicken, folding the ends in to enclose the butter completely. Secure with wooden toothpicks.
5 Season the flour with salt and pepper, add the chicken and turn until coated. Dip in beaten egg, then in breadcrumbs. Pat the crumbs firmly so that the chicken is well coated. Chill for at least 1 hour or until required.
6 Heat the oil to 325°F. Place two chicken portions in a frying basket and carefully lower into the oil. Deep-fry for about 15 minutes, then drain on kitchen paper towels while frying the rest. Serve immediately.

CHICKEN AND BROCCOLI PIE

SERVES 4–6

2 tablespoons butter	1 pound boneless cooked chicken, cut into strips
2 carrots, diced	6 ounces broccoli, blanched
8 pearl onions, skinned	grated rind of ½ lemon
¼ pound button mushrooms	2 tablespoons light cream
¼ cup wholewheat flour	salt and pepper
2 cups milk, plus extra to glaze	½ pound frozen puff pastry, thawed

1 Melt the butter in a large saucepan, add the carrots, onions and mushrooms and fry lightly for 8 minutes, stirring occasionally.

2 Stir in the flour and cook for 1–2 minutes. Gradually add the milk, stirring continuously, until the sauce thickens, boils and is smooth. Simmer for 3–4 minutes.

3 Add the chicken, broccoli, lemon rind and cream to the sauce. Season to taste and pour into a 5-cup pie dish.

4 Roll out the pastry on a lightly floured surface to a round large enough to fit the dish. Cover the pie with the pastry and moisten the edges so the pastry is well sealed. Use any pastry trimmings to decorate. Brush with milk to glaze.

5 Bake in a preheated oven at 400°F for 25 minutes or until the crust is golden brown.

CHICKEN POT PIES

SERVES 4

1 lemon	6 ounces pearl onions, skinned
2½ pound oven-ready broiler/fryer chicken, with separate giblets	6 ounces button mushrooms, halved or sliced if large
a few sprigs of fresh tarragon	3 tablespoons all-purpose flour
1 bay leaf	¼ cup heavy cream
salt and pepper	13 ounces frozen puff pastry, thawed
2 leeks, sliced	a little beaten egg, to glaze
2 large carrots, thinly sliced	
3 tablespoons butter	

1 Prick the lemon all over with a skewer, then place inside the chicken. Put the chicken in a saucepan with the tarragon, bay leaf and seasoning. Add the giblets (except the liver), then pour in water to cover and bring to a boil. Simmer for 1¼ hours or until tender.

2 Thirty minutes before the end of cooking, add the leeks and carrots. Remove from the heat and leave to cool.

3 Remove the chicken from the cooking liquid. Cut the flesh from the bird, dice and set aside.

4 Melt the butter and lightly brown the onions.

5 Strain the chicken cooking liquid and reserve 1¼ cups. Add the mushrooms, leeks and carrots to the onions. Fry gently for 1–2 minutes, then add the chicken.

6 Mix the flour to a paste with the cream. Gradually blend in the reserved cooking liquid, then add to the chicken. Season. Simmer, stirring, for 2–3 minutes, then turn into four 1½-cup pie dishes.

7 Use the pastry to cover the pies. Brush with beaten egg. Bake at 400°F for 25 minutes or until the pastry is golden brown.

CORONATION CHICKEN

SERVES 8

5-pound roasting chicken, cooked	juice of ½ lemon
2 tablespoons butter	4 canned apricots, drained and finely chopped
1 small onion, finely chopped	1¼ cups mayonnaise
1 tablespoon curry paste	⅔ cup heavy cream
1 tablespoon tomato paste	salt and pepper
½ cup red wine	sliced cucumber, for garnish
1 bay leaf	

1 Remove all the flesh from the chicken and dice. Discard all skin and bones.

2 Heat the butter in a small saucepan, add the onion and cook for 3 minutes or until softened. Add the curry paste, tomato paste, wine, bay leaf and lemon juice. Simmer, uncovered, for about 10 minutes or until well reduced. Strain and cool.

3 Sieve the chopped apricots to produce a purée. Beat the cooked sauce into the mayonnaise with the apricot purée.

4 Whip the cream until softly stiff and fold into the mixture. Season to taste, adding a little more lemon juice if necessary.

5 Toss the chicken pieces into the sauce and garnish with sliced cucumber.

DEVILED SQUABS

SERVES 6

1 tablespoon dry mustard	1 tablespoon lemon juice
1 tablespoon mild paprika	⅓ cup butter, melted
4 teaspoons ground turmeric	three 1½-pound squabs or Rock Cornish game hens
4 teaspoons ground cumin	1 tablespoon poppy seeds
¼ cup ketchup	

1 Spoon the dry mustard, paprika, turmeric and cumin into a small bowl. Add the ketchup and lemon juice and beat well to form a thick, smooth paste. Slowly pour in the melted butter, stirring all the time.

2 Place the squabs or game hens on a chopping board, breast side down. With a small sharp knife, cut right along the backbone of each bird through skin and flesh.

3 With scissors, cut through the backbone to open the birds up. Turn the birds over, breast side up.

4 Continue cutting along the breast bone, splitting the birds into two equal halves.

5 Lie the birds, skin side uppermost, on a large edged baking sheet. Spread the spice paste evenly over the surface of the birds and sprinkle with the poppy seeds. Cover loosely with plastic wrap and leave in a cool place for at least 1–2 hours.

6 Cook the birds (uncovered on the baking sheet) in a preheated oven at 425°F for 15 minutes.

7 Remove the birds from the oven and place under a preheated hot broiler until the skin is well browned and crisp.

8 Return to the oven, reduce the temperature to 350°F and cook for a further 20 minutes or until the birds are tender. Serve immediately.

BONED STUFFED SQUABS

SERVES 6

three 1½ pound squabs or Rock Cornish game hens boned (bones reserved)	3 cups fresh white breadcrumbs
2 large onions, skinned	juice and grated rind of 1 lemon
1 carrot	2 small eggs, beaten
1 bay leaf	pepper
6 black peppercorns	⅔ cup dry white wine
salt	1 tablespoon cornstarch
½ cup butter	a dash of gravy coloring
1½ cups chopped nuts	
two 8-ounce packets frozen chopped spinach, thawed	

1 To make the stock, place the bones, 1 onion, quartered, the carrot, bay leaf, peppercorns and a little salt in a pan. Add 4 cups water and simmer, uncovered, for 30 minutes. Strain and reserve 2½ cups.

2 Chop the remaining onion. Heat ¼ cup butter, fry the onion and nuts for 2–3 minutes, then add the spinach. Cool slightly, then add the breadcrumbs, lemon juice and rind, egg to bind and seasoning.

3 Lay the birds flesh side up and divide the stuffing among them. Fold the skin over and sew up. Push a skewer through the leg and wing joints and tie the knuckle ends together. Place in a roasting pan and spread over the remaining butter. Pour over half the stock and the wine. Roast at 400°F for 1 hour.

4 Remove the skewers and twine and cut each bird in half lengthwise. Place on a serving dish. Mix the cornstarch with a little water and add to the pan with the stock. Cook for 2 minutes, season, add gravy coloring and serve.

ROAST TURKEY

SERVES 6–12

	FOR THE HERB STUFFING
6–8 pound oven-ready turkey, thawed if frozen	3 large onions, chopped
1 onion, skinned	⅓ cup butter
1 lemon wedge	3 cups fresh breadcrumbs
butter	3 tablespoons chopped fresh parsley
salt and pepper	salt and pepper
lemon juice	

1 Wash the turkey inside and out, and dry thoroughly.

2 To make the stuffing, fry the onion in the butter until softened, then stir in the remaining ingredients and mix well. Use to stuff the neck end only of the turkey. Fold the neck skin over and truss to secure.

3 Place the bird in a large roasting pan and place the onion, lemon wedge and a knob of butter inside the body. Spread butter over the turkey skin and season well with salt, pepper and a squeeze of lemon juice. Roast in a preheated at 350°F for 2–3 hours. To test if the turkey is cooked, pierce the deepest part of the thigh with a skewer. If the juices that run out are colorless, the bird is cooked; if pink-tinged cook a little longer.

4 Transfer the turkey to a warmed serving platter and leave to rest before carving. Serve with gravy and bread sauce. Small sausage links, rolls of bacon and watercress may be used to garnish the turkey. Cranberry sauce is the traditional accompaniment.

ROAST TURKEY WITH LEMON STUFFING

8–11¼ POUND SERVES 10–15; 11¼–15 POUND
SERVES 15–20; 15–20 POUND SERVES 20–30

2 tablespoons butter	finely grated rind of 2 lemons
2 medium onions, finely chopped	salt and pepper
2 celery stalks, finely chopped	1 egg, beaten
4 cups wholewheat breadcrumbs	1 oven-ready turkey, thawed if frozen
4 tablespoons chopped parsley	bacon slices

1 To make the stuffing, melt the butter in a large saucepan, add the onions and celery, cover and cook gently for about 10 minutes or until very soft, stirring occasionally.
2 Remove from the heat and add the breadcrumbs, parsley and lemon rind. Season to taste and stir in the egg.
3 Wash the inside of the bird and stuff at the neck end only before folding the neck skin over. Make the turkey plump and as even in shape as possible, then truss it with the wings folded under the body and the legs tied together.
4 Weigh the turkey and calculate the cooking time, allowing 20 minutes per pound plus 20 minutes.
5 Place the turkey in a roasting pan, then sprinkle with salt and pepper.
6 Place the bacon slices over the breast to prevent it from becoming dry. Roast in a preheated oven at 350°F, basting occasionally. Put a piece of foil over the bird if it shows signs of becoming too brown.
7 Let the turkey rest for 10 minutes, then carve. Serve with thin gravy, bread sauce, small sausage links and bacon rolls.

TURKEY BREAST WITH ASPARAGUS

SERVES 4

½ pound thin asparagus spears	1 tablespoon vegetable oil
two ½ pound turkey breast fillets, skinned and halved	1¼ cups chicken bouillon
2 tablespoons all-purpose flour	1 teaspoon chopped fresh sage or ¼ teaspoon dried
salt and pepper	¼ cup dry white wine
1 tablespoon butter	⅔ cup dairy sour cream

1 Cut off the ends of the asparagus if they are tough and woody. Trim them all to the same length, cut off the tips and cut the spears into three pieces.
2 Put the turkey pieces on a wooden board and beat out slightly with a rolling pin or meat mallet. Season the flour with salt and pepper, add the turkey pieces and turn until coated. Shake off any excess flour. Heat the butter and oil in a large skillet, add the turkey and fry until lightly browned on both sides. Add the chicken bouillon, asparagus spears, reserving the tips, the sage and wine, cover and cook gently for 15–20 minutes or until tender.
3 Five minutes before the end of the cooking time, add the reserved asparagus tips and the cream. Season to taste.

TURKEY SCALLOPS WITH DAMSONS

SERVES 4

two ½-pound turkey breast fillets, skinned and cut widthwise into 2-inch slices	1 teaspoon chopped fresh thyme or ¼ teaspoon dried
⅓ cup unsweetened apple cider	1 tablespoon butter
3 tablespoons soy sauce	1 tablespoon vegetable oil
3 tablespoons dry sherry	½ pound damsons, halved and pitted
1 small garlic clove, crushed	pepper

1 Place the turkey slices between two sheets of dampened baker's parchment and beat out with a rolling pin or meat mallet until about 1-inch thick.

2 Place the turkey slices in a large shallow dish and pour over the apple cider, soy sauce, sherry, garlic and thyme. Cover and leave in the refrigerator to marinate for 3–4 hours or overnight.

3 Remove the turkey from the marinade, reserving the marinade. Heat the butter and oil in a skillet, add the turkey and fry quickly until browned on both sides. Add the damsons, reserved marinade and pepper to taste.

4 Cover and simmer gently for 10–15 minutes or until tender, stirring occasionally.

VARIATION

Turkey Scallops with Plums

Substitute plums for damsons in the above recipe if damsons are not available.

TURKEY SCALLOPS WITH HAZELNUT CREAM SAUCE

SERVES 4

1 pound turkey breast fillets, thinly sliced	⅓ cup finely chopped hazelnuts
¼ cup butter	salt and pepper
¼ cup sweet sherry	mild paprika, for garnish
¼ cup heavy cream	

1 Place the turkey slices between two sheets of dampened baker's parchment and beat out with a rolling pin or meat mallet into small scallops.

2 Melt the butter in a skillet and cook the scallops quickly for 4–5 minutes, turning once. Remove from the pan and keep warm.

3 Reduce the heat and stir the sherry, cream and hazelnuts into the pan. Season to taste and cook, stirring, for 1 minute. Pour over the scallops and serve immediately with a light dusting of paprika.

TURKEY SCALLOPS WITH CRANBERRY AND COCONUT

SERVES 4

1 pound turkey breast fillets, skinned	1 egg, beaten
salt and pepper	3 tablespoons flaked coconut
4 teaspoons Dijon mustard	⅔ cup fresh breadcrumbs
¼ cup cranberry sauce	¼ cup butter or margarine
2 tablespoons all-purpose flour	

1 Thinly slice the turkey breasts to give four portions.
2 Place the turkey pieces between two sheets of dampened baker's parchment and beat out with a rolling pin or meat mallet to make thin scallops. Season to taste, then spread each portion with mustard and cranberry sauce.
3 Roll up the scallops, starting from the thin end, and secure with a toothpick. Dust each portion with flour, then brush with egg. Combine the coconut and breadcrumbs, then coat the turkey scallops with the mixture.
4 Melt the butter or margarine in a skillet, add the turkey portions, and fry until brown on both sides. Transfer to a baking pan just large enough to take the turkey in a single layer and baste with more fat. Bake in a preheated oven at 350°F for about 40 minutes or until the turkey is tender.

COOK'S TIP

Cranberry sauce is traditionally associated with turkey. The fresh fruit have a limited season (September to February) but they can also be bought frozen or canned throughout the year. The sauce is available bottled, from supermarkets.

TURKEY SAUTÉ WITH LEMON AND WALNUTS

SERVES 4

1 pound turkey breast fillets, skinned	¼ cup chicken bouillon
2 tablespoons cornstarch	2 tablespoons lemon juice
2 tablespoons vegetable oil	3 tablespoons lemon marmalade
1 sweet green pepper, thinly sliced	1 teaspoon white wine vinegar
⅓ cup walnut halves or pieces	¼ teaspoon soy sauce
2 tablespoon butter	salt and pepper

1 Cut the turkey flesh into 2-inch pencil thin strips. Add to the cornstarch and toss until coated.
2 Heat the oil in a large sauté pan or deep skillet, add the pepper strips and walnuts and fry for 2–3 minutes. Remove from the pan with a slotted spoon.
3 Add the butter to the oil remaining in the pan and fry the turkey strips for 10 minutes or until golden. Add the bouillon and lemon juice, stirring well to scrape up any sediment at the bottom of the pan. Add the lemon marmalade, vinegar and soy sauce. Season to taste.
4 Return the walnuts and green pepper to the pan. Cook gently for a further 5 minutes or until the turkey is tender. Taste and adjust the seasoning and serve immediately.

VARIATION

Turkey Sauté with Orange and Walnuts
Substitute 2 tablespoons orange juice and 3 tablespoons orange marmalade for the lemon juice and marmalade in the above recipe. Garnish with thin slices or wedges of orange.

CASSEROLED TURKEY IN RED WINE

SERVES 4

2 tablespoons butter	1 bay leaf
2 tablespoons vegetable oil	⅔ cup red wine
1½ pounds turkey casserole meat	salt and pepper
12 bacon slices, diced	12 pearl onions or shallots, skinned
2 tablespoons all-purpose flour	chopped fresh parsley and pastry crescents or croûtons, for garnish
good pinch of dried thyme	

1 Heat half the butter with half the oil in a large skillet. When foaming, add the turkey meat and fry until well browned. Remove with a slotted spoon and place in a casserole.
2 Add the bacon to the fat remaining in the skillet and fry until beginning to brown. Remove the bacon with a slotted spoon and add to the turkey.
3 Stir the flour, thyme and bay leaf into the fat in the skillet and cook gently for a few minutes. Slowly stir in the red wine and 1¼ cups water. Season to taste. Bring to a boil, stirring, then pour over the turkey.
4 Cover the casserole tightly and cook in a preheated oven at 300°F for about 2 hours.
5 Thirty minutes before the end of the cooking time, melt the remaining butter and oil in a skillet. Add the onions or shallots and cook slowly until golden brown and tender. Add the onions to the casserole, re-cover and cook for a further 20 minutes. Garnish with parsley and pastry crescents or croûtons and serve hot.

TURKEY IN SPICED YOGURT

SERVES 6

about 2½ pounds turkey leg meat on the bone	2 tablespoons lemon juice
1½ teaspoons ground cumin	3 tablespoons corn oil
1½ teaspoons ground coriander	2 cups sliced onion
½ teaspoon ground turmeric	3 tablespoons flaked coconut
½ teaspoon ground ginger	2 tablespoons all-purpose flour
salt and pepper	⅔ cup chicken bouillon
1¼ cups plain yogurt	chopped parsley, for garnish

1 Cut the turkey meat off the bone into large fork-size pieces, discarding the skin. There should be about 2 pounds of meat.
2 In a large bowl, mix the spices with the seasoning, yogurt and lemon juice. Stir well until evenly blended
3 Fold the turkey meat into the yogurt mixture, turning until coated. Cover tightly with plastic wrap and refrigerate for several hours.
4 Heat the oil in a medium flameproof casserole, add the onion and fry for 5–10 minutes or until lightly browned. Add the coconut and flour and fry gently, stirring, for about 1 minute.
5 Remove from the heat and stir in the turkey with its marinade and the bouillon. Return to the heat and bring slowly to a boil, stirring all the time. Cover tightly and cook in a preheated oven at 325°F for 1–1¼ hours or until the turkey is tender.
6 Adjust the seasoning and serve garnished with parsley.

QUICK TURKEY CURRY

SERVES 4–6

2 tablespoons vegetable oil	½ teaspoon chili powder
3 bay leaves	salt and pepper
2 cardamom pods, crushed	½ cup unsalted cashews
1 cinnamon stick, broken into short lengths	1½ pounds turkey breast fillets, skinned and cut into bite-size pieces
1 medium onion, thinly sliced	2 medium potatoes, blanched, peeled and cut into chunks
1 sweet green pepper, chopped (optional)	4 tomatoes, peeled and chopped
2 teaspoons mild paprika	bay leaves, for garnish
1½ teaspoons garam masala	
½ teaspoon ground turmeric	

1 Heat the oil in a Dutch oven, add the bay leaves, cardamom and cinnamon and fry over a moderate heat for 1–2 minutes. Add the onion and green pepper (if using), with the spices and salt and pepper to taste. Pour in enough water to moisten, then stir to mix for 1 minute.

2 Add the cashews and turkey, cover and simmer for 20 minutes. Turn the turkey occasionally during this time to ensure even cooking.

3 Add the potatoes and tomatoes and continue cooking for a further 20 minutes or until the turkey and potatoes are tender. Taste and adjust the seasoning before serving. Garnish with bay leaves.

TURKEY TETRAZZINI

SERVES 6

½ pound spaghetti	¼ teaspoon grated nutmeg
6 tablespoons butter or margarine	salt and pepper
3 tablespoons all-purpose flour	1 cup sliced button mushrooms
1¼ cups hot turkey or chicken bouillon	¾-1 pound cooked turkey, sliced or cut into bite-size pieces
½ cup heavy cream	2 tablespoons grated Parmesan cheese
3 tablespoons dry sherry	

1 Cook the spaghetti in boiling salted water for about 11 minutes or until just tender.

2 Meanwhile, make the sauce. Melt half the butter or margarine in a heavy-based saucepan, sprinkle in the flour and stir over gentle heat for 1–2 minutes. Gradually stir in the hot bouillon, then bring to a boil. Simmer, stirring all the time, until thick and smooth.

3 Remove the sauce from the heat and leave to cool for about 5 minutes, then stir in the cream, sherry and nutmeg. Season to taste.

4 Melt the remaining butter or margarine in a separate pan. Add the mushrooms and fry gently until soft.

5 Drain the spaghetti and arrange half of it in the base of a greased baking dish.

6 Arrange the turkey and mushrooms over the top. Cover with the remaining spaghetti, then coat with the sauce.

7 Sprinkle with the Parmesan and bake in a preheated oven at 375°F for 30 minutes or until golden and bubbling.

STUFFED TURKEY LEGS

SERVES 6

2 turkey legs (drumsticks) (at least 2 pounds total weight)	¼ cup all-purpose flour
½ pound bulk pork sausage	1 egg white, beaten
1 tablespoon chopped fresh tarragon or ½ teaspoon dried	3 cups fresh white breadcrumbs
2 teaspoons chopped parsley	½ cup butter or margarine, softened
salt and pepper	1 tablespoon Dijon mustard
½ cup sliced button mushrooms	watercress, for garnish

1 Skin the turkey legs, slit the flesh and carefully ease out the bone and large sinews.

2 Mix the bulk sausage and herbs, season to taste and spread one quarter of the mixture over each boned leg. Cover with a layer of sliced mushrooms, then top with more sausage stuffing.

3 Reshape the stuffed turkey legs, then sew them up neatly, using fine twine.

4 Dip the legs in flour, brush with beaten egg white and place, seam side down, in a greased roasting pan.

5 Beat together the breadcrumbs, butter or margarine and mustard. Spread over the tops and sides only of the legs.

6 Bake in a preheated oven at 375°F for about 1 hour 40 minutes or until the turkey is tender with a crisp, golden crust. Remove the twine, slice, and serve garnished with watercress.

TURKEY BALLS WITH CRANBERRY AND ORANGE SAUCE

SERVES 4

1 tablespoon butter	1½ cups fresh breadcrumbs
1 onion, chopped	
1 garlic clove, crushed	FOR THE SAUCE
2 tablespoons chopped fresh thyme or 2 teaspoons dried	¼ cup superfine sugar
	⅔ cup fresh orange juice
¾ pound lean ground turkey	1½ cups fresh cranberries
	1 teaspoon grated orange rind

1 Melt the butter in a small saucepan. Add the onion, garlic and thyme and sauté for 3–5 minutes, then leave to cool.

2 Place the turkey and breadcrumbs in a medium bowl, add the onion mixture and mix thoroughly.

3 Divide the mixture into walnut-size balls and place on a lightly greased baking sheet. Bake in a preheated oven at 400°F for 30–40 minutes or until cooked through.

4 Meanwhile, to make the sauce, place the sugar and fresh orange juice in a medium saucepan and heat gently, stirring, until the sugar has dissolved. Add the cranberries and grated orange rind and bring to a boil. Cover and simmer for 5–10 minutes or until the cranberries have softened. Serve with the turkey balls.

TURKEY AND BACON KABOBS

SERVES 4

2 tablespoons cranberry sauce	salt and pepper
6 tablespoons vegetable oil	1½ pounds boneless turkey scallops
3 tablespoons fresh orange juice	1 small onion
1 garlic clove, crushed	6 bacon slices, halved
½ teaspoon ground allspice	1 large sweet red pepper, cut into chunks

1 Put the cranberry sauce, oil and orange juice in a shallow dish with the garlic, allspice and seasoning to taste. Whisk with a fork until well combined.

2 Cut the turkey into bite-size pieces and place in the dish. Stir to coat in the oil and orange juice mixture, then cover and leave to marinate for at least 4 hours, stirring occasionally.

3 Cut the onion into squares or even-size chunks. Form the bacon slices into small rolls. Drain the turkey from the marinade, reserving the marinade.

4 Thread the turkey, onion and red pepper onto oiled skewers with the bacon, dividing the ingredients as evenly as possible.

5 Cook under a preheated moderate broiler for about 20 minutes, turning the skewers frequently and basting with the remaining marinade. Serve hot.

--- COOK'S TIP ---

Don't be tempted to reduce the marinating time suggested above as the longer the turkey is marinated the more tender and succulent it will be. If marinating in the refrigerator overnight, allow the turkey to come to room temperature before broiling.

MARINATED TURKEY WITH ASPARAGUS

SERVES 4–6

2 pounds turkey breast fillets	4 teaspoons ground ginger
4 cups chicken bouillon	2 cups French dressing
salt and pepper	1 pound fresh asparagus, scraped and trimmed
2 tablespoons chopped parsley	1 teaspoon salt
½ cup chopped walnuts	celery leaves, for garnish
1 garlic clove, crushed	

1 Put the turkey fillets in a large saucepan and add enough chicken bouillon to cover. Season to taste. Poach for about 20 minutes or until tender. Leave to cool in the liquid.

2 Meanwhile, to make the marinade, stir the parsley, walnuts, garlic and ginger into the French dressing.

3 Tie the asparagus spears into two neat bundles. Wedge upright in a large deep saucepan and cover the tips with foil.

4 Pour in enough boiling water to come three-quarters of the way up the asparagus spears. Add salt, return to a boil, lower the heat and simmer gently for about 10 minutes.

5 Lift the bundles carefully out of the water, place in a dish and remove the twine. While still hot, pour over half the dressing. Leave the asparagus to cool.

6 Cut the turkey into ¼-inch wide strips. Marinate in the remaining dressing for 3–4 hours.

7 To serve, arrange the turkey strips and asparagus in a serving dish and garnish with celery leaves. Serve chilled.

DUCKLING WITH GREEN PEAS

SERVES 4

4½ pound oven-ready duckling	3 cups fresh or frozen peas
salt and pepper	few sprigs of fresh herbs, such as savory, thyme or mint
16 pickling or small onions, chopped	
6 bacon slices, diced	¼ cup chicken bouillon

1 Weigh the duckling, prick the skin all over with a sharp skewer or fork and rub with salt. Place the duckling on a wire rack or trivet in a roasting pan and roast in a preheated oven at 350°F for 30–35 minutes per pound.

2 Thirty minutes before the end of the cooking time, drain off the fat from the roasting pan, transferring 2 tablespoons of it to a saucepan, and discarding the remainder. Add the onions to the pan and cook, turning frequently, until lightly browned. Add the bacon and cook for 2 minutes or until the fat starts to run.

3 If using fresh peas, blanch them for 3 minutes in boiling water, then refresh and drain well. Do not blanch frozen peas. Mix the peas with the onions, bacon and herbs and season to taste with pepper.

4 Stir the bouillon into the sediment in the roasting pan, then stir in the pea mixture. Return the duckling to the roasting pan, still on the rack, and continue cooking for the remaining 30 minutes. Serve the duckling on a large platter surrounded by the vegetables and cooking juice.

ROAST DUCK WITH APPLE STUFFING

SERVES 4

1 tablespoon butter	salt and pepper
1 celery stalk, finely chopped	1 egg, beaten
2 small onions, chopped	4 pound oven-ready duckling (with separate giblets)
2 cups fresh white breadcrumbs	
1 small dessert apple, peeled, cored and grated	1 bay leaf
	1 tablespoon all-purpose flour
1 tablespoon chopped fresh sage or 1 teaspoon dried	watercress, for garnish

1 Melt the butter in a saucepan, add the celery and half the chopped onions and sauté gently for about 5 minutes.

2 Mix the breadcrumbs, apple, sage, celery and onion. Season, then bind with egg. Cool for 15 minutes.

3 Stuff the neck cavity of the duck with the apple stuffing, then sew or truss the duck to keep in the stuffing.

4 Weigh the stuffed duck and calculate the cooking time, allowing 30–35 minutes per pound. Put the duck on a wire rack in a roasting pan. Prick the skin of the duck all over and sprinkle with salt and pepper. Roast at 350°F for the calculated time.

5 To make the gravy, put the giblets in a saucepan with the remaining onion, 2½ cups water, the bay leaf and seasoning. Simmer for 1 hour, then strain.

6 When the duck is cooked, remove from the pan and keep warm. Pour off any excess fat from the pan, leaving about 2 tablespoons. Transfer to the hob and blend in the flour. Cook until browned, stirring continuously. Stir in the stock and boil, stirring. Taste and season.

7 To serve, joint the duck into four portions and arrange on a warmed dish. Pour gravy round, garnish and serve.

DUCKLING ROULADES WITH PEACHES

SERVES 6

six ¾-pound duckling wing portions, skinned	¼ cup chopped hazelnuts
slices of onion and carrot	2 firm, ripe peaches, skinned and chopped
1 bay leaf	2 tablespoons brandy
salt and pepper	1 cup wholewheat breadcrumbs
5 tablespoons butter	2 tablespoons all-purpose flour
1 small onion, finely chopped	

1 Carefully fillet the duckling flesh in one piece away from the breastbone. Place the breast meat between two sheets of dampened baker's parchment and beat out thinly. Cut any meat off the wings, chop finely and set aside.

2 To make the stock, place the wing bones in a saucepan with the slices of onion and carrot, the bay leaf and seasoning. Just cover with water and bring to a boil. Simmer, uncovered, for 30–40 minutes or until about 1¼ cups stock remains. Strain the stock.

3 To make the stuffing, melt 2 tablespoons butter in a skillet and sauté the onion, chopped duckling flesh and hazelnuts for 3–4 minutes, turning frequently. Stir in the peaches and sauté until soft. Remove from the heat, stir in the brandy, breadcrumbs and seasoning, and cool.

4 Divide the stuffing among the duckling fillets and roll up tightly. Secure with wooden toothpicks, then sprinkle with flour.

5 Melt the remaining butter in a large flameproof casserole and cook the duckling rolls until lightly browned. Sprinkle in any remaining flour, then pour in 1¼ cups stock. Season to taste. Bring to a boil, cover and bake in the oven at 350°F for 40 minutes. Adjust the seasoning and skim the juices before serving.

DUCKLING WITH BRANDY AND GREEN PEPPERCORN SAUCE

SERVES 6

6 duckling portions	2 tablespoons all-purpose flour
salt and pepper	1¼ cups chicken bouillon
3 large oranges	2 tablespoons brandy
3 tablespoons vegetable oil	a dash of gravy coloring
1 onion, chopped	
2 tablespoons green peppercorns, lightly crushed	

1 Wipe the duckling portions all over and pat dry with kitchen paper towels. Place on a rack in a roasting pan.

2 Prick the skin well with a fork and sprinkle with salt. Roast in a preheated oven at 350°F for about 1 hour or until the juices run clear, basting occasionally.

3 Meanwhile, to make the sauce, remove the rind from one orange and cut it into fine shreds. Blanch in boiling water for 1 minute, then drain. Squeeze the juice from the orange and reserve. Thinly slice the remaining oranges.

4 Heat the oil in a medium saucepan, add the chopped onion and fry gently until golden.

5 Stir in the lightly crushed peppercorns and flour and cook gently, stirring, for 1–2 minutes. Blend in the bouillon with the orange juice. Season to taste and bring to a boil, stirring all the time, then simmer for about 4 minutes.

6 Warm the brandy slightly in a small saucepan, ignite and, when the flames die down, add to the sauce with a dash of gravy coloring and a few orange shreds. Adjust the seasoning.

7 Heat the sauce to boiling point and pour into a warmed sauceboat. Garnish the duckling portions with orange slices and the remaining orange shreds.

DUCK WITH CUMBERLAND SAUCE

SERVES 4

4 duckling portions	4 tablespoons currant jelly
salt and pepper	2 teaspoons cornstarch
finely shredded rind and juice of 1 large orange	¼ cup port
	2 tablespoons brandy
finely shredded rind and juice of 1 lemon	lemon balm sprigs, for garnish

1 Prick the duckling portions all over with a sharp skewer or fork, then sprinkle with salt and pepper.

2 Place the duckling portions on a wire rack in a roasting pan and roast in a preheated oven at 375°F for 45–60 minutes or until the skin is crisp and the juices run clear when the thickest parts of the duckling portions are pricked with a skewer.

3 Meanwhile, to make the sauce, put the orange and lemon juices in a small saucepan, add the shreds of orange and lemon rind, cover and simmer gently for 5 minutes.

4 Add the currant jelly to the citrus juices and let it melt slowly over a gentle heat. Mix the cornstarch with the port, then stir into the sauce and bring to a boil, stirring, until the sauce thickens.

5 When the duckling portions are cooked, put them on a warmed serving dish and keep hot while you finish the sauce. Pour off the fat from the roasting pan, leaving the cooking juices behind. Add the brandy and stir over a gentle heat, scraping up the sediment from the bottom of the pan.

6 Add the sauce to the brandy, stir well and serve with the duckling. Garnish with lemon balm.

DUCK JULIENNE EN CROÛTE

SERVES 4

2 tablespoons butter	2 carrots, peeled
2 garlic cloves, crushed	2 zucchini
2 tablespoons chopped fresh parsley or 2 teaspoons dried	1 pound frozen puff pastry, thawed
	salt and pepper
four 7-ounce duckling breasts, boned and skinned	1 egg, beaten

1 Melt the butter in a large skillet, add the garlic and parsley and fry for 2 minutes. Add the duck breasts and fry until browned. Drain and cool.

2 Cut the carrots and zucchini into thin 2-inch strips. Blanch in boiling water for 1–2 minutes, then drain and rinse under cold running water.

3 Roll out one third of the pastry to a 16 x 6-inch rectangle. Divide into four 4 x 6-inch bases and place on a lightly greased baking sheet. Roll the remaining two thirds to a 20 x 6-inch rectangle. Divide into four 5 x 6-inch lids.

4 Divide the vegetables among the bases, leaving a ¼-inch border. Place the duck breasts on the vegetables and season well. Brush the border with egg. Add the lids and seal.

5 Brush with beaten egg and bake in a preheated oven at 400°F for 45–55 minutes.

TO MICROWAVE

Complete step 1. Cut the carrots and zucchini into thin 2-inch strips. Place in a medium bowl and cover with boiling water. Cook on HIGH for 1–1½ minutes, drain and rinse under cold running water. Complete steps 3–5, baking the filled pastry cases conventionally.

DUCK WITH MANGO

SERVES 4

1 ripe, but still firm mango	½ teaspoon ground allspice
four 10-ounce duckling portions	3 tablespoons plum jam
¼ cup peanut oil	4 teaspoons wine vinegar
	salt and pepper

1 Skin and thickly slice the mango on either side of the large central stone.

2 Remove any excess fat from the duck portions. Divide each portion into three and place in a saucepan. Cover with cold water and bring to a boil. Lower the heat and simmer gently for 15–20 minutes. Drain well and pat dry with kitchen paper towels. Trim the bones.

3 Heat the oil in a wok or large skillet until hot and smoking. Add the duck pieces and allspice and cook until well browned on all sides.

4 Stir in the jam and vinegar. Cook for a further 2–3 minutes, stirring constantly, until well glazed. Stir in the mango slices and season to taste. Heat through, then turn into a warmed serving dish and serve immediately.

VARIATION
Tropical Duck
Other tropical fruits could be used instead of the mango in the above recipe. Try guava, papaya or lychees.

SWEET AND SOUR DUCK JOINTS

SERVES 4

4 duckling portions	2 tablespoons dry sherry
salt and pepper	juice of 1 orange
¼ cup soy sauce	½ teaspoon ground ginger
3 tablespoons soft light brown sugar	a few orange slices and watercress sprigs, for garnish
3 tablespoons honey	
3 tablespoons wine or cider vinegar	

1 Prick the duck portions all over with a fork, then sprinkle the skin liberally with salt and pepper.

2 Place on a rack in a roasting pan and roast in a preheated oven at 375°F for 45–60 minutes or until the skin is crisp and the juices run clear when the thickest part of each joint is pierced with a skewer.

3 Meanwhile, to make the sauce, mix together all the remaining ingredients except the garnish in a saucepan, add ⅔ cup water and bring to a boil. Simmer, stirring constantly, for about 5 minutes to allow the flavors to blend and the sauce to thicken slightly. Add salt and pepper to taste.

4 Trim the duck joints neatly by cutting off any knuckles or wing joints. Arrange the duck on a warmed serving platter and coat with some of the sauce. Garnish with orange and watercress.

RABBIT CASSEROLE WITH SAGE DUMPLINGS

SERVES 4

12 bacon slices	2½ cups chicken bouillon
4 rabbit portions	salt and pepper
4 celery stalks, chopped	¾ cup self-rising flour
2 leeks, sliced	¼ cup shredded beef suet
1 bay leaf	1 teaspoon chopped fresh sage or ½ teaspoon dried
1½ cups sliced carrots	
2 tablespoons all-purpose flour	

1 Using a sharp pair of kitchen scissors, snip the bacon into a flameproof casserole. Fry for 5 minutes or until the fat runs. Add the rabbit and fry gently, then add the celery, leeks, bay leaf and carrots.

2 Sprinkle over the all-purpose flour and stir well, then gradually add the bouillon and bring to a boil, stirring. Season to taste.

3 Cover the casserole and cook in a preheated oven at 325°F for about 1½ hours or until the rabbit is tender.

4 To make the dumplings, combine the self-rising flour, shredded suet, sage and salt and pepper in a bowl. Stir in just enough water to mix to a soft dough.

5 Divide the dough into four portions, then shape evenly into balls and place on top of casserole. Re-cover and cook for 20–25 minutes or until the dumplings are well risen and cooked through.

RABBIT CASSEROLE WITH CIDER AND MUSTARD

SERVES 4

2 tablespoons butter or margarine	¼ cup all-purpose flour
12 bacon slices, diced	1 rabbit, jointed
12–18 small pearl onions, skinned	2 teaspoon Dijon mustard
salt and pepper	1¼ cups hard cider
	2 cups chicken bouillon

1 Melt the butter or margarine in a skillet, add the bacon and onions and sauté for 5 minutes or until lightly browned. Remove to a casserole with a slotted spoon.

2 Season the flour with salt and pepper, add the rabbit portions and turn until coated. Shake off and reserve any excess flour. Add the rabbit to the fat remaining in the pan and fry for about 8 minutes or until golden brown. Arrange in the casserole.

3 Stir the remaining flour and the Dijon mustard into the pan. Gradually add the cider and bouillon, season to taste, then bring to a boil and pour over the rabbit.

4 Cover and cook in a preheated oven at 325°F for about 2 hours or until the rabbit is tender. Adjust the seasoning before serving.

COOK'S TIP

Small pearl onions can be very difficult to skin. Soak them in boiling water for 1–2 minutes first, then the skins should slip off easily. Leave the root ends intact so the onions stay whole during cooking.

GAME PIE

SERVES 4–6

ROAST PHEASANT WITH HERBY SAUSAGE MEATBALLS

SERVES 4

1 pound boneless game (pigeon, venison, partridge, hare or pheasant)	3 tablespoons vegetable oil
	1¼ cups red wine
2 tablespoons all-purpose flour	6 juniper berries, lightly crushed
2 teaspoons dried thyme	¾ pound bulk pork sausage
½ teaspoon ground cinnamon	½ pound frozen puff pastry, thawed
salt and pepper	1 egg, beaten, to glaze

1 Cut the meat into even-size cubes. Mix the flour with the thyme, cinnamon and seasoning, add the meat and toss until coated.

2 Heat the oil in a flameproof casserole, add the meat and fry over a moderate heat for 5 minutes or until browned on all sides. Pour in the wine, add the juniper berries, then cover and simmer gently for 1–1½ hours or until tender. Leave until cold, preferably overnight.

3 Put half the sausage in the bottom of an ovenproof pie dish. Put the game mixture on top, then cover with the remaining sausage and level the surface.

4 Roll out the pastry on a lightly floured surface to 2 inches wider than the pie dish. Cut a 1-inch strip from the outer edge and use to line the dampened rim of the dish.

5 Moisten the strip of dough, then place the pastry lid on top and press to seal. Flute the edge. Use pastry trimmings to decorate.

6 Brush the pastry with beaten egg, then bake in a preheated oven at 400°F for 30 minutes or until the pastry is golden brown and crisp. Let stand for 15 minutes before serving, or serve cold.

2 young oven-ready pheasants	2 tablespoons shredded beef suet
10 tablespoons butter	1 tablespoon chopped fresh parsley
2 teaspoons dried thyme	1 tablespoon chopped fresh lemon thyme or 2 teaspoons dried thyme
salt and pepper	
4 bacon slices	
2 cups chicken bouillon	1 tablespoon chopped sage
½ lb bulk pork sausage	1 onion, finely chopped
1 cup fresh white breadcrumbs	1 egg, beaten
finely grated rind of ½ lemon	

1 Wash the insides of the pheasants, then dry. Put 1 tablespoon butter and 1 teaspoon thyme inside each bird. Season the birds inside, then truss.

2 Spread the breast of each bird with 2 tablespoons softened butter and sprinkle with salt and pepper. Use two bacon slices to cover each pheasant breast. Stand the pheasants on a rack in a roasting pan, then pour in the bouillon. Roast at 400°F for 25 minutes.

3 Mix the sausage, breadcrumbs, lemon rind, suet, parsley, lemon thyme and sage together.

4 Melt 4 tablespoons butter in a small pan, add the onion and fry gently for 5 minutes or until soft. Mix into the sausage, season, then bind with beaten egg. Form into small balls.

5 Remove the bacon slices, roll them up and pierce them on to small metal skewers. Arrange on the rack around the pheasants, together with the sausage meatballs.

6 Return to the oven and roast for a further 20 minutes or until the pheasants are tender. Serve hot.

PHEASANT BREASTS WITH VERMOUTH

SERVES 4

2 pheasants	⅔ cup chicken bouillon
salt and pepper	2 tablespoons chopped fresh sage or 1 teaspoon dried
2 tablespoons all-purpose flour	
2 tablespoons vegetable oil	2 tablespoons light cream
½ cup finely chopped onion	1 cup seedless green grapes, halved
⅔ cup dry vermouth	sage leaves, for garnish

1 Using a sharp knife, cut all the breast flesh off the bone of each pheasant, keeping each fillet in one piece. You will have four breast fillets, two from each bird. (Use the legs and carcase for a casserole.) Ease off the skin of the fillets, and trim away any fat.

2 Season the flour with salt and pepper, add the breast fillets and turn until coated. Shake off and reserve any excess flour. Heat the oil in a medium skillet, add the pheasant and fry until well browned. Remove from the pan with a slotted spoon.

3 Add the onion and any remaining flour to the fat remaining in the pan and cook, stirring, for 1–2 minutes. Blend in the vermouth, bouillon, sage and seasoning. Bring to a boil, stirring, then return the pheasant to the pan.

4 Cover tightly and simmer for about 30 minutes, turning once. Lift the pheasant out of the juices and place on a warmed serving dish. Cover and keep warm.

5 Stir the cream and grapes into the juices and simmer for 1 minute. Adjust the seasoning. Spoon over the pheasant and garnish with sage leaves.

PHEASANT WITH CHESTNUTS

SERVES 4

2 tablespoons butter	2 cups chicken bouillon
1 tablespoon vegetable oil	⅔ cup dry red wine
2 oven-ready pheasants, jointed	salt and pepper
2 medium onions, sliced	juice and grated rind of ½ orange
½ pound peeled chestnuts	2 teaspoons currant jelly
3 tablespoons wholewheat flour	bouquet garni

1 Heat the butter and oil in a large skillet, add the pheasant joints and fry for about 5 minutes or until browned. Remove from the pan and put into an ovenproof casserole.

2 Add the onions and chestnuts to the oil and butter remaining in the pan and fry for a few minutes or until brown, then add to the pheasant.

3 Stir the flour into the fat remaining in the pan and cook, stirring, for 2–3 minutes. Remove from the heat and gradually stir in the bouillon and wine. Bring to a boil, stirring continuously, until thickened and smooth. Season to taste and pour over the pheasant in the casserole. Add the orange juice and rind, currant jelly and bouquet garni.

4 Cover the casserole and cook in a preheated oven at 350°F for about 1 hour or until the pheasant is tender. Remove the bouquet garni.

PHEASANT AU PORTO

SERVES 6

2 tablespoons vegetable oil	⅓ cup golden raisins
3 young oven-ready pheasants	salt and pepper
1¼ cups chicken bouillon	4 teaspoons cornstarch
½ cup port	¼ cup slivered almonds, toasted, for garnish
juice and finely grated rind of 2 oranges	

1 Heat the oil in a Dutch oven. When hot, add the pheasants and cook, turning, until brown all over.
2 Pour the bouillon and port over the birds. Add the orange juice and rind with the golden raisins and season well. Bring to a boil. Cover tightly and cook in a preheated oven at 325°F for 1–1½ hours.
3 Remove the pheasants from the casserole, then joint each into two or three pieces, depending on size, and arrange on a warmed serving dish. Keep warm.
4 Mix the cornstarch to a smooth paste with a little water, stir into the juices in the casserole and bring to a boil, stirring. Adjust the seasoning and spoon over the pheasant. Garnish with toasted almonds.

ROAST GOOSE WITH APPLES AND PRUNES

SERVES 8

9–11 pound oven-ready goose, with separate giblets	1 tablespoon chopped fresh sage or 1 teaspoon dried
salt and pepper	2 cups wholewheat breadcrumbs
1 tablespoon butter	6 small juicy apples
1 large onion, chopped	1¼ cups dry white wine
1 pound no-soak prunes	
¼ cup port	

1 Prick the skin of the goose all over with a sharp skewer. Pull the inside fat out and reserve. Rub salt over the skin.
2 To make the stuffing, melt the butter in a large skillet, add the onion and cook for 5–6 minutes or until softened. Separate the goose liver from the giblets and chop, then add to the onion and cook for 2–3 minutes.
3 Remove the stones from half of the prunes and discard. Chop the prunes roughly and stir into the onion with the port. Cover and simmer gently for 5 minutes. Add the sage and breadcrumbs and mix thoroughly together. Season.
4 Spoon the stuffing into the neck end of the goose, then truss with strong cotton or fine twine. Weigh the bird.
5 Put the goose on a wire rack in a roasting pan. Cover the breast with the reserved fat and then with foil. Roast in a preheated oven at 400°F for 15 minutes per pound plus 15 minutes, basting frequently.
6 Thirty minutes before the end of the cooking time, drain the fat from the roasting pan and discard. Core the apples and cut into eighths, then add to the pan with the remaining prunes and wine. Remove the foil and goose fat and cook, uncovered, for the last 30 minutes.
7 Serve with the cooking juices and fruit.

CASSEROLED SQUABS WITH CIDER AND APPLE

SERVES 4

3 medium carrots	sprig of thyme
3 celery stalks	1 bay leaf
4 small dessert apples	pinch of cayenne
salt and pepper	pinch of grated nutmeg
4 oven-ready squabs	4 teaspoons currant jelly
3 tablespoons vegetable oil	Worcestershire sauce (optional)
3 tablespoons butter	watercress sprigs, for garnish
1 medium onion, chopped	
2 cups hard cider	
⅔ cup chicken bouillon	

I Roughly chop one carrot and one celery stalk. Peel, core and chop two apples. Season the squabs and brown in 2 tablespoons oil and 2 tablespoons butter.

2 Fry the chopped onion, carrot, celery and apples. Transfer to a casserole and add the squabs. Pour the cider and bouillon into a pan and bring to a boil. Add to the casserole with the herbs and spices. Cover and cook at 300°F for 1½–2 hours or until tender.

3 Meanwhile, cut the remaining apples in half crosswise and scoop out the centers. Place a little currant jelly in the center of each and place on a greased baking sheet. Bake the apples for about 20 minutes or until tender.

4 Cut the remaining carrots and celery into julienne strips and sauté in the remaining oil and butter until soft.

5 When the squabs are cooked, remove them from the casserole and keep warm. Strain the juices into a saucepan and cook until syrupy. Season to taste and add a dash of Worcestershire if the sauce is too sweet.

6 Serve the squabs on a pool of the sauce and garnish.

VENISON SCALLOPS WITH RED WINE

SERVES 6

six 6-ounce venison scallops cut from the haunch (leg)	8 juniper berries
	1¼ cups dry red wine
1 small onion, finely chopped	1 tablespoon butter
	1 tablespoon vegetable oil
1 bay leaf	2 tablespoons currant jelly
2 parsley sprigs	salt and pepper

I Put the scallops in a large shallow dish and sprinkle with the onion, bay leaf, parsley and juniper berries. Pour on the wine, cover and marinate in the refrigerator for 3–4 hours or overnight, turning the scallops occasionally.

2 Remove the scallops from the marinade, reserving the marinade. Heat the butter and oil in a large skillet, add the scallops and fry for 3–4 minutes on each side. Transfer to a warmed serving dish and keep warm while making the sauce.

3 Strain the reserved marinade into the skillet and stir to loosen any sediment. Increase the heat and boil rapidly for 3–4 minutes or until reduced. Stir in the currant jelly and season to taste. Cook for 1–2 minutes, stirring, then pour over the scallops. Serve immediately.

——— COOK'S TIP ———

Gourmet markets sell fresh game in season; frozen venison is available all year round. When buying fresh venison, look for dark, fine-grained flesh, with firm white fat.

FISH AND SHELLFISH

Fish is both nutritious and flavorsome and can be cooked in a wonderful variety of ways. Shellfish always adds a touch of luxury, whether cooked on its own or used to add variety to a Gratin of Seafood or a champagne sauce to serve with pasta.

COD WITH CORIANDER IN CREAM

SERVES 4

1 pound thick-cut cod fillet	¼ cup butter
2 tablespoons all-purpose flour	1–2 tablespoons lemon juice
2 teaspoons ground coriander	1 tablespoon capers
salt and pepper	1 egg yolk
	6 tablespoons light cream

I Skin the fish and divide into four portions. Mix the flour, coriander and seasoning and use to coat the fish.
2 Heat the butter in a medium skillet, add the fish pieces and sauté gently until golden, turning only once.
3 Add 1 tablespoon lemon juice to the pan with the capers, cover tightly and continue cooking for a further 4–5 minutes. Place the fish on a warmed serving dish.
4 Mix the egg yolk and cream together, stir into the pan juices and heat gently, without boiling, until the sauce thickens. Adjust the seasoning and spoon over the fish.

TANDOORI COD

SERVES 4

four 7-ounce cod fillets	1 tablespoon chopped fresh cilantro or 1 teaspoon ground coriander
4 tablespoons plain yogurt	
2 tablespoons lemon juice	1 tablespoon vegetable oil
1 tablespoon tandoori paste	cilantro sprigs, for garnish

I Place the fish fillets in a shallow dish. Mix all the remaining ingredients, except the garnish.
2 Spread the yogurt mixture evenly over the fish, turning the fillets to ensure they are evenly coated. Cover and refrigerate for 8 hours or overnight.
3 Cover the broiler pan with foil and add the fillets, leaving any excess marinade in the dish.
4 Cook the fillets under a preheated broiler for 5–7 minutes, basting them with the remaining marinade. Turn over and broil for a further 5 minutes or until the fish is firm and flakes easily, basting frequently. Transfer the fillets to a warmed serving dish and garnish with cilantro sprigs.

COD IN CREAM AND CELERY SAUCE

SERVES 4

4 cod steaks or cutlets	5 tablespoons heavy cream
1 tablespoon lemon juice	½ teaspoon dried thyme
salt and pepper	½ cup crumbled Lancashire cheese
2 tablespoons butter	2 tomatoes, sliced
3 celery stalks, chopped	parsley, for garnish
¼ cup all-purpose flour	
1 cup milk	

1 Sprinkle the fish with lemon juice and season to taste. Cook under a preheated broiler or bake in a preheated oven at 400°F for 20 minutes. Place in a warmed, shallow, heatproof serving dish and keep warm.

2 Melt the butter in a saucepan, add the celery and fry for about 10 minutes or until tender. Stir in the flour and cook gently for 1 minute, stirring. Remove the pan from the heat and gradually stir in the milk and cream. Bring slowly to a boil, lower the heat and simmer gently, stirring constantly, until the sauce thickens.

3 Season the sauce to taste, then add the thyme and ¼ cup cheese. Pour the sauce over the fish and sprinkle with the remaining cheese.

4 Arrange the tomatoes on the dish and place under the broiler to brown. Serve hot, garnished with parsley.

VARIATION

Haddock in Cream and Leek Sauce
Substitute haddock for the cod in the above recipe and use 1 large leek instead of the celery. Any other white fish would also be suitable.

HADDOCK AU GRATIN

SERVES 6

6 ounces fresh haddock fillet	1 cup sliced button mushrooms
6 ounces finnan haddie	2 tablespoons all-purpose flour
¼ cup dry white wine	pepper
6 peppercorns	½ cup shredded Red Leicester cheese or Monterey Jack
1 bay leaf	
1 small onion, sliced	½ cup fresh breadcrumbs
¼ cup butter	

1 Place the fresh and smoked fish in a saucepan with 1¼ cups water and the wine. Add the peppercorns, bay leaf and onion and bring to a boil. Cover and poach gently for about 15 minutes.

2 Strain off the liquid and reserve. Flake the fish, discarding skin and bones. Discard the flavoring ingredients.

3 Melt the butter in a saucepan, add the mushrooms and sauté for 2 minutes. Stir in the flour and cook gently for 1 minute, stirring. Remove the pan from the heat and gradually stir in the strained cooking liquid. Bring to a boil and continue to cook, stirring, until the sauce thickens. Add the fish, half the shredded cheese and season to taste with pepper.

4 Spoon the mixture into six individual soufflé dishes. Top with the remaining cheese and the breadcrumbs.

5 Bake in a preheated oven at 425°F for about 15 minutes or until golden brown. Serve hot.

HADDOCK AND CARAWAY CHEESE SOUFFLÉ

SERVES 4

1 pound mealy potatoes	¼ cup all-purpose flour
1 pound fresh haddock fillets	½ teaspoon caraway seeds
1 cup thinly sliced button mushrooms	1 cup shredded sharp Cheddar cheese
1¼ cups milk	2 eggs, separated
1 bay leaf	salt and pepper
2 tablespoons butter	

1 Scrub the potatoes, then cook in boiling salted water for about 20 minutes or until tender. Drain and peel, then mash three-quarters of the potatoes. Grate the remaining quarter into a bowl and set aside.

2 Meanwhile, place the haddock, mushrooms, milk and bay leaf in a small saucepan. Cover and poach for 15–20 minutes or until tender. Drain, reserving the milk and mushrooms. Flake the fish, discarding the skin and bay leaf.

3 To make the sauce, melt the butter in a saucepan, stir in the flour and cook gently for 1 minute, stirring. Remove from the heat, add the caraway seeds and gradually stir in the milk. Bring to a boil, stirring, lower the heat and simmer for 2–3 minutes or until thickened and smooth.

4 Stir the mashed potato into the sauce with ¾ cup cheese, the egg yolks, fish and mushrooms. Season well.

5 Stiffly whisk the egg whites and fold into the fish. Turn into a buttered 7-cup soufflé dish.

6 Sprinkle over the reserved grated potato and remaining grated cheese. Bake in a preheated oven at 375°F for about 1 hour or until just set and golden brown.

CREAMY COD BAKE

SERVES 4

	FOR THE CHEESE SAUCE
1 pound frozen leaf spinach	2 tablespoons butter or margarine
¼ cup butter or margarine	¼ cup all-purpose flour
4 frozen cod steaks	2 cups milk
½ teaspoon grated nutmeg	1 cup shredded Cheddar or Brick cheese
salt and pepper	1 teaspoon dry mustard
1 cup shredded Cheddar cheese	salt and pepper
two 1-ounce packets sour cream and chive flavored potato chips, crushed	

1 To make the cheese sauce, melt the butter in a saucepan, add the flour and cook gently, stirring, for 2 minutes. Remove from the heat and blend in the milk. Bring to a boil and cook, stirring, until thick.

2 Simmer the sauce gently for 2–3 minutes, then add the cheese and stir until melted. Add the mustard and season.

3 Put the frozen spinach in a heavy-based saucepan and heat gently until thawed, adding a few spoonfuls of water if necessary to prevent the spinach sticking. Meanwhile, melt half the butter in a skillet and fry the cod until golden.

4 Transfer the spinach to the base of an ovenproof dish and mix in the remaining butter or margarine with half the nutmeg and seasoning to taste. Arrange the steaks on top of the spinach and pour over any cooking juices.

5 Stir the remaining nutmeg into the cheese sauce, then pour the sauce evenly over the fish to cover it completely. Mix the grated cheese with the chips and sprinkle over.

6 Bake in a preheated oven at 375°F for 30 minutes until golden brown and bubbling. Serve hot.

SPANISH COD WITH PEPPERS, TOMATOES AND GARLIC

SERVES 4

1½ pounds cod fillets	1–2 garlic cloves, crushed
1 quart mussels (about 1 pound)	2½ cups chopped peeled tomatoes
2 tablespoons vegetable oil	1¼ cups white wine
2 onions, sliced	½ teaspoon hot pepper sauce
1 sweet red pepper, sliced	1 bay leaf
1 sweet green pepper, sliced	salt and pepper

1 Using a sharp knife, skin the cod and cut it into chunks.
2 Scrub the mussels, discarding any which are open. Place in a pan, cover and cook over a high heat for about 8 minutes or until the mussels have opened. Discard any that do not open.
3 Shuck all but four of the mussels. Heat the oil in a skillet and cook the onions, peppers and garlic for about 5 minutes or until starting to soften. Add the tomatoes and wine, bring to a boil and simmer for 5 minutes, then add the red pepper sauce.
4 Using a slotted spoon, remove the vegetables from the wine sauce and layer them with the fish chunks in a casserole. Add the bay leaf and seasoning and pour over the sauce. Push the four unshucked mussels into the top layer. Cover and cook in a preheated oven at 350°F for 1 hour.

COD IN A SPICY YOGURT CRUST

SERVES 4

2 tablespoons chopped mint	2 teaspoons ground cumin
1 medium onion or 2 large scallions, roughly chopped	2 teaspoons dried dill
2 garlic cloves, crushed	⅔ cup plain yogurt
1 teaspoon mild paprika	salt and pepper
2 tablespoons coriander seeds	four 8-ounce thick cod steaks or fillets

1 First make the marinade mixture. Put the mint, onion, garlic, paprika, coriander, cumin, dill and yogurt in a blender or food processor and process until a thick paste is formed. Season the mixture to taste with salt and pepper.
2 Place the fish in a single layer in a shallow heatproof dish. Spread the paste all over the top of the fish and leave in a cool place to marinate for 2–3 hours.
3 Cook under a preheated hot broiler, basting occasionally, until the fish is cooked and the yogurt mixture has formed a crust. Serve immediately.

───────────── **VARIATION** ─────────────
Haddock in a Spicy Yogurt Crust
Substitute haddock for cod in the above recipe. Steaks or fillets are equally suitable.

HALIBUT CREOLE

SERVES 4

SOLE BONNE FEMME

SERVES 4

2 tablespoons vegetable oil	¼ teaspoon hot pepper sauce
1 onion, chopped	2 tablespoons chopped fresh parsley or 2 teaspoons dried
2 garlic cloves, crushed	
1 celery stalk, chopped	salt and pepper
1 sweet green pepper, chopped	butter, for greasing
1-pound can chopped tomatoes	four 10-ounce halibut steaks
1 teaspoon soft light brown sugar	

1 Heat the oil in a medium saucepan, add the onion and garlic and sauté for 3 minutes. Add the celery and pepper and cook for 5 minutes or until softened.

2 Add the tomatoes, sugar, hot pepper sauce and parsley and season to taste. Cook for 15–20 minutes or until the vegetables have softened and the sauce has thickened.

3 Butter a large shallow dish and lay the halibut steaks in it. Pour the creole sauce over the fish and cover with foil. Bake in a preheated oven at 400°F for 25–30 minutes or until the fish is firm and flakes easily.

4 Transfer the fish to a warmed serving platter and spoon the remaining sauce over the top.

TO MICROWAVE

Place the oil, onion and garlic in a medium bowl. Cover and cook on HIGH for 3 minutes. Add the celery, sweet green pepper, tomatoes, sugar, hot pepper sauce, parsley and seasoning. Cook, uncovered, on HIGH for 9–10 minutes. Arrange the fish in a buttered shallow dish and pour over the sauce. Cover and microwave on HIGH for 12–14 minutes or until the fish is firm and flakes easily. Complete step 4.

2 sole fillets	1 bay leaf
2 shallots, or 2–3 slices of onion, finely chopped	3 tablespoons butter
¼ pound button mushrooms	2 tablespoons all-purpose flour
3 tablespoons dry white wine	about ⅔ cup milk
salt and pepper	3 tablespoons light cream

1 Trim off the fins, wash and wipe the fillets and fold each into three. Put the shallots or onion in the bottom of an ovenproof dish with the stalks from the mushrooms, (finely chopped). Cover with the fish, pour round the wine and 1 tablespoon water, season to taste and add the bay leaf.

2 Cover with foil or a lid and bake in a preheated oven at 350°F for about 15 minutes or until tender. Strain off the cooking liquid and keep the fish warm.

3 Melt half the butter in a skillet, add the mushrooms and fry gently until just beginning to soften, then drain well.

4 Melt the remaining butter in a saucepan, stir in the flour and cook gently for 1 minute, stirring. Remove from the heat and gradually stir in the cooking liquid from the fish, made up to 1¼ cups with milk.

5 Bring to a boil and continue to cook, stirring, until the sauce thickens, then remove from the heat and stir in the cream. Pour the sauce over the fish and serve garnished with the mushroom caps.

SOLE 'STEWED' IN CREAM

SERVES 4

4 sole fillets, skinned and cut in half lengthwise	FOR THE GARNISH
2 tablespoons butter	lobster coral or salmon eggs (optional)
1 tablespoon minced shallots	cooked crayfish or shrimp (optional)
1¼ cups fish stock	puff pastry fleurons or bread croûtes
blade of mace	parsley sprigs
1 cup heavy cream	lemon twists
salt and white pepper	

1 Tie each strip of sole into a loose knot in the center.
2 Melt half the butter in a large skillet, add the shallot, cover and cook for about 5 minutes or until softened, shaking the pan occasionally. Stir in the stock and mace and boil rapidly until reduced to ¼ cup. Remove the mace.
3 Stir half the cream into the shallots and bring to a boil. Lower the heat, season lightly and gently lower the fish into the pan. Spoon cream over the fish. Cover with buttered baker's parchment and poach gently for about 3 minutes, or until the fish just flakes.
4 Carefully transfer the fish to a warmed plate using a fish slice, cover and keep warm. Boil the cooking liquid until slightly thickened. Stir in the remaining butter and adjust the seasoning, if necessary.
5 Spoon the sauce over four warmed serving plates. Arrange the fish on top and garnish attractively.

MOUSSELINES OF SOLE WITH SHRIMP

SERVES 6

1 pound sole fillets, skinned and chopped	3 egg yolks, beaten
2 ounces shelled shrimp	⅓ cup butter, softened
1 egg white	2 teaspoons lemon juice
¼ teaspoon salt	1 teaspoon tomato paste
½ teaspoon white pepper	fresh dill sprigs and whole shell-on shrimp, for garnish
2 cups heavy cream	

1 Combine the chopped fish with the shrimp and egg white and season to taste. Put the mixture in a blender or food processor with 1¼ cups cream and blend until smooth.
2 Butter six ⅔-cup ovenproof ramekin dishes and press the mixture well down into the dishes. Cover and chill for 3 hours.
3 Place the ramekins in a roasting pan and pour in enough boiling water to come halfway up the dishes. Cook in a preheated oven at 300°F for 30–40 minutes. Turn out on to a wire rack to drain. Keep warm.
4 Put the egg yolks, a knob of butter and the lemon juice in the top of a double boiler or in a heatproof bowl over a pan of simmering water. Heat gently, stirring, until of a coating consistency.
5 Remove from the heat and slowly beat in the remaining butter and the tomato paste. Whip the remaining cream until softly stiff and fold into the sauce. Return to the heat to thicken without boiling.
6 Place the molds in a warmed serving dish and coat with the sauce. Garnish with dill and whole shrimp and serve hot.

MUSHROOM-STUFFED FLOUNDER

SERVES 4

¼ cup butter	4 large flounder fillets, skinned
1 small onion, finely chopped	¼ cup all-purpose flour
2 cups finely chopped mushrooms	⅔ cup milk
grated nutmeg	a few drops of lemon juice
salt and pepper	1 tablespoon heavy cream
2 tablespoons finely chopped parsley	chopped parsley, for garnish

1 Melt half the butter in a skillet, add the onion and fry gently for 5–10 minutes or until soft and golden. Add the mushrooms and cook for about 20 minutes or until all the juices have evaporated.

2 Remove from the heat, season with nutmeg, salt and pepper, then transfer all but 2 tablespoons of the mixture to a bowl and mix with 1 tablespoon of the parsley.

3 Cut the fish fillets in half lengthwise and spread an equal quantity of the mushroom mixture on the skinned side of each piece of fish. Roll up the fillets from the head to tail and place close together in a baking dish.

4 Pour in ⅔ cup water and place a piece of buttered foil on top of the fish. Bake in a preheated oven at 350°F for 20–25 minutes or until tender. Strain off the cooking liquid and transfer the fish to a warmed serving dish. Keep warm.

5 Melt the remaining butter in a saucepan, stir in the flour and cook for 2 minutes, stirring continuously. Remove from the heat and gradually stir in the cooking liquid and milk. Bring to a boil, stirring. Add the remaining mushroom mixture, season with salt, pepper and lemon juice and stir in the cream. Pour over the fish and garnish.

STUFFED PLAICE WITH LEMON SAUCE

SERVES 4

4 small whole plaice (fluke), cleaned	¼ teaspoon dry mustard
5 tablespoons butter	salt and pepper
1 cup finely chopped mushrooms	1 egg, beaten
2 cups white breadcrumbs	⅔ cup dry white wine
6 tablespoons chopped parsley	¼ cup all-purpose flour
3 tablespoons green peppercorns, crushed	¼ cup light cream
juice and finely grated rind of 2 lemons	lemon slices and parsley sprigs, for garnish

1 With the white skin uppermost, cut down the backbone of each of the four plaice. Carefully make a pocket on each side of the backbone by easing up the white flesh.

2 To make the stuffing, beat 1 tablespoon butter until softened, then add the mushrooms, breadcrumbs, parsley, 2 tablespoons peppercorns, lemon rind and mustard. Season to taste. Moisten with egg and a little lemon juice.

3 Spoon the stuffing into the pockets in the fish. Place in a buttered ovenproof dish, pour in the wine, cover with foil and cook at 375°F for 30 minutes.

4 Remove the fish and place on a serving dish. Cover and keep warm. Strain and reserve the cooking liquid.

5 To make the sauce, melt the remaining butter in a saucepan, add the flour and cook for 1–2 minutes. Gradually stir in the fish cooking juices, ⅔ cup water and the remaining lemon juice. Bring to a boil, stirring, then stir in the remaining peppercorns and the cream. Season.

6 Garnish the fish and serve with the sauce.

TROUT IN CREAM

SERVES 4

4 trout	⅔ cup light cream
juice of 1 lemon	2 tablespoons fresh breadcrumbs
1 tablespoon chopped chives	a little butter, melted
1 tablespoon chopped parsley	

1 Clean the fish, leaving the heads on if wished. Wash and wipe the fish and lay them in a buttered shallow flameproof dish.

2 Sprinkle over the lemon juice, herbs and about 1 tablespoon water. Cover with foil.

3 Cook in a preheated oven at 350°F for 10–15 minutes or until tender.

4 Heat the cream gently and pour over the fish. Sprinkle with breadcrumbs and melted butter and brown under a hot broiler. Serve immediately.

BAKED TROUT WITH HAZELNUTS AND DILL

SERVES 4

four 10-ounce trout, cleaned	1 shallot, finely chopped
3 tablespoons lemon juice	¾ cup hazelnuts
salt and pepper	¼ cup butter
4 dill sprigs	lemon slices and dill, for garnish
½ cup dry white wine	

1 Cut the fins from the fish, then sprinkle 2 tablespoons of the lemon juice over the skin and the cavities. Season to taste inside and out and put a sprig of dill in each cavity.

2 Place the trout in a baking dish large enough to hold them tightly in one layer. Pour over the wine and add the shallot. Cover the dish with greased baker's parchment, then bake in a preheated oven at 350°F for 20–25 minutes or until the flesh flakes easily.

3 Meanwhile, place the hazelnuts under a moderately hot broiler for about 5 minutes or until the skins dry out and flake. Rub off the skins and chop the nuts. Melt the butter in a saucepan, add the hazelnuts and cook over a moderately high heat, stirring frequently, until golden brown. Add the remaining lemon juice and season to taste.

4 Carefully transfer the trout to four warmed serving plates. Boil the cooking juices rapidly until reduced to about 3 tablespoons. Spoon the juices, hazelnuts and butter over the fish. Garnish and serve at once.

BAKED TROUT WITH CUCUMBER SAUCE

SERVES 4

four 10-ounce trout, cleaned	1¼ cups dairy sour cream
salt and pepper	1 teaspoon tarragon vinegar
1¼ cups fish or vegetable stock	1 teaspoon chopped tarragon
½ small cucumber	tarragon, for garnish

1 Arrange the trout in a single layer in a shallow ovenproof dish. Season to taste and pour over the stock.

2 Cover and bake in a preheated oven at 350°F for about 25 minutes or until the trout are tender.

3 Remove the fish from the cooking liquor and carefully peel off the skin, leaving the head and tail intact. Leave to cool.

4 Just before serving, make the sauce. Coarsely grate the cucumber into a bowl, then add the cream, vinegar and chopped tarragon. Season to taste.

5 Coat the trout in some of the sauce, leaving the head and tail exposed. Garnish with tarragon. Serve the remaining sauce separately in a bowl.

TO MICROWAVE

Cook two trout at a time. Arrange in a shallow dish, cover and cook on HIGH for 5–7 minutes or until tender. Repeat with the remaining two trout. Complete the recipe as above.

TROUT STUFFED WITH SPINACH AND WALNUTS

SERVES 4

4 small trout, cleaned, boned and heads removed	juice of 1 lemon
½ cup butter	2 tablespoons chopped fresh parsley or 2 teaspoons dried
1 onion, finely chopped	1 teaspoon grated nutmeg
12 ounces frozen chopped spinach, thawed	salt and pepper
1 cup fresh breadcrumbs	parsley sprigs and lemon and lime slices, for garnish
½ cup chopped walnuts	

1 Butter a large, shallow ovenproof dish and lay the trout in it.

2 Melt ¼ cup of the butter in a deep skillet, add the onion and cook for 4–5 minutes or until soft. Stir in the spinach and cook for 5 minutes, stirring frequently.

3 Add the breadcrumbs, walnuts, lemon juice, parsley and nutmeg. Stir well to combine and continue to cook over a gentle heat for 10 minutes, stirring frequently. Remove from the heat and let cool.

4 Spoon the stuffing into the cavity of each fish. Lay the fish on their sides and dot with the remaining butter. Season and cover with buttered foil.

5 Cook in a preheated oven at 350°F for 40–60 minutes or until the fish is firm and flakes easily. Skin the fish, transfer to a warmed serving dish, garnish and serve.

GRAY MULLET COOKED IN LEMON AND RED WINE

SERVES 4

1 tablespoon butter	salt and pepper
1 pound dessert apples, peeled, cored and sliced	four 10-ounce gray mullet, cleaned
6 scallions, sliced	2 lemons, sliced
juice and finely grated rind of 1 lemon	1¼ cups dry red wine
1–2 garlic cloves, crushed	¼ cup heavy cream

1 To make the stuffing, melt the butter in a medium saucepan and add the apples, scallions, lemon rind, 2 tablespoons of the lemon juice and the garlic. Fry lightly, then season to taste.

2 Make three slashes across both sides of each gray mullet and insert the lemon slices. Sprinkle the cavity of each fish with the remaining lemon juice and fill with the stuffing. Put into a large ovenproof dish.

3 Pour over the red wine and bake in a preheated oven at 350°F for 20–30 minutes or until tender. Remove the fish and place on a serving dish. Keep hot.

4 Pour the cooking liquid into a small saucepan, stir in the cream and reheat gently. Pour over the fish and serve.

--- **TO MICROWAVE** ---

Melt the butter in a medium bowl on HIGH for 30 seconds. Add the apples, scallions, lemon rind, 2 tablespoons of the lemon juice and the garlic. Cook on HIGH for 8 minutes. Complete step 2. Put the fish into a shallow dish and pour over the red wine. Cook on HIGH for 10 minutes or until tender, rearranging once. Complete step 4. Stir the cream into the cooking liquid and cook on HIGH for 1 minute. Serve poured over the fish.

STEAMED MULLET WITH CHILI SAUCE

SERVES 2

one 1¼-pound gray mullet, cleaned	1 small sweet green pepper, cut into matchsticks
⅓ cup ketchup	1 teaspoon cornstarch
1 tablespoon soy sauce	1 tablespoon chopped parsley
pinch of chili powder	salt and pepper
⅓ cup white wine	
1 small sweet red pepper, cut into matchsticks	

1 Place the mullet in a shallow dish.

2 Whisk together the ketchup, soy sauce, chili powder and wine. Make three deep slashes in the side of each fish. Pour over the marinade, cover and leave for 2 hours.

3 Drain off the marinade and reserve. Place the fish on a rack over a roasting pan half full of water and cover tightly with foil. Steam the fish over a medium heat for 20–25 minutes or until the fish is cooked. (When cooked, the eyes should be white.)

4 To make the chili sauce, place the marinade and peppers in a saucepan. Mix the cornstarch to a smooth paste with 1 tablespoon water and stir into the sauce. Bring to a boil, then simmer for 4–5 minutes, stirring. Stir in the parsley and season to taste.

5 Carefully lift the steamed mullet onto a warmed serving plate. Spoon over the sauce and serve.

SKATE WITH CAPERS

SERVES 4

ANGLER FISH WITH LIME AND SHRIMP

SERVES 4

two 1¼-pound skate wings, halved	3 tablespoons drained capers
salt	2 tablespoons vinegar from the capers
¼ cup butter	

1 Put the skate in a roasting pan and cover with salted water. Bring to a boil, then simmer for 10–15 minutes or until tender.
2 Meanwhile, melt the butter in a small saucepan and cook until it turns golden brown. Add the capers and vinegar and cook until bubbling.
3 Drain the fish and place on warmed serving plates. Pour over the sauce and serve at once.

─────────── **COOK'S TIP** ───────────
The 'wings' are the only edible part of the skate. They may look bony but in fact the bones are soft and gelatinous, and the flesh is easily picked off them when the fish is cooked.

1¼ pound angler fish	⅔ cup dry white wine
salt and pepper	juice and finely grated rind of 1 lime
1 tablespoon all-purpose flour	pinch of sugar
2 tablespoons vegetable oil	4 ounces shelled shrimp
1 small onion, chopped	lime slices, for garnish
1 garlic clove, chopped	
1½ cups chopped peeled tomatoes	

1 Using a sharp knife, skin the fish, if necessary, then cut the flesh into 1-inch chunks. Season the flour with salt and pepper, add the fish and toss until coated.
2 Heat the oil in a flameproof casserole, add the onion and garlic and sauté gently for 5 minutes. Add the fish and fry until golden.
3 Stir in the tomatoes, wine, lime rind and juice, sugar and seasoning. Bring to a boil.
4 Cover and cook in a preheated oven at 350°F for 15 minutes. Add the shrimp and continue to cook for a further 15 minutes or until the fish is tender. Garnish with lime.

FRICASSÉE OF ANGLER FISH WITH CILANTRO

SERVES 6

1½ pounds angler fish fillets	3 tablespoons butter
1 pound halibut steaks	3 tablespoons all-purpose flour
⅔ cup dry vermouth	2 tablespoons chopped cilantro
1 small onion, sliced	¼ cup light cream
salt and pepper	cilantro sprigs, for garnish
¼ pound small button mushrooms	

1 Cut the angler fish and halibut into large, fork-size pieces, discarding skin and bone.
2 Place the fish in a medium saucepan, cover with cold water and bring slowly to a boil. Strain the fish in a colander and rinse off any scum.
3 Return the fish to the clean pan and pour over the vermouth and 1¼ cups water. Add the onion, season to taste and bring to a boil. Cover the pan, reduce the heat and simmer gently for 8–10 minutes or until the fish is just tender and beginning to flake, adding the mushrooms after 6 minutes' cooking.
4 Strain off the cooking liquor and reserve.
5 Melt the butter in a separate saucepan, stir in the flour and cook for 1–2 minutes. Gradually add the cooking liquor. Bring slowly to a boil, stirring all the time, and bubble for 2 minutes or until thickened and smooth.
6 Stir in the chopped cilantro, cream, mushrooms, onion and fish and adjust the seasoning. Warm through gently, being careful not to break up the fish. Serve hot, garnished with sprigs of cilantro.

ANGLER FISH AND MUSSEL SKEWERS

SERVES 6

12 bacon slices, halved	juice and finely grated rind of 1 large lemon
2 pounds angler fish, skinned, boned and cut into 1-inch cubes	4 garlic cloves, crushed
36 frozen cooked mussels, thawed	salt and pepper
2 tablespoons butter	shredded lettuce, to serve
4 tablespoons chopped parsley	lemon slices, for garnish

1 Roll the bacon slices up neatly. Thread the cubed fish, mussels and bacon alternately onto 12 oiled skewers.
2 Melt the butter in a saucepan, remove from the heat, then add the parsley, lemon juice and rind and garlic. Season to taste. (Take care when adding salt as both the mussels and the bacon are naturally salty.)
3 Place the skewers on an oiled broiler rack. Brush with the butter mixture, then cook under a preheated moderate broiler for 15 minutes. Turn the skewers frequently during cooking and brush with the butter mixture with each turn.
4 Arrange the hot skewers on a serving platter lined with shredded lettuce. Garnish with lemon slices and serve at once with any remaining flavored butter.

COOK'S TIP

Keep the skewers well brushed with butter while broiling to prevent the fish from drying out.

SALMON WITH HERB SAUCE

SERVES 4

2 pounds salmon, cleaned	3 tablespoons chopped parsley
3 tablespoons lemon juice	2 tablespoons chopped chervil
¼ cup butter	1 teaspoon chopped dill
salt and pepper	⅔ cup mayonnaise
1 bunch of watercress, roughly chopped	fresh herbs and lemon rind shapes, for garnish (optional)
¼ pound fresh spinach leaves, roughly chopped	

1 Place the fish in the center of a large piece of foil. Add 2 tablespoons of the lemon juice, then dot with 2 tablespoons of the butter. Season to taste.

2 Seal the foil, weigh the fish and place on a baking sheet. Calculate the cooking time at 10 minutes per pound. Bake in a preheated oven at 350°F until tender.

3 Remove the fish from the foil, reserving the cooking liquor, then carefully remove the skin while still warm. Place the fish on a serving dish and let cool.

4 To make the sauce, put the cooking liquor and the remaining butter in a saucepan and heat gently. Add the watercress, spinach, parsley, chervil and dill, then cook for 2–3 minutes or until softened.

5 Put the sauce in a blender or food processor and blend until smooth. Transfer to a bowl, add the remaining lemon juice and season to taste. Let cool, then fold in the mayonnaise. Turn into a small serving pitcher and refrigerate until required.

6 Garnish the fish decoratively with herbs and lemon rind shapes, and serve with the herb sauce.

SUMMER POACHED SALMON

SERVES 15

4 pound salmon, tail and fins trimmed and eyes removed	salt and pepper
	1¼ cups liquid aspic
⅔ cup dry white wine	whole shrimp, cucumber slices, endive and chicory, for garnish
1 onion, sliced	
1 bay leaf	mayonnaise, to serve

1 Place the salmon in a fish kettle. Pour over the wine and enough water just to cover the fish. Add the onion and bay leaf and season to taste. Bring slowly to a boil, cover and simmer for 25 minutes.

2 Lift the salmon out of the cooking liquid and leave to cool for 2–3 hours. Ease off the skin and place the fish on a serving platter.

3 As the aspic begins to set, brush some over the fish. Leave to set in a cool place for 1–1½ hours. Coat with several layers of aspic.

4 Garnish the salmon with shrimp and cucumber slices and brush more aspic on top. Arrange endive, chicory, sliced cucumber and lemon on the side of the dish and serve with mayonnaise.

— COOK'S TIP —

This is an ideal dish to serve for a summer buffet. Pay particular attention to the garnishing and allow yourself a little extra time for those important finishing touches. The result can look spectacular.

SALMON WITH FENNEL SAUCE

SERVES 4

6-ounce salmon steaks	2 egg yolks
2 shallots, chopped	½ cup butter, softened
1 small fennel bulb, finely chopped	salt and pepper
1 bay leaf	lemon juice, to taste
2 parsley stalks, crushed	fennel sprigs, for garnish
⅔ cup dry white wine	

1 Place the salmon steaks in a shallow ovenproof dish. Scatter the shallots, fennel, bay leaf and parsley over the top. Pour in the wine, cover tightly and bake in a preheated oven at 350°F for 15 minutes or until the fish is tender.
2 Strain off ½ cup of the cooking liquor into a saucepan. Reserve 2 teaspoons of the chopped fennel. Turn off the oven, re-cover the salmon and keep warm.
3 Boil the strained liquor until reduced to 1 tablespoon. Beat the egg yolks together in a medium heatproof bowl, then stir in the reduced liquor and work in half the butter.
4 Place the bowl over a saucepan of hot water and whisk with a balloon whip until the butter has melted. Gradually whisk in the remaining butter, whisking well after each addition, to make a thick, fluffy sauce. Remove the bowl from the heat.
5 Add the reserved cooked fennel to the sauce and season to taste, adding a little lemon juice, if necessary.
6 Transfer the salmon to a warmed serving plate. Spoon the sauce over and garnish with fennel sprigs.

SOUR CREAM SALMON PIE

SERVES 8

1 pound salmon	3 eggs, hard-cooked and chopped
¼ cup dry white wine	
salt and pepper	⅔ cup dairy sour cream
¾ cup butter plus 1 tablespoon	2 tablespoons chopped parsley
6 tablespoons all-purpose flour	4 cups self-rising flour
2 cups shredded Cheddar cheese	5 tablespoons shortening
	milk, to bind
	beaten egg, to glaze

1 Place the salmon in a large saucepan and just cover with cold water. Add the wine, season to taste and simmer for about 20 minutes. Remove the fish from the stock and flake, discarding bones and skin. Reserve the stock.
2 Melt 3 tablespoons butter in a saucepan and stir in the all-purpose flour. Remove the pan from the heat and gradually stir in 1¼ cups reserved fish stock. Bring to a boil and continue to cook, stirring, for 2 minutes. Remove from the heat and stir in 1¾ cups shredded cheese, the chopped eggs, sour cream and parsley. Season and cool.
3 To make the dough, mix the self-rising flour and remaining cheese in a bowl, add the remaining butter and the shortening and cut or rub in until the mixture resembles fine breadcrumbs. Add a little milk to bind the mixture.
4 Roll out one third of the dough on a lightly floured surface to a 12 x 4-inch rectangle and place on a baking sheet. Top with some of the sauce mixture, the salmon, then more sauce.
5 Roll out the remaining dough and use to cover the pie, sealing the edges well. Brush with beaten egg and bake at 375°F for about 40 minutes. Serve warm.

FISH WELLINGTON

SERVES 6–8

2 tablespoons butter	salt and pepper
1 cup chopped mushrooms	13 ounces frozen puff pastry, thawed
½ cup finely chopped onion	2 large cod or haddock fillets, (about 2 pounds), skinned
6 ounces smooth liver pâté or liver sausage	
¼ cup heavy cream	beaten egg, to glaze

1 Melt the butter in a skillet, add the mushrooms and onion and sauté for about 5 minutes or until soft.

2 Mash the liver pâté or sausage in a bowl and stir in the cream, onion and mushrooms. Season to taste.

3 Roll out the pastry on a lightly floured surface to a 14 x 12-inch rectangle. Place one fish fillet in the center of the pastry, spread the filling mixture over the fillet, then top with the other fillet. Trim the pastry, allowing a good 4-inch border. Reserve the trimmed pastry.

4 Brush round the edges of the pastry with beaten egg, then carefully fold it over the fish and neatly wrap it up like a parcel.

5 Place the parceled fish on a baking sheet with the sealed edges underneath. Brush with beaten egg. Roll and cut the pastry trimmings into decorative fish shapes and place on top of the pastry parcel.

6 Bake in a preheated oven at 425°F for about 25 minutes or until the pastry is golden brown and the fish is cooked through.

INDONESIAN FISH CURRY

SERVES 4

1 small onion, chopped	salt
1 garlic clove, chopped	1½ pounds haddock fillets, skinned and cut into bite-size pieces
1-inch piece of fresh root ginger, chopped	
1 teaspoon ground turmeric	½ pound shelled shrimp
½ teaspoon laos powder	1¼ cups coconut milk
¼ teaspoon chili powder	juice of 1 lime
2 tablespoons vegetable oil	flaked coconut and lime wedges, for garnish

1 Put the first seven ingredients in an electric blender or food processor with ½ teaspoon salt and blend to a paste.

2 Transfer the mixture to a flameproof casserole and fry gently, stirring, for 5 minutes. Add the haddock pieces and shrimp and fry for a few minutes more, tossing the fish to coat with the spice mixture.

3 Pour in the coconut milk, shake the pan and turn the fish gently in the liquid. (Take care not to break up the pieces of fish.) Bring slowly to a boil, then lower the heat, cover and simmer for 10 minutes or until tender.

4 Add the lime juice, taste and adjust the seasoning, then transfer to a warmed serving dish and sprinkle with coconut. Serve hot, garnished with lime wedges.

— COOK'S TIP —

Loas powder is used extensively in the cooking of South-East Asia. It comes from a root rather like ginger and has a peppery hot taste.

To make 1¼ cups coconut milk, break 4-ounce block creamed coconut into a liquid measure and pour in 1¼ cups boiling water. Stir, then strain.

FISH IN SPICY SAUCE WITH TOMATOES

SERVES 4

1½ pounds white fish (cod, halibut or haddock), skinned and filleted	1 teaspoon ground turmeric
4 tablespoons ghee or vegetable oil	¼ teaspoon chili powder
1½ teaspoons coriander seeds	1 teaspoon salt
1 teaspoon black peppercorns	4 tomatoes, peeled and roughly chopped
1 garlic clove, crushed	½ teaspoon garam masala
	chopped cilantro, for garnish

1 Wash the fish under cold running water and pat dry with kitchen paper towels. Cut into 1-inch cubes.
2 Heat the ghee or oil in a heavy-based skillet. Add the fish, a few pieces at a time, and fry gently for 2–3 minutes. Remove the fish carefully from the pan with a slotted spoon and set aside on a plate.
3 Put the coriander seeds, peppercorns and garlic in a small electric mill or pestle and mortar and grind to a smooth paste.
4 Add the spice paste to the skillet with the turmeric, chili powder and salt, and fry gently for 2 minutes.
5 Stir in the tomatoes and 1¼ cups water. Bring to a boil, then lower the heat and cook over a medium heat for 5 minutes. Add the fish and simmer, shaking the pan occasionally, for a further 10 minutes or until the fish is tender. *Do not stir*. Remove from the heat.
6 Sprinkle the garam masala over the fish, cover the pan and let the fish stand for 2 minutes, then turn into a warmed serving dish. Garnish with chopped cilantro and serve immediately.

ITALIAN FISH STEW

SERVES 4

a good pinch of saffron strands	2½ cups chopped peeled tomatoes
about 2 pounds mixed fish fillets (cod, flounder, red snapper, sea bass, angler fish)	2 canned anchovy fillets, drained
10–12 shell-on cooked shrimp	⅔ cup dry white wine
¼ cup olive oil	2 bay leaves
1 large onion, finely chopped	3 tablespoons chopped basil
3 garlic cloves, crushed	salt and pepper
2 slices of canned pimiento, drained and sliced	10–12 mussels, unshucked
	4 slices of hot toast, to serve

1 To prepare the saffron water, soak the saffron strands in a little boiling water for 30 minutes. Meanwhile, skin the fish and cut into bite-size pieces. Shell the shrimp.
2 Heat the oil in a large heavy-based pan, add the onion, garlic and pimiento and fry for 5 minutes or until soft.
3 Add the tomatoes and anchovies and stir with a wooden spoon to break them up. Pour in the wine and ⅔ cup water and bring to a boil, then lower the heat and add the bay leaves and half the basil. Simmer, uncovered, for 20 minutes, stirring occasionally.
4 Add the firm fish to the tomato mixture, then strain in the saffron water and season to taste. Cook for 10 minutes, then add the delicate fish and cook for a further 5 minutes.
5 Add the shrimp and mussels, cover and cook for 5 minutes or until the mussels open. Discard the bay leaves and any mussels that do not open.
6 To serve, put one slice of toast in each of four individual bowls. Spoon over the stew and sprinkle with basil.

MEDITERRANEAN FISH STEW WITH AÏOLI

SERVES 4

10 garlic cloves	1 small onion, thinly sliced
1 egg yolk	1 leek, thinly sliced
1¼ cups olive oil	1–2 parsley sprigs
juice of 1 lemon	1 bay leaf
salt and pepper	1 thin strip of orange rind
2 pounds firm white fish fillets (sea bass, pollock, whiting, angler fish or halibut), skinned	1 small baguette (French loaf), sliced, to serve
5 cups fish stock	chopped parsley, for garnish

1 First make the aïoli. Roughly chop eight of the garlic cloves and put in a mortar with the egg yolk. Crush with a pestle. Add the oil a drop at a time and work until the ingredients emulsify and thicken. Continue adding the oil in a thin, stready stream, beating vigorously until the mayonnaise is very thick and smooth.

2 Beat in the lemon juice and 1 teaspoon lukewarm water. Season to taste and set aside in a cool place.

3 Cut the fish into thick chunks and place in a large saucepan. Pour in the stock, then add the next five ingredients, with the remaining garlic, halved. Season to taste, cover and simmer for 15 minutes or until tender.

4 Transfer the fish and vegetables to a warmed serving dish with a slotted spoon. Keep warm.

5 Strain the cooking liquid into a pitcher and blend a few spoonfuls into the aïoli. Toast the baguette and keep warm.

6 Put the aïoli in a heavy-based saucepan, then gradually whisk in the remaining cooking liquid. Heat through gently, stirring constantly. Adjust the seasoning. Pour over the fish and sprinkle with parsley. Serve with the toast.

SPECIAL PARSLEY FISH PIE

SERVES 4

1 pound whiting fillet	2 eggs, hard-cooked and chopped
1¾ cups milk	⅔ cup light cream
1 bay leaf	2 tablespoons chopped parsley
6 peppercorns	
1 onion, sliced	4 ounces shelled shrimp
salt and pepper	2 pounds potatoes, peeled
5 tablespoons butter	1 egg, beaten, to glaze
3 tablespoons all-purpose flour	

1 Place the whiting in a saucepan and pour over 1¼ cups of the milk. Add the bay leaf, peppercorns, onion and a pinch of salt. Simmer for 10 minutes. Lift the fish from the pan, flake the flesh and remove the skin and bones. Strain the cooking liquid and reserve.

2 To make the sauce, melt 3 tablespoons of the butter in the saucepan, add the flour and cook gently, stirring, for 1–2 minutes. Off the heat, gradually blend in the reserved cooking liquid. Bring to a boil, stirring constantly, then simmer until thickened. Season.

3 Add the eggs to the sauce with the cream, fish, parsley and shrimp. Taste and adjust the seasoning, then spoon the mixture into a 11-inch oval baking dish.

4 Meanwhile, boil the potatoes, drain and mash without any liquid. Heat the remaining milk and butter and beat into the potatoes. Season to taste. Pipe or spoon over the fish mixture.

5 Bake at 400°F for 10–15 minutes or until the potato is set. Brush the beaten egg over the pie. Return to the oven for a further 15 minutes.

FISHERMAN'S HOT POT

SERVES 4

1 pound cod fillet, skinned	1 medium onion, thinly sliced
6 tablespoons all-purpose flour	2 cups sliced mushrooms
1½ pounds potatoes, peeled	1 tablespoon butter
1–2 tablespoons lemon juice	⅔ cup milk
salt and pepper	1 cup shredded Cheddar cheese

1 Cut the cod into ¾-inch squares and toss in 4 tablespoons of the flour.

2 Cook the potatoes in boiling salted water for about 15 minutes or until tender, but not soft, then slice them thinly. Arrange one third in the bottom of a buttered ovenproof casserole. Cover with half the cod, sprinkle with half the lemon juice and season well.

3 Combine the onion and mushrooms and arrange half the mixture over the fish. Cover with the remaining cod, lemon juice, one third of the potatoes and the remaining onions and mushrooms.

4 Melt the butter in a saucepan, stir in the remaining flour and cook gently for 1 minute, stirring. Remove the pan from the heat and gradually stir in the milk. Bring to a boil and continue to cook, stirring, until the sauce thickens, then add half the cheese and season to taste.

5 Pour the sauce over the ingredients in the casserole, put the remaining potato slices on top, and sprinkle with the remaining cheese.

6 Bake, uncovered, in a preheated oven at 400°F for about 40 minutes or until golden.

TOMATO FISH BAKE

SERVES 4

1 cup fresh breadcrumbs	2 tablespoons butter
½ cup shredded Cheddar cheese	½ cup sliced mushrooms
1 small onion, finely chopped	¼ cup all-purpose flour
½ teaspoon dried mixed herbs	2 tablespoons tomato paste
1½ cups milk	1 teaspoon lemon juice
salt and pepper	pinch of sugar
1 pound white fish	1 pound potatoes, peeled
	chopped parsley or watercress, for garnish

1 To make the stuffing, mix the breadcrumbs, shredded cheese, onion and herbs with 3 tablespoons of the milk. Season to taste.

2 Wash and skin the fish. Place half on the base of a buttered shallow flameproof dish. Spread the stuffing over the fish and top with the remaining fish.

3 Melt the butter in a saucepan and sauté the mushrooms for about 5 minutes or until soft. Add the flour, the remaining milk, the tomato paste, lemon juice, sugar and seasoning. Heat, whisking continuously, until the sauce thickens. Pour over the fish. Bake in a preheated oven at 375°F for 20 minutes.

4 Meanwhile, cook the potatoes in boiling salted water for about 20 minutes or until tender. Drain and mash. Remove the fish from the oven and pipe a border of mashed potato around the dish. Return to the oven or place under a preheated hot broiler to brown. Garnish with chopped parsley or watercress.

HOT FISH TERRINE WITH GRUYÈRE SAUCE

SERVES 6

6 tablespoons butter	3 eggs
1 garlic clove, crushed	1 egg yolk
¼ cup all-purpose flour	salt and pepper
3 cups milk	2 teaspoons chopped parsley
1¼ pounds whiting fillets, skinned and chopped	4 ounces shelled cooked shrimp, chopped
⅔ cup heavy cream	1 cup shredded Gruyère cheese
2 teaspoons anchovy essence	

1 Lightly butter and base-line a 7-cup shallow loaf pan or terrine.

2 Melt 3 tablespoons butter and add the garlic. Stir in 3 tablespoons flour and cook, stirring, for 1–2 minutes. Off the heat, blend in 2 cups milk. Bring to a boil, stirring, then simmer for 2 minutes or until thick.

3 Turn the sauce into a blender or food processor. Add the fish, cream, anchovy essence, eggs and egg yolk and blend to a purée. Season lightly.

4 Spoon half the fish mixture into the pan. Sprinkle with parsley and half the shrimp, then spoon in the rest of the fish mixture. Cover with buttered baker's parchment. Place in a roasting pan and pour in hot water to come halfway up the sides. Cook at 300°F for 1¾ hours.

5 Just before the terrine is cooked, make the sauce. Melt 2 tablespoons butter, add the remaining flour and cook, stirring, for 1–2 minutes. Off the heat, blend in the remaining milk. Cook, stirring, for 2 minutes until thick. Stir in the cheese and remaining shrimp. Season to taste.

6 Invert the terrine on to a warmed serving dish and drain off the juices. Spoon over a little sauce before serving.

FISH MOUSSES WITH CILANTRO AND TOMATO SAUCE

SERVES 4

½ pound haddock or cod fillets, skinned	pinch of cayenne
	FOR THE SAUCE
4 ounces shelled shrimp	2 tablespoons butter
1 egg	3 scallions, chopped
⅔ cup heavy cream	1-pound can chopped tomatoes
⅔ cup plain yogurt	1 tablespoon tomato paste
2 tablespoons chopped fresh cilantro or 2 teaspoons ground coriander	1 teaspoon sugar
	1 tablespoon chopped fresh cilantro or 1 teaspoon ground coriander
2 teaspoons lemon juice	
salt and pepper	cilantro sprigs, for garnish

1 Put the fish and shrimp in a blender or food processor and blend to a purée. Blend in the egg, cream, yogurt, cilantro/coriander and lemon juice and season to taste with salt, pepper and cayenne.

2 Butter four ¾-cup ovenproof ramekin dishes and divide the fish mixture among them. Cover loosely with foil, place in a roasting pan and pour in enough hot water to come halfway up the sides. Cook in a preheated oven at 350°F for 20–30 minutes or until firm.

3 For the sauce, melt the butter in a small saucepan, add the scallions and cook for 3 minutes. Put the tomatoes in a food processor or blender and purée until smooth. Add the tomatoes to the onions and stir in the tomato paste and sugar. Cook for 5–6 minutes. Sieve the sauce and stir in the chopped cilantro. Unmold the mousses and serve with the sauce. Garnish with cilantro sprigs.

FISH MEDALLIONS WITH DILL SAUCE

SERVES 4

HERRING IN OATMEAL

SERVES 2

	FOR THE SAUCE
½ pound salmon fillets, skinned	2 tablespoons butter
¾ pound plaice (fluke) fillets, skinned	1 small onion, minced
⅔ cup dry white wine	1 tablespoon all-purpose flour
2 tablespoons lemon juice	1¼ cups light cream
pepper	1 bay leaf
a few dill sprigs	2 tablespoons chopped fresh dill or 2 teaspoons dried
	salt and pepper

2 medium herring, cleaned, heads and tails removed	1 tablespoon vegetable oil
salt and pepper	1 tablespoon butter
⅓ cup medium oatmeal	lemon wedges, to serve

1 To remove the backbone of the fish, open out on a board, cut side down, and press lightly with the fingers along the middle of the back. Turn the fish over and ease the backbone up with your fingers. Fold the fish in half. Season well and coat with the oatmeal.

2 Heat the oil and butter in a large skillet and fry the herring for about 5 minutes on each side. Drain well before serving hot with lemon wedges.

TO MICROWAVE

Complete step 1. Heat a large browning skillet on HIGH for 5–8 minutes or according to the manufacturer's instructions. Put the oil and butter into the browning skillet, then quickly add the herring. Cook on HIGH for 1 minute, then turn over and cook on HIGH for 1–2 minutes or until tender. Serve hot with lemon wedges.

1 Cut the fish fillets lengthwise into ¼-inch thick strips. Using two of one color and one of the other, lay alternate colors alongside each other and coil round to form a spiral, securing with a wooden toothpick. Continue to make eight medallions.

2 Place the wine and lemon juice in a skillet. Add the medallions, season with pepper and scatter over the dill sprigs. Poach gently for 5–7 minutes or until the fish is firm and moist. Remove the dill sprigs and toothpicks. Transfer the medallions to a warmed serving dish and cover with foil to keep warm.

3 For the sauce, melt the butter in a saucepan and cook the onion for 2–3 minutes or until softened. Stir in the flour and cook, stirring continuously, for a further minute. Remove from the heat and gradually stir in the cream. Add the bay leaf. Heat gently, without boiling, for 3–5 minutes or until the sauce is thickened, stirring continuously. Remove the bay leaf and stir in the dill. Season to taste.

4 Serve the fish medallions with the dill sauce.

STUFFED HERRING

SERVES 4

5 tablespoons butter	juice and finely grated rind of 1 lemon
1 medium onion, finely chopped	3 tablespoons chopped fresh mixed herbs (chives, parsley, rosemary, thyme)
1 cup wholewheat breadcrumbs	salt and pepper
½ cup chopped walnut pieces	four 10-oz herring, cleaned, boned and heads and tails, removed
1 tablespoon prepared English mustard	

1 Melt 1 tablespoon of the butter in a saucepan, add the onion and fry gently for about 5 minutes or until softened, stirring occasionally.

2 Meanwhile, mix together the breadcrumbs, walnuts, mustard, lemon rind, 1 tablespoon lemon juice and the mixed herbs. Season to taste. Add the onion and mix together well.

3 Open the herring fillets and lay skin side down. Press the stuffing mixture evenly over each fillet. Fold the herring fillets back in half and slash the skin several times.

4 Melt the remaining butter in a large skillet, add the fish and fry for about 10 minutes or until they are tender and browned on each side, turning the fish once.

VARIATION
Stuffed Mackerel
Substitute four mackerel for the herring in the above recipe if preferred.

MACKEREL PARCELS

SERVES 4

four 6-ounce fresh mackerel	2 tablespoons chopped mint
about 2 tablespoons margarine	1 teaspoon sugar
½ large cucumber, sliced	salt and pepper
¼ cup white wine vinegar	plain yogurt and mint leaves, to serve

1 With the back of a knife and working from the tail toward the head, scrape off the scales from the skin of the mackerel. Cut off the heads just below the gills with a sharp knife. Cut off the fins and tails with kitchen scissors.

2 Slit the underside of each fish open from head to tail end with a sharp knife or scissors. With the flat of the knife blade, scrape out the entrails of the fish, together with any membranes and blood. Wash the fish thoroughly.

3 Lay the fish flat on a board or work surface with the skin uppermost. Press firmly along the backbone with your knuckles to flatten the fish and loosen the backbone.

4 Turn the fish over and lift out the backbone. Cut each fish lengthwise into two fillets. Dry thoroughly.

5 Grease eight squares of kitchen foil with a little margarine. Put a mackerel fillet in the center of each square, skin side down.

6 Arrange cucumber slices down one half of the length of each fillet, then sprinkle with vinegar, mint and sugar. Season. Dot with the remaining margarine.

7 Fold the mackerel fillets over lengthwise to enclose the cucumber filling, then wrap in the foil. Place the foil parcels in a single layer in an ovenproof dish. Cook at 400°F for 30 minutes or until tender.

8 To serve, unwrap the foil parcels and carefully place the mackerel fillets in a circle on a warmed platter. Spoon the yogurt in the center and garnish with mint.

BROILED MACKEREL WITH SAGE SAUCE

SERVES 4

4 mackerel, cleaned	⅓ cup dry white wine
salt and pepper	⅓ cup dry vermouth
⅔ cup olive oil	1 teaspoon minced sage
2 tablespoons lemon juice	

1 Cut the fins from the mackerel and cut three diagonal slits in the skin across both sides of each fish. Season the fish inside and out, then place in a dish large enough to hold them in a single layer.

2 Mix the oil, lemon juice and wine together and pour over the fish. Cover and leave to marinate in a cool place for 1½ hours, turning the fish occasionally.

3 Remove the mackerel from the marinade. Cook under a preheated hot broiler for 5–8 minutes on each side, depending on the thickness of the fish, until the flesh flakes easily. Transfer the mackerel to a warmed serving dish, cover and keep hot.

4 Carefully remove the oil from the top of the marinade and pour the marinade into a saucepan with the cooking juices from the broiler pan. Add the vermouth and sage leaves and simmer for 2–3 minutes. Season to taste and pour over the mackerel.

SMOKED MACKEREL SOUFFLÉ

SERVES 4

1 cup milk	2 tablespoons butter
a few onion and carrot slices	salt and pepper
1 bay leaf	4 eggs, separated
6 black peppercorns	3 ounces cooked smoked mackerel, skinned, boned and finely flaked
2 tablespoons all-purpose flour	

1 Grease a 6-cup soufflé dish.

2 Put the milk in a medium saucepan with the onion and carrot slices, bay leaf and peppercorns. Bring slowly to a boil, remove from the heat, cover and leave to infuse for 30 minutes. Strain and reserve the milk.

3 Put the flour, butter and reserved milk in a medium saucepan. Heat, whisking continuously, until the sauce thickens, boils and is smooth. Simmer for 1–2 minutes. Season to taste, then let cool slightly.

4 Beat the egg yolks into the cooled sauce, one at a time. Sprinkle the fish over the sauce and stir in until evenly blended. Whisk all the egg whites until stiff.

5 Mix one large spoonful of egg white into the sauce to lighten its texture. Gently pour the sauce over the remaining egg whites and fold the ingredients lightly together.

6 Pour the soufflé mixture gently into the prepared dish and smooth the surface.

7 Place the soufflé on a baking sheet and bake in a preheated oven at 350°F for about 30 minutes or until golden brown on top, well risen and just firm to the touch. Serve immediately.

CHEESY SMOKED SALMON ROULADE

SERVES 4–6

ITALIAN SQUID STEW

SERVES 4

FOR THE ROULADE	FOR THE FILLING
½ cup butter	1½ cups finely shredded smoked salmon
1 cup all-purpose flour	⅓ cup heavy cream
1¼ cups milk	1 teaspoon lemon juice
1 cup shredded Gruyère cheese	1 tablespoon chopped fresh dill or 1 teaspoon dried
4 eggs, separated	dill sprigs and lemon slices, for garnish
2 tablespoons freshly grated Parmesan cheese	

1 Grease and line a 9 x 13-inch jelly roll pan. Grease the paper.

2 To make the roulade, melt the butter in a saucepan, stir in the flour and cook for 1 minute. Remove from the heat and gradually stir in the milk. Gently bring to a boil, stirring continuously. Beat in the Gruyère and egg yolks.

3 Whisk the egg whites until stiff. Fold into the cheese mixture and pour into the prepared pan. Bake in a preheated oven at 375°F for 25–30 minutes or until firm to the touch and golden.

4 Lay a sheet of wax paper on a work surface and sprinkle with the Parmesan cheese. Turn the roulade on to the paper and remove the lining paper. Cover with a damp cloth.

5 To make the filling, place the smoked salmon in a small saucepan and stir in the cream, lemon juice and chopped dill. Heat very gently for 1–2 minutes. Spread the filling over the roulade and roll up, using the wax paper to assist. Serve immediately, cut into slices and garnished with dill sprigs and lemon slices.

2¼ pounds small squid	2 garlic cloves, crushed
⅓ cup olive oil	juice of ½ lemon
salt and pepper	1 tablespoon chopped parsley
⅓ cup dry white wine	

1 Wash the squid in plenty of cold water. Grip the head and tentacles firmly and pull them away from the body. The entrails will follow. Discard these and pull out the transparent quill.

2 With your hands, carefully peel the skin from the body and fins of each squid.

3 Cut the tentacles from the head and remove the skin. Reserve two ink sacs, being careful not to pierce them. Discard the rest of the head.

4 Cut the squid bodies into ¼-inch rings. Place in a bowl with the tentacles and spoon over 3 tablespoons of the oil. Season well and leave for 3 hours.

5 Pour the squid and marinade into a large skillet and cook the squid for 5 minutes, turning frequently. Add the wine and garlic and cook for a further 5 minutes. Add the ink sacs, breaking them up with a spoon.

6 Cover and cook over a low heat for about 40 minutes or until the squid is tender.

7 Add the remaining oil, the lemon juice and parsley. Stir for 3 minutes over a high heat, taste and adjust the seasoning and serve.

SCALLOPS IN CREAMY BASIL SAUCE

SERVES 4

2 pounds sea scallops, thawed if frozen	⅔ cup dry white wine
2 tablespoons vegetable oil	4 tablespoons chopped basil
1 tablespoon butter	salt and pepper
1 small onion, finely chopped	⅔ cup heavy cream
2 garlic cloves, crushed	a few fresh basil sprigs, for garnish

1 Cut the scallops (including the coral) into fairly thick slices. Pat dry with kitchen paper towels and set aside.
2 Heat the oil and butter in a large skillet, add the onion and garlic, and fry gently for 5 minutes or until soft and lightly colored.
3 Add the scallops to the pan and toss to coat in the oil and butter. Stir in the wine and basil and season to taste.
4 Sauté the scallops over a moderate heat for 10 minutes or until they are tender, turning them constantly so that they cook evenly on all sides. Do not overcook or they will become tough and rubbery.
5 Remove the scallops from the liquid with a slotted spoon and set aside on a plate. Boil the liquid until reduced by about half, then stir in the cream, a little at a time, and simmer until the sauce is thick.
6 Return the scallops to the pan and heat gently. Taste and adjust the seasoning and serve garnished with basil.

MUSSEL AND ONION STEW

SERVES 4

3 dozen fresh mussels in the shell, scrubbed and bearded	¼ cup wholewheat flour
⅔ cup dry white wine	1¼ cups milk
2 tablespoons butter	2 tablespoons chopped parsley
2 large onions, chopped	2 tablespoons light cream

1 Discard any mussels that are cracked or do not close when tapped sharply with a knife.
2 Put the wine in a large saucepan and bring to a boil. Add the mussels, cover and cook over a high heat for 3–4 minutes or until the mussels open, shaking the pan occasionally. Discard any mussels that have not opened.
3 Drain the mussels, reserving the cooking liquid in a bowl. Remove the mussels from the shells, working over the bowl to catch the mussel liquor.
4 Melt the butter in a saucepan, add the onions and sauté lightly for about 5 minutes or until soft but not colored. Stir in the flour and cook for 1 minute.
5 Gradually add the milk and the mussel cooking liquid, stirring, until the sauce thickens, boils and is smooth. Simmer for 1–2 minutes.
6 Return the mussels to the pan with the parsley and cream. Reheat gently and serve at once.

MUSSELS AND CLAMS WITH TOMATOES

SERVES 2–3

1½ dozen fresh mussels in the shell, scrubbed and bearded	⅔ cup dry white wine
1½ dozen cherrystone clams	1½ cups chopped ripe tomatoes
2 tablespoons butter	finely grated rind of 1 lemon
1–2 large garlic cloves, crushed	2 tablespoons chopped parsley
1 small onion, finely chopped	salt and pepper

1 Discard any cracked mussels, or any that do not close when tapped sharply with a knife. Scrub the clams thoroughly and discard any that are cracked or open.

2 Melt the butter in a saucepan and cook the garlic and onion until soft. Add the wine, tomatoes, lemon rind and half the parsley. Bring to a boil.

3 Add the mussels and clams to the pan, cover and cook over a high heat for 3–4 minutes or until the mussels and clams are open, shaking the pan occasionally. Discard any mussels or clams that have not opened.

4 Season to taste. Transfer to two or three large bowls or soup plates and sprinkle with the remaining parsley.

TAGLIATELLE WITH SEAFOOD AND CHAMPAGNE SAUCE

SERVES 4

16 fresh mussels in the shell, scrubbed and bearded	½ pound fresh tagliatelle
8 fresh clams, scrubbed	⅓ cup butter
⅔ cup fish stock	salt and pepper
one 11-ounce red mullet, filleted	1 leek, cut into fine julienne strips
6 ounces salmon fillets, skinned	⅔ cup champagne or sparkling dry white wine
4 jumbo shrimp, shelled and deveined	1¼ cups heavy cream
4 fresh sea scallops	pinch of cayenne
	12 fresh basil leaves

1 Discard any open mussels or clams which do not close when tapped. Place in a pan with the stock, cover and cook until the shells open. Discard any closed shells. Let cool, then remove the mussels and clams from their shells. Strain the stock and reserve.

2 Cut the fish into ½-inch strips. Cut each shrimp in half. Separate the coral from each scallop and cut the scallops in half crosswise.

3 Cook the tagliatelle in boiling salted water for 2–3 minutes. Drain and toss in half the butter. Season.

4 Melt the remaining butter in a saucepan and fry the leeks, shrimp and scallop coral for 30 seconds. Add the fish fillets, champagne and reserved stock and simmer for 1 minute. Remove the fish from the pan and keep warm.

5 Boil the cooking liquid rapidly until reduced by half. Add the cream and boil until thick. Season and add the cayenne. Return the fish to the sauce with the seafood and basil. Warm and serve with the tagliatelle.

LIMA BEAN AND TUNA GRATIN

SERVES 4

1 cup dried lima (butter) beans	1 pound fresh or frozen broccoli
2 cups milk	7-ounce can tuna, drained
a small piece of onion	salt and pepper
a small piece of carrot	3 tablespoons butter
1 bay leaf	¼ cup all-purpose flour
6 peppercorns	½ cup shredded Cheddar cheese
a blade of mace	

1 Soak the beans overnight in cold water.
2 Put the milk, vegetables, bay leaf and spices in a saucepan and bring slowly to a boil. Remove from the heat, cover and leave to infuse for 30 minutes, then strain and reserve.
3 Drain the beans and cook in a pan of gently boiling water for 1¼ hours or until tender. Drain well.
4 Meanwhile, break the broccoli into flowerets and cook in a little boiling salted water for about 5 minutes or until just tender. Drain and arrange in a buttered shallow ovenproof dish.
5 Flake the tuna and combine with the cooked beans. Season to taste and pile in the center of the dish.
6 To make the sauce, melt the butter in a saucepan, stir in the flour and cook gently for 1 minute, stirring. Remove the pan from the heat and gradually stir in the strained milk. Bring to a boil and continue to cook, stirring, until the sauce thickens, then season to taste. Pour over the tuna and broccoli mixture.
7 Sprinkle with the cheese and bake in a preheated oven at 400°F for 15–20 minutes or until golden.

FISHERMAN'S PIE

SERVES 4

5 tablespoons butter or margarine	¼ pound button mushrooms, halved
1 cup thinly sliced sweet red pepper	2 cups tomato juice
1 cup thinly sliced sweet green pepper	1¼ pounds cod fillet, skinned
½ cup sliced onion	3 cups thinly sliced potatoes
salt and pepper	½ cup shredded Edam cheese

1 Melt 2 tablespoons of the butter or margarine in a skillet, add the peppers and onion and sauté gently for 10 minutes or until soft but not colored. Transfer to a 10-cup ovenproof dish. Season well.
2 Cook the mushrooms in the fat remaining in the skillet, stirring frequently, for 3–4 minutes or until evenly colored.
3 Pour the tomato juice evenly over the pepper and onion mixture in the dish.
4 Cut the fish into large cubes. Arrange the cubes on top of the tomato juice, pressing them down gently into the juice. Top with the mushrooms. Season again with salt and pepper.
5 Arrange the sliced potatoes on top of the mushrooms. Melt the remaining butter or margarine and brush over the potatoes. Bake in the oven at 375°F for 25 minutes.
6 Sprinkle the shredded cheese over the pie, return to the oven and bake for a further 15 minutes or until melted and bubbling. Serve hot, straight from the dish.

SEAFOOD STIR-FRY

SERVES 4

2 celery stalks, trimmed	1 garlic clove, crushed
1 medium carrot	¼ pound shelled shrimp
¾ pound haddock, cod or wolffish fillets, skinned	1 pound can whole baby corn cobs, drained
2 Iceberg or Romaine lettuces	1 teaspoons anchovy essence
3 tablespoons peanut oil	salt and pepper

1 Slice the celery and carrot into thin matchsticks, 2 inches long. Cut the fish into 1-inch chunks.

2 Shred the lettuce finely with a sharp knife, discarding the core and any thick stalks.

3 Heat 1 tablespoon of the oil in a wok or large skillet until smoking. Add the lettuce and fry for about 30 seconds or until lightly cooked. Transfer to a warmed serving dish with a slotted spoon and keep warm.

4 Heat another 2 tablespoons oil in the wok until smoking. Add the celery, carrot, white fish and garlic and stir-fry over a high heat for 2–3 minutes, adding more oil if necessary.

5 Lower the heat and add the shrimp, baby corn and anchovy essence. Toss well together for 2–3 minutes to heat through and coat all the ingredients in the sauce (the fish will flake apart).

6 Season to taste, spoon on top of the lettuce and serve immediately.

CURRIED SHRIMP CRÊPES

SERVES 4

	FOR THE FILLING
1 cup all-purpose flour	2 tablespoons butter
salt	1 tablespoon curry powder
1 egg, beaten	¼ cup all-purpose flour
1¼ cups milk	1¼ cups milk
vegetable oil, for frying	½ pound shelled shrimp
1 cup shredded sharp Cheddar cheese	2 tablespoons chopped fresh parsley or 2 teaspoons dried
parsley sprigs and lemon wedges, for garnish	salt and pepper

1 To make the crêpes, sift the flour and salt into a bowl. Add the egg and ⅔ cup of the milk and beat well. Gradually beat in the remaining milk.

2 Heat a small skillet or crêpe pan and brush with oil. Add about 3 tablespoons of the batter and swirl to coat the pan. Cook for 1–2 minutes or until the underside is golden, then flip over and cook the other side until golden. Turn on to a plate and repeat the process, making eight to ten crêpes.

3 To make the filling, melt the butter in a saucepan, stir in the curry powder and flour and cook for 1 minute. Remove from the heat and gradually stir in the milk. Return to the heat and slowly bring to a boil, stirring continuously. Add the shrimp and parsley and season.

4 Divide the filling among the crêpes, placing it toward one edge. Roll up the crêpes and arrange, side by side, in an ovenproof dish. Sprinkle over the cheese.

5 Bake in a preheated oven at 350° for 15–20 minutes. Garnish with parsley and lemon.

VEGETARIAN DISHES

Full of goodness and flavor, vegetarian dishes can be both satisfying and simple for family meals, yet special enough for entertaining. Carefully selected combinations of vegetables, herbs, nuts and seeds are delicious served in a wide range of wholesome dishes.

GRANDMA'S CHEESE PUDDING

SERVES 8

5 cups milk	8 eggs
2 cups fresh breadcrumbs	1 teaspoon Dijon mustard
4 cups shredded Cheddar cheese or Monterey Jack	salt and pepper

1 Put the milk in a saucepan and bring to a boil. Place the breadcrumbs in a bowl and pour the hot milk over. Stir in the cheese.
2 Lightly beat the eggs with the mustard and the milk and breadcrumb mixture. Season to taste.
3 Butter a shallow 3-quart ovenproof dish and pour in the cheese pudding mixture. Bake in a preheated oven at 350°F for about 45 minutes or until lightly set and golden. Serve at once.

STUFFED EGGPLANTS

SERVES 4

2 eggplants	1 shallot, chopped
2 tablespoons butter	1 onion, chopped
4 small tomatoes, peeled and chopped	1 cup wholewheat breadcrumbs
2 teaspoons chopped fresh marjoram or 1 teaspoon dried	salt and pepper
	½ cup shredded cheese
	parsley sprigs, for garnish

1 Steam or boil the eggplants for 30 minutes or until tender. Cut in half lengthwise, scoop out the flesh and chop finely. Reserve the shells.
2 Melt the butter in a saucepan, add the tomatoes, marjoram, shallot and onion and cook for 10 minutes. Stir in the eggplants and a few breadcrumbs, then season.
3 Stuff the eggplant shells with this mixture, then sprinkle with the remaining breadcrumbs and the shredded cheese. Broil until golden brown. Garnish and serve.

CHEESE SOUFFLÉ

SERVES 4

3 tablespoons butter	2 teaspoons Dijon mustard
1 cup milk	salt and pepper
1 onion, sliced	4 eggs, separated, plus 1 egg white
1 carrot, sliced	
1 bay leaf	1¼ cups shredded Brick cheese
6 peppercorns	
2 tablespoons all-purpose flour	

1 Grease the inside of a 7-cup soufflé dish with 1 teaspoon butter.

2 Place the milk, onion, carrot, bay leaf and peppercorns in a saucepan, bring slowly to a boil, then remove from the heat. Leave to infuse for 15 minutes, then strain and reserve the milk.

3 Melt the remaining butter in a saucepan, stir in the flour and cook gently for 1 minute, stirring. Remove from the heat and gradually stir in the reserved milk. Bring to a boil and continue to cook, stirring, until the sauce thickens, then add the mustard and season to taste. Let the mixture cool slightly.

4 Beat the egg yolks into the sauce, one at a time. Add the cheese, reserving 1 tablespoon, and stir until well blended.

5 Whisk the egg whites until stiff. Mix in one spoonful of sauce, then pour the remaining sauce over the egg whites and fold the ingredients lightly together.

6 Turn the mixture gently into the prepared dish. Smooth the top and sprinkle over the remaining cheese. Place on a baking sheet and bake in the center of the oven at 350°F for 30 minutes. Serve at once.

ZUCCHINI, PARMESAN AND TOMATO BAKE

SERVES 4

1½ pounds zucchini	2 tablespoons tomato paste
salt and pepper	1 tablespoon chopped fresh marjoram or 1 teaspoon dried
about ⅔ cup vegetable oil	
1 medium onion, finely chopped	¾ pound Mozzarella cheese, thinly sliced
2⅔ cups chopped peeled tomatoes	1 cup freshly grated Parmesan cheese
1 large garlic clove, crushed	

1 Cut the zucchini into ¼-inch thick slices. Put in a colander, sprinkling each layer generously with salt, and leave for at least 20 minutes.

2 Heat 2 tablespoons of the oil in a saucepan, add the onion and sauté for about 5 minutes or until just beginning to brown.

3 Stir in the tomatoes, garlic and tomato paste and season to taste. Simmer for about 10 minutes, stirring to break down the tomatoes. Stir in the marjoram and remove from the heat.

4 Rinse the zucchini and pat dry with kitchen paper towels. Heat half the remaining oil in a skillet, add half the zucchini and fry until golden brown. Drain well on kitchen paper towels while frying the remaining zucchini in the remaining oil.

5 Layer the zucchini, tomato sauce and Mozzarella cheese in a shallow ovenproof dish, finishing with a layer of Mozzarella. Sprinkle with the Parmesan cheese.

6 Bake in a preheated oven at 350°F for about 40 minutes or until brown and bubbling. Serve hot, straight from the dish.

ITALIAN STUFFED TOMATOES

SERVES 4–6

1 tablespoon olive oil	3 tablespoons pignoli (pine nuts)
4 scallions, finely chopped	1-pound can flageolet beans, drained
2 garlic cloves, crushed	
1 tablespoon tomato paste	salt and pepper
12 pimiento-stuffed green olives, sliced	4 large beefsteak tomatoes or 6 medium tomatoes
2 tablespoons chopped fresh basil or 1 tablespoon dried	basil sprigs, for garnish

1 Heat the oil in a large saucepan and cook the scallions and garlic for 2–3 minutes or until soft.
2 Add the tomato paste, olives, basil and nuts and cook for 2 minutes. Stir in the beans. Season.
3 Slice the tops off the tomatoes, reserving them for the lids, and scoop out the seeds and flesh to make them hollow. Chop the flesh and add to the filling mixture. Arrange the tomato shells in a buttered ovenproof dish and divide the filling among them. Add the lids and cover with foil.
4 Bake in a preheated oven at 350°F for 15–20 minutes. Garnish and serve.

JERUSALEM ARTICHOKE GRATIN

SERVES 4

2 pounds Jerusalem artichokes	3 medium leeks, thickly sliced
salt and pepper	1½ cups fresh or frozen peas
⅓ cup butter	
1 tablespoon olive oil	⅔ cup heavy cream
½ pound pearl onions	¾ cup shredded Swiss cheese
2 garlic cloves, crushed	¾ cup shredded Cheddar cheese
⅔ cup dry white wine or vegetable stock	½ cup dried wholewheat breadcrumbs
¼ teaspoon grated nutmeg	

1 Parboil the artichokes in salted water for 10 minutes. Remove with a slotted spoon and leave to cool.
2 Peel the artichokes and slice thickly. Set aside.
3 Heat ¼ cup butter with the oil in a saucepan, add the onions and garlic and toss until well coated.
4 Pour in the wine or stock and ⅔ cup water and bring to a boil. Add the nutmeg, cover and simmer for 10 minutes. Add the artichokes, leeks and peas and continue simmering for 5 minutes or until tender. Transfer the vegetables to a flameproof gratin dish.
5 Boil the cooking liquid rapidly until reduced by about half, then lower the heat and stir in the cream.
6 Mix the two cheeses together. Stir half into the sauce, season and stir until melted.
7 Pour the cheese sauce over the vegetables. Mix the remaining cheese and breadcrumbs, then sprinkle on top.
8 Dot the remaining butter over the gratin, then bake at 425°F for 10 minutes or until golden.

CYPRUS STUFFED PEPPERS

SERVES 4

8 sweet peppers	1 teaspoon sugar
⅓ cup olive oil	salt and pepper
2 onions, chopped	3 tablespoons chopped cilantro
4 garlic cloves, crushed	1 cup Italian risotto rice
2 cups peeled chopped tomatoes	½ teaspoon ground cinnamon
1 tablespoon tomato paste	

1 Cut the stalk end off each pepper and reserve. Remove the cores and seeds and discard. Wash and pat dry.
2 Heat ¼ cup oil in a skillet, add the peppers and fry for 10 minutes, turning frequently. Remove from the pan with a slotted spoon and drain.
3 To make the stuffing, drain off all but 2 tablespoons oil from the pan, then add the onions and garlic and fry very gently for about 15 minutes. Add the tomatoes and fry gently to soften, stirring constantly. Increase the heat and cook rapidly until thick and pulpy.
4 Lower the heat and add the tomato paste and sugar. Season to taste and simmer gently for 5 minutes. Remove from the heat and stir in the cilantro and rice. Spoon into the peppers, dividing it equally among them.
5 Stand the peppers close together in a large heavy-based pan or flameproof casserole. Sprinkle with the cinnamon, then the remaining oil. Put the reserved 'lids' on top.
6 Pour ⅔ cup water into the base of the pan, then bring to a boil. Lower the heat, cover with a plate which just fits inside the pan, then place weights on top.
7 Simmer gently for 1 hour, then remove from the heat and leave to cool. Chill in the refrigerator overnight, still with the weights on top. Serve the peppers chilled.

CABBAGE AND HAZELNUT ROLLS

MAKES 16

1 pound potatoes, peeled	½ cup chopped toasted hazelnuts
salt and pepper	2 eggs, beaten
2 pounds green cabbage, roughly chopped	1 cup breadcrumbs
3 tablespoons milk, if necessary	vegetable oil, for deep frying
¼ cup butter	lemon twists, for garnish
½ cup all-purpose flour	

1 Cook the potatoes in boiling salted water for 20 minutes or until tender. Drain and mash without adding liquid.
2 Cook the cabbage in boiling salted water for 5–10 minutes or until just tender. Drain well, then put in a blender or food processor and blend to a purée, adding the milk if necessary – you should have 2 cups purée.
3 Melt the butter in a saucepan, add the flour and cook gently, stirring, for 1–2 minutes. Gradually blend in the cabbage purée, bring to a boil, then simmer for 5 minutes.
4 Stir the mashed potatoes and hazelnuts into the sauce, season to taste and mix well. Transfer to a bowl, cool, cover and chill for at least 1½ hours or until firm.
5 With dampened hands, shape the mixture into 16 rolls. Place on a greased baking sheet and chill again for at least 20 minutes.
6 Coat the rolls in beaten egg, then roll in the breadcrumbs. Heat the oil to 350°F in a deep-fat fryer. Deep-fry the rolls in batches for about 4 minutes or until crisp and golden. Remove with a slotted spoon and drain on kitchen paper towels while frying the remainder. Serve the rolls hot, garnished with lemon twists.

BAKED POTATOES WITH CHICK-PEAS

SERVES 4

four 10-ounce baking potatoes	½ teaspoon ground cumin
3 tablespoons vegetable oil	1-pound can chick-peas, drained
salt and pepper	4 tablespoons chopped parsley
1 medium onion, roughly chopped	⅔ cup plain yogurt
½ teaspoon ground coriander	chopped parsley, for garnish

1 Scrub the potatoes and pat dry. Brush them with 1 tablespoon of the vegetable oil and sprinkle lightly with salt.

2 Run thin skewers through the potatoes to help conduct the heat through them. Place them directly on the oven shelves and bake in a preheated oven at 400°F for 1¼ hours or until tender.

3 Meanwhile, heat the remaining oil in a large saucepan, add the onion, coriander and cumin and fry for 4 minutes, stirring occasionally. Add the chick-peas and cook for a further 1–2 minutes, stirring all the time.

4 Halve the potatoes and scoop out the flesh, keeping the skin intact. Add the potato flesh to the chick-pea mixture with the parsley and yogurt. Mash until smooth, then season to taste.

5 Place the potato skins on a baking sheet and fill with the potato and chick-pea mixture. Return to the oven and bake for a further 10–15 minutes. Serve hot, sprinkled with chopped parsley.

CAULIFLOWER AND ZUCCHINI BAKE

SERVES 4

1 large cauliflower	3 tablespoons wholewheat flour
salt and pepper	⅔ cup milk
¼ cup butter or margarine	3 eggs, separated
2 cups thinly sliced zucchini	1 tablespoon grated Parmesan cheese

1 Divide the cauliflower into small flowerets, trimming off thick stalks and leaves. Cook in boiling salted water for 10–12 minutes or until tender.

2 Meanwhile, in a separate pan, melt 2 tablespoons of the butter or margarine, add the zucchini and cook until beginning to soften. Remove from the pan with a slotted spoon and drain on kitchen paper towels.

3 Melt the remaining butter or margarine in the pan, stir in the flour and cook, stirring, for 1–2 minutes. Remove from the heat and add the milk, a little at a time, whisking constantly after each addition. Return to the heat and bring to a boil, stirring. Simmer until thickened.

4 Drain the cauliflower well and place in a blender or food processor with the warm sauce, egg yolks and plenty of seasoning. Stir together until evenly mixed, then turn into a large bowl.

5 Whisk the egg whites until stiff and carefully fold into the cauliflower mixture.

6 Spoon half the mixture into a 7-cup soufflé dish. Arrange the zucchini on top, reserving a few for garnish, then cover with the remaining cauliflower mixture. Top with the reserved zucchini.

7 Sprinkle over the Parmesan cheese and bake in a preheated oven at 375°F for 35–40 minutes or until golden. Serve immediately.

LEEK AND MACARONI GRATIN

SERVES 4

¼ pound short-cut macaroni	1½ cups shredded Brick cheese or Double Gloucester with chives
salt and pepper	
¼ cup butter	½ cup breadcrumbs
2 cups chopped leeks	2 tablespoons chopped chives
¼ cup all-purpose flour	
2½ cups milk	

1 Cook the macaroni in boiling salted water for 8–10 minutes or until tender, but not soft. Drain well.

2 Melt the butter in a skillet, add the leeks and sauté for 2 minutes. Stir in the flour and cook gently for 1 minute, stirring. Remove the pan from the heat and gradually stir in the milk. Bring to a boil and continue to cook, stirring for 2 minutes. Remove from the heat and stir in the macaroni and all but 2 tablespoons cheese. Season to taste.

3 Spoon the mixture into a buttered 5-cup shallow ovenproof dish. Mix together the breadcrumbs, chives and remaining cheese and sprinkle evenly in lines across the dish.

4 Bake in a preheated oven at 375°F for 30–35 minutes or until golden. Serve immediately.

PASTA AND MUSHROOMS BAKED WITH TWO CHEESES

SERVES 2–3

½ pound tagliatelle or linguine	½ cup crumbled Stilton cheese
2 tablespoons butter	¼ cup heavy cream
1 garlic clove, crushed	salt and pepper
2 cups thinly sliced mushrooms	1 egg, lightly beaten
	¼ pound Mozzarella cheese

1 Cook the noodles in boiling salted water for about 7 minutes or until just tender.

2 Meanwhile, melt the butter in a large skillet, add the garlic and mushrooms and fry for about 5 minutes or until just softened, stirring frequently. Add the Stilton cheese and cook for 1–2 minutes, stirring continuously. Stir in the cream and season to taste.

3 Drain the pasta and season with lots of pepper. Mix into the mushroom sauce. Stir in the egg and mix thoroughly.

4 Turn the mixture into a buttered ovenproof dish and shred the Mozzarella on top. Cover with foil and bake in a preheated oven at 350°F for 10 minutes, then remove the foil and bake at 425°F for a further 10–15 minutes or until brown and crusty on top.

TO MICROWAVE

Complete step 1. Meanwhile, put the butter, garlic and mushrooms in a large bowl, cover and cook on HIGH for 3–4 minutes or until the mushrooms are softened, stirring occasionally. Stir in the Stilton cheese and the cream and cook on HIGH for 2 minutes, stirring once. Complete step 3. Turn the mixture into a buttered flameproof dish and shred the Mozzarella on top. Cook on HIGH for 3–4 minutes or until heated through. Brown the top under a hot broiler.

VEGETABLE LASAGNE

SERVES 4

1½ cups thinly sliced carrots	2 chicken bouillon cubes
2 cups thinly sliced, zucchini	2 tablespoons butter
1 onion, thinly sliced	2 tablespoons all-purpose flour
1 cup thinly sliced sweet green pepper	1¼ cups milk
1 cup thinly sliced celery	salt and pepper
	6 ounces lasagne
	1½ cups shredded Cheddar cheese

1 Place the vegetables in a saucepan with the bouillon cubes and pour over ⅔ cup boiling water. Bring to a boil, cover and simmer for 10 minutes.

2 Melt the butter in a pan, stir in the flour and cook gently for 1 minute, stirring. Remove from the heat and gradually stir in the milk. Bring to a boil and continue to cook, stirring, until the sauce thickens, then season to taste. If the sauce is too thick, add a little stock from the vegetables.

3 Meanwhile, cook the lasagne in fast boiling salted water until tender, but not soft, or according to packet instructions. Drain, being careful not to break up the lasagne sheets.

4 Make alternate layers of lasagne, vegetables and cheese (use 1 cup) in a 7-cup shallow ovenproof dish, finishing with a layer of lasagne. Top with the sauce, then sprinkle over the remaining cheese.

5 Bake in a preheated oven at 375°F for about 30 minutes.

SPAGHETTI WITH RATATOUILLE SAUCE

SERVES 4

1 eggplant	3 medium zucchini, cut into thin strips
salt and pepper	2 cups finely chopped peeled tomatoes
1 onion, finely chopped	
1 garlic clove, crushed	2 teaspoons chopped basil
1 sweet green pepper, cut into thin strips	14 ounces wholewheat spaghetti
1 sweet red pepper, cut into thin strips	freshly grated Parmesan cheese, to serve

1 Dice the eggplant, then spread out on a plate and sprinkle with salt. Leave for 30 minutes or until the juices flow.

2 Tip the diced eggplant into a sieve and rinse under cold running water. Put into a large, heavy-based saucepan with the prepared vegetables and basil. Season to taste, cover and cook over a moderate heat for 30 minutes. Shake the pan and stir the vegetables frequently during this time, to encourage the juices to flow.

3 Meanwhile, plunge the spaghetti into a large saucepan of boiling salted water. Simmer, uncovered, for 12 minutes or according to packet instructions, until *al dente* (tender but firm to the bite).

4 Drain the spaghetti thoroughly and turn into a warmed serving dish. Taste and adjust the seasoning of the ratatouille sauce, then pour over the spaghetti. Serve immediately, with the Parmesan cheese.

FRESH TAGLIATELLE WITH LEEK AND ROQUEFORT SAUCE

SERVES 4

6 tablespoons butter	1½ pounds fresh tagliatelle
1 garlic clove, crushed	1 teaspoon olive oil
4 cups sliced leeks	pepper
1 cup roughly chopped Roquefort cheese	⅔ cup heavy cream
2 tablespoons chopped fresh chervil or 2 teaspoons dried	1–2 tablespoons grated Parmesan cheese
	chervil sprigs, for garnish

1 Melt 4 tablespoons of the butter in a medium saucepan, add the garlic and leeks and fry for 2–3 minutes or until softened.

2 Stir in the Roquefort cheese and chervil. Cook for 2–3 minutes or until the cheese has melted, stirring constantly.

3 Meanwhile, add the tagliatelle to a large saucepan of boiling water, with the olive oil added, and cook for 3–4 minutes. Drain and return to the clean pan. Add the remaining butter, toss well and season with pepper.

4 Pour the cream into the sauce, whisking vigorously. Cook, stirring, for a few minutes or until thick.

5 Serve the tagliatelle on warmed individual serving plates with the sauce poured over. Sprinkle with Parmesan cheese and garnish with chervil sprigs.

TO MICROWAVE

Dice the butter into a medium bowl. Cover and cook on HIGH for 1 minute. Add the garlic and leeks. Cover and cook on HIGH for 2–3 minutes. Add the cheese and chervil and cook for 1–1½ minutes. Whisk in the cream and cook on HIGH for 1–1½ minutes. Complete steps 3 and 5 as above.

TAGLIATELLE WITH CHEESE AND NUT SAUCE

SERVES 4

14 ounces wholewheat or green (spinach) tagliatelle	1 teaspoon chopped fresh sage or ½ teaspoon dried
salt and pepper	⅓ cup olive oil
1 cup crumbled Gorgonzola cheese	1 tablespoon chopped parsley, for garnish
1 cup chopped walnuts	

1 Plunge the tagliatelle into a large saucepan of boiling salted water. Simmer, uncovered, for 10 minutes, or according to packet instructions, until *al dente* (tender but firm to the bite).

2 Meanwhile, put the cheese into a blender or food processor. Add two thirds of the walnuts and the sage and blend to combine.

3 Add the oil gradually through the funnel (as when making mayonnaise) and blend until the sauce is evenly incorporated.

4 Drain the tagliatelle well and return to the pan. Add the nut sauce and fold in gently to mix. Season to taste.

5 Transfer the pasta and sauce to a warmed serving bowl and sprinkle with the remaining walnuts. Serve immediately, garnished with chopped parsley.

RATATOUILLE PASTA BAKE

SERVES 4–6

2 tablespoons olive oil	2 tablespoons chopped fresh basil or 1 teaspoon dried
1 large onion, thinly sliced	
1 sweet red pepper, cut into 2-inch strips	pinch of sugar
1 sweet yellow pepper, cut into 2-inch strips	salt and pepper
½ lb zucchini, cut into 2-inch strips	2 cups vegetable stock
	¾ pound tri-colored pasta twists
3 cups chopped ripe tomatoes	2 tablespoons butter
2 garlic cloves, crushed	1½ cups shredded sharp Cheddar cheese
2 tablespoons tomato paste	

1 Heat the oil in a large pan, add the onion and peppers, and cook for 5 minutes or until softened, stirring. Add the zucchini and cook for 5 minutes.

2 Stir in the tomatoes, garlic, tomato paste, basil and sugar. Season to taste and simmer for 25–30 minutes, stirring occasionally and gradually adding the stock.

3 Meanwhile, bring a large saucepan of salted water to a boil and add the pasta twists. Cook for 15–20 minutes, stirring occasionally. Drain, then return to the pan, add the butter, toss well and season to taste. Transfer to a deep flameproof dish.

4 Pour the ratatouille sauce over the pasta and sprinkle over the cheese. Broil until golden.

WHOLEWHEAT MACARONI BAKE

SERVES 4–6

6 ounces wholewheat macaroni	1 teaspoon dried oregano
salt and pepper	2 tablespoons wholewheat flour
1 onion, chopped	1¼ cups milk
2 tablespoons vegetable oil	½ cup low-fat cream cheese
½ pound button mushrooms	1 egg, beaten
2 cups chopped peeled tomatoes	1 teaspoon dry English mustard
1¼ cups vegetable stock	2 tablespoons wholewheat breadcrumbs
1 tablespoon tomato purée	2 tablespoons grated Parmesan cheese
1 teaspoon dried mixed herbs	

1 Cook the macaroni in boiling salted water for 10 minutes. Drain. Sauté the onion in the oil for 5 minutes.

2 Cut the small mushrooms in half and slice the larger ones. Add to the pan and toss with the onion for 1–2 minutes.

3 Add the tomatoes and stock and bring to a boil, stirring constantly. Lower the heat, add the tomato paste and herbs and season to taste. Simmer for 10 minutes.

4 Put the flour and milk in a blender and blend for 1 minute. Transfer to a pan and simmer, stirring constantly, for 5 minutes or until thick. Remove from the heat and beat in the cheese, egg and mustard. Season.

5 Mix the macaroni with the mushroom and tomato sauce, then pour into a baking dish. Pour over the cheese sauce and sprinkle with breadcrumbs and Parmesan.

6 Bake in a preheated oven at 375°F for 20 minutes or until golden brown and bubbling. Serve hot.

SPINACH AND LENTIL ROULADE

SERVES 4

1 cup red lentils	salt and pepper
1 small onion, finely chopped	1 pound spinach
2 tablespoons ketchup	½ cup all-purpose flour
1 tablespoon horseradish sauce	1¼ cups milk
½ cup butter	2 eggs, separated
	dry breadcrumbs

1 Butter and line an 11-inch jelly roll pan.
2 Cook the lentils with the onion in a large saucepan of boiling salted water until tender. Drain well, then return to the pan and heat to evaporate excess moisture. Add the ketchup, horseradish and ¼ cup butter. Rub through a sieve, season to taste and set aside.
3 Trim and wash the spinach but do not dry. Pack into a large saucepan, sprinkle with salt, cover tightly and cook gently for 3–4 minutes.
4 To make the roulade, melt the remaining butter in a saucepan, stir in the flour and cook gently for 1 minute, stirring. Remove from the heat and gradually stir in the milk. Bring to a boil and continue to cook, stirring, until the sauce thickens. Remove from the heat. Stir in the spinach and egg yolks. Season to taste.
5 Whisk the egg whites until stiff and gently fold into the spinach mixture. Spoon into the prepared pan and level the surface. Bake in a preheated oven at 400°F for 20 minutes or until well risen and golden.
6 Turn out onto a sheet of wax paper sprinkled with the breadcrumbs. Peel off the lining paper. Spread the lentil purée over the surface and roll up jelly-roll style. Return to the oven to heat through before serving.

SPINACH AND STILTON CRÊPES

SERVES 8

2 pounds fresh spinach	8 teaspoons all-purpose flour
salt and pepper	⅔ cup light cream
¼ cup butter	8 crêpes (see page 119)
½ cup chopped salted peanuts	1¼ cups milk
½ teaspoon mild paprika	½ cup crumbled Blue Stilton cheese

1 Tear the stalks off the spinach and wash, but do not dry. Place in a large saucepan, sprinkle with salt, cover tightly and cook for 10 minutes. Drain well and chop.
2 Heat 2 tablespoons butter in a small saucepan, add the peanuts and paprika and fry gently for 1 minute. Stir in the spinach, 4 teaspoons flour and the cream. Season to taste. Bring to a boil and cook for 2–3 minutes, stirring. Divide the filling among the crêpes, roll up and place, side by side, in a buttered ovenproof dish.
3 Melt the remaining butter in a saucepan, stir in the remaining flour and cook for 1 minute, stirring. Remove from the heat and gradually stir in the milk. Bring to a boil, stirring all the time, until the sauce thickens. Stir in the cheese and season to taste. Pour over the crêpes, cover lightly with foil and bake in a preheated oven at 350°F for 25–30 minutes.

VARIATION

Spinach and Ricotta Crêpes

Ricotta is a fragrant Italian cheese made from the whey left over when producing other cheeses. It has a delicate, smooth flavor and is often mixed with spinach in stuffings for ravioli or cannelloni. It would make an ideal substitute for Stilton in the above recipe.

VEGETARIAN MEDLEY

SERVES 4

2 tablespoons butter	2 cups cooked lentils (1 cup raw lentils)
2 carrots, sliced	1 tablespoon raisins
1 large onion, chopped	2 tablespoons unsalted peanuts
1 sweet green pepper, sliced	salt and pepper
2 tomatoes, chopped	1¼ cups plain yogurt
1 large tart apple, peeled, cored and chopped	2 tablespoons cream cheese
1 garlic clove, crushed	
1 tablespoon chopped fresh sage or 1 teaspoon dried	

1 Melt the butter in a large skillet, add the carrots, onion, green pepper, tomatoes, apple, garlic and sage and fry lightly for 15 minutes or until softened

2 Add the lentils, raisins and peanuts. Season to taste. Stir the yogurt into the cream cheese and mix well to blend. Stir into the mixture. Reheat gently for 5 minutes.

TO MICROWAVE

Melt the butter in a large bowl on HIGH for 45 seconds. Add the carrots, onion, green pepper, tomatoes, apple, garlic and sage and cook on HIGH for 7 minutes, stirring occasionally. Add the remaining ingredients, as in step 2, and cook on HIGH for 2 minutes. Serve at once.

VEGETABLE CURRY

SERVES 4

2 tablespoons vegetable oil	2 potatoes, peeled and roughly chopped
2 teaspoons ground coriander	2 carrots, sliced
1 teaspoon ground cumin	1 sweet green pepper, chopped
½–1 teaspoon chili powder	1½ cups roughly chopped tomatoes
½ teaspoon ground turmeric	⅔ cup plain yogurt
2 garlic cloves, crushed	salt and pepper
1 medium onion, chopped	
1 small cauliflower, cut into small flowerets	

1 Heat the oil in a large saucepan, add the coriander, cumin, chili, turmeric, garlic and onion and sauté for 2–3 minutes, stirring continuously.

2 Add the cauliflower, potatoes, carrots and green pepper and stir to coat in the spices. Stir in the tomatoes and ⅔ cup water. Bring to a boil, cover and simmer gently for 25–30 minutes or until the vegetables are tender.

3 Remove from the heat, stir in the yogurt and season.

TO MICROWAVE

Put the oil, coriander, cumin, chili, turmeric, garlic and onion in a large bowl and cook on HIGH for 2 minutes, stirring once. Add the cauliflower, potatoes, carrots and green pepper and stir to coat in the spices. Stir in the tomatoes and ⅔ cup water. Cover and cook on HIGH for 20 minutes or until the vegetables are tender, stirring occasionally. Complete step 3.

MOONG DAL AND SPINACH

SERVES 6

1¼ cups moong dal (split, washed mung beans)	1 garlic clove, crushed
2 pounds fresh spinach, washed and trimmed, or 1 pound frozen chopped spinach	2 teaspoons ground coriander
	1 teaspoon ground turmeric
⅓ cup ghee or clarified butter	½ teaspoon chili powder
	¼ teaspoon asafoetida (optional)
1 cup finely chopped onion	salt and pepper
½ ounce fresh root ginger, finely chopped	lemon wedges, for garnish

1 Rinse the dal under cold running water. Place in a bowl, cover with cold water and leave to soak for about 2 hours, then drain.

2 Place the fresh spinach in a saucepan with only the water that clings to the leaves. Cover and cook gently for about 5 minutes or until tender. Drain well and chop roughly. If using frozen spinach, place in a saucepan and cook for 7–10 minutes to thaw and to remove as much liquid as possible.

3 Heat the ghee or butter in a large skillet, add the onion, ginger and garlic and fry for 2–3 minutes.

4 Stir in the coriander, turmeric, chili powder, asafoetida (if using) and the dal. Fry, stirring, for 2–3 minutes.

5 Pour in 1¼ cups water, season to taste and bring to a boil. Cover and simmer for about 15 minutes or until the dal is almost tender. Add a little more water if necessary, but the mixture should be almost dry.

6 Stir in the spinach and cook, stirring for 2–3 minutes or until heated through. Taste and adjust the seasoning before serving, garnished with lemon wedges.

VEGETABLE BIRYANI

SERVES 4

1½ cups Basmati rice	½ teaspoon chili powder
salt and pepper	3 medium carrots, thinly sliced
½ cup ghee or clarified butter	½ pound fresh or frozen green beans, cut in two lengthwise
1 large onion, chopped	
1-inch piece of fresh root ginger, grated	½ pound cauliflower flowerets, divided into small sprigs
1–2 garlic cloves, crushed	1 teaspoon garam masala
1 teaspoon ground coriander	juice of 1 lemon
2 teaspoons ground cumin	hard-cooked egg slices and cilantro sprigs, for garnish
1 teaspoon ground turmeric	

1 Rinse the rice and put in a saucepan with 2½ cups water and 1 teaspoon salt. Bring to a boil, then simmer for 10 minutes or until only just tender.

2 Meanwhile, heat the ghee or butter in a large heavy-based saucepan, add the onion, ginger and garlic and fry gently for 5 minutes or until soft but not colored. Add the coriander, cumin, turmeric and chili powder and fry for 2 minutes more, stirring constantly.

3 Remove the rice from the heat and drain. Add 4 cups water to the onion and spice mixture and season to taste. Stir well and bring to a boil. Add the carrots and beans and simmer for 15 minutes, then add the cauliflower and simmer for a further 10 minutes. Lastly, add the rice. Fold gently to mix and simmer until reheated.

4 Stir the garam masala and lemon juice into the biryani and simmer for a few minutes more to reheat and allow the flavors to develop. Season, garnish and serve.

VEGETABLE HOT POT

SERVES 4

3 cups thinly sliced carrots	salt and pepper
2 large onions, thinly sliced	1-pound can butter beans or cannellini beans, drained
3 celery stalks, thinly sliced	
3 cups peeled and sliced potatoes	⅔ cup frozen peas
1 cup thinly sliced rutabaga	3 cups fresh breadcrumbs
2 cups vegetable stock	1½ cups grated Romano cheese
bouquet garni	

1 Layer the carrots, onions, celery, potato and rutabaga in a 9-cup casserole.

2 Pour the vegetable stock into the casserole and add the bouquet garni. Season to taste.

3 Cover the casserole, and cook in a preheated oven at 350°F for 1 hour.

4 Remove the bouquet garni. Add the beans and peas to the casserole. Mix the breadcrumbs and cheese together and spoon over the hot pot. Return to the oven and cook, uncovered, for about 20 minutes.

VARIATION

The vegetables used in this satisfying dish can be varied according to the season. Other root vegetables, such as parsnips or turnips could replace the rutabaga, and any canned beans could be used instead of butter beans. When available, replace the frozen peas with fresh.

BUCKWHEAT AND LENTIL CASSEROLE

SERVES 4

salt and pepper	3 bay leaves
1¼ cups buckwheat	2 tablespoons lemon juice
2 tablespoons vegetable oil	1 garlic clove, crushed
1 sweet red or green pepper, cut into strips	2 rosemary sprigs
1 onion, finely chopped	1 teaspoon cumin seeds
2 cups sliced zucchini	2½ cups vegetable stock
1½ cups sliced mushrooms	2 tablespoons butter
1 cup red lentils	chopped parsley, for garnish

1 Put 2 cups water in a saucepan, add a pinch of salt, then bring to a boil. Sprinkle in the buckwheat and return to a boil. Boil rapidly for 1 minute, reduce the heat, cover and cook gently for 12 minutes or until the water has been absorbed. Do not stir. Transfer to a buttered casserole.

2 Heat the oil in a flameproof casserole, add the pepper and onion and sauté for 5 minutes. Add the zucchini and mushrooms and fry for a further 5 minutes. Stir in the lentils, bay leaves, lemon juice, garlic, rosemary, cumin and stock. Add to the buckwheat and stir well.

3 Simmer for about 45 minutes or until the lentils are cooked, stirring occasionally. Add the butter, adjust the seasoning and sprinkle with parsley. Serve hot.

COUSCOUS

SERVES 6

1 pound couscous	5 cups vegetable stock
4 zucchini, cut into ½-inch slices	salt and pepper
1 sweet red pepper, diced	1 cup chick-peas, soaked overnight, then drained
1 sweet green pepper, diced	¼ cup blanched almonds
2 onions, diced	1 teaspoon ground turmeric
2 carrots, diced	2 teaspoons mild paprika
2 cups diced turnips	½ teaspoon ground coriander
1 small cauliflower, cut into small flowerets	⅓ cup melted butter
4 large tomatoes, peeled and chopped	⅔ cup dried apricots, soaked overnight
2 garlic cloves, crushed	

1 Place the couscous in a large bowl with 2 cups lukewarm water and leave to soak for 1 hour.
2 Place the prepared vegetables in a large saucepan with the garlic, stock, pepper to taste, chick-peas, almonds and spices. Bring to a boil, cover, then simmer for 30 minutes.
3 Drain the couscous and place in a steamer over the vegetables. Cover and cook for a further 40 minutes, then remove the steamer and cover the saucepan.
4 Place the couscous in a large mixing bowl. Beat the butter into the couscous with ¼ cup salted water.
5 Drain and quarter the apricots, add them to the vegetables and simmer for 15 minutes. Stir the couscous well to remove any lumps, return it to the steamer over the simmering vegetables, cover and cook for 20 minutes.
6 Season the vegetables and serve with the couscous.

VEGETABLE CHILI

SERVES 4

2 tablespoons olive oil	⅔ cup dry red wine
1 large onion, chopped	2 tablespoons chopped fresh oregano or 1 teaspoon dried
2 garlic cloves, crushed	
1–2 teaspoons chili powder	1-pound can red kidney beans, drained
2 cups diced zucchini	
⅔ cup sliced carrots	1 tablespoon cornstarch
1 sweet red pepper, diced	⅔ cup Greek strained yogurt and chopped parsley, to serve
1-pound can tomatoes, chopped	

1 Heat the oil in a large saucepan, add the onion, garlic and chili powder and cook for 2–3 minutes or until softened. Add the zucchini and carrots and cook for a further 3–4 minutes.
2 Add the sweet red pepper and chopped tomatoes. Cook for 5 minutes. Stir in the wine, oregano and kidney beans, cover and cook for 25–30 minutes.
3 Mix 3 tablespoons water with the cornstarch to give a smooth paste. Stir the paste into the chili and bring to a boil. Simmer for 2–3 minutes, stirring. Serve with yogurt and parsley.

SOUTHERN BAKED BEANS

SERVES 4

1½ cups dried navy beans, soaked overnight	2 tablespoons molasses
1 tablespoon vegetable oil	1¼ cups tomato juice
2 onions, chopped	3 tablespoons tomato paste
1½ cups chopped carrots	1¼ cups beer
1 tablespoon dry mustard powder	salt and pepper

1 Drain the beans, place in a saucepan and cover with fresh water. Bring to a boil and simmer for 25 minutes, then drain.

2 Meanwhile, heat the oil in a flameproof casserole, add the onions and carrots and sauté for 5 minutes or until lightly golden.

3 Remove from the heat and add the mustard, molasses, tomato juice, tomato paste, beer and beans. Stir well.

4 Bring to a boil, cover and cook in a preheated oven at 275°F for about 5 hours or until the beans are tender and the sauce is the consistency of syrup, stirring occasionally. Season well.

VARIATION

If navy beans are not available, cannellini beans can be used instead.

VEGETARIAN ROAST

SERVES 4–6

1 cup long grain brown rice	2 cups wholewheat breadcrumbs
1 tablespoon butter	1 cup finely chopped almonds
1 medium onion, chopped	
1 garlic clove, crushed	1 cup shredded sharp Cheddar cheese
2 carrots, grated	
1 cup finely chopped button mushrooms	2 eggs
	salt and pepper

1 Cook the rice in boiling salted water for 30–35 minutes or until tender. Drain well.

2 Meanwhile, heat the butter in a medium skillet, add the onion, garlic, carrots and mushrooms and sauté for 5–10 minutes or until softened, stirring frequently. Stir in the breadcrumbs, almonds, cooked rice, cheese and eggs. Season to taste and mix thoroughly together.

3 Pack the mixture into a greased 7-cup loaf pan and bake in a preheated oven at 350°F for 1–1¼ hours or until firm to the touch and brown on top. Serve sliced, hot or cold.

VARIATION

Any type of chopped nuts can be used in the above recipe. Try substituting brazils or unsalted peanuts or cashews for the almonds.

CURRIED EGGS

SERVES 4

2 tablespoons corn oil	8-ounce can tomatoes
1 onion, chopped	1 tablespoon tomato paste
1 medium tart apple, peeled, cored and chopped	½ teaspoon chili powder
2 teaspoons garam masala	salt and pepper
1¼ cup vegetable stock or water	1¼ cups plain yogurt
	4 eggs, hard-cooked

1 Heat the oil in a deep, heavy-based saucepan. Add the onion, apple and garam masala and fry gently for about 5 minutes or until soft, stirring frequently.
2 Pour in the stock or water and tomatoes with their juice and bring to a boil, stirring to break up the tomatoes as much as possible. Stir in the tomato paste with the chili powder. Season to taste. Lower the heat and simmer, uncovered, for 20 minutes to allow the flavors to develop.
3 Cool the sauce slightly, then pour into a blender or food processor. Add half the yogurt and blend to a purée. Return to the rinsed-out pan.
4 Shell the eggs and cut them in half lengthwise. Add them to the sauce, cut side up, then simmer very gently for 10 minutes. Taste the sauce and adjust the seasoning if necessary. Serve hot, with the remaining yogurt drizzled over the top.

MIXED VEGETABLE RING

SERVES 4

½ cup butter	salt and pepper
1 large onion, sliced	1 cup milk
½ cup halved mushrooms	1 cup all-purpose flour
2 zucchini, sliced	3 eggs, beaten
1 eggplant, quartered and sliced	⅓ cup chopped walnut pieces
1 sweet red pepper, sliced	1 cup shredded Brick cheese
3 tomatoes, peeled and chopped	

1 Melt 2 tablespoons of the butter in a large saucepan, add the onion and mushrooms and sauté lightly for 5 minutes or until softened.
2 Add the zucchini, eggplant and sweet red pepper and cook for 5 minutes, stirring occasionally. Add the tomatoes and season to taste.
3 Melt the remaining butter in a medium saucepan with the milk, then bring to the boil. Remove the pan from the heat, tip in all the flour and beat thoroughly with a wooden spoon. Let cool slightly, then beat in the eggs, a little at a time. Stir in the walnuts. Pipe or spoon the mixture around the edge of a well-greased 4-cup ovenproof serving dish.
4 Fill the center with the vegetables and bake in a preheated oven at 400°F for 35–40 minutes or until the pastry is risen and golden. Sprinkle with the cheese, then return to the oven until the cheese has melted. Serve at once.

VEGETABLE JALOUSIE

SERVES 4

1¼ pounds fresh fava beans, hulled	3 tablespoons grated Parmesan cheese
4 baby carrots, thinly sliced	¼ teaspoon ground mace
3 medium leeks, thickly sliced	salt and pepper
2 tablespoons butter or margarine	14 ounces frozen puff pastry, thawed
½ cup all-purpose flour	2 teaspoons chopped fresh summer savory or 1 teaspoon dried
1¼ cups milk	
1 cup shredded Wensleydale cheese or Cheddar	a little beaten egg, to glaze

1 Parboil the beans for 4 minutes, the carrots for 2 minutes and the leeks for 1 minute. Remove with a slotted spoon and reserve 2 tablespoons of the blanching water.

2 Melt the butter in a clean pan, add the flour and cook, stirring, for 1–2 minutes. Off the heat, blend in the milk. Bring to a boil, stirring, then simmer for 3 minutes or until thick. Add the cheeses and mace and season.

3 Remove the cheese sauce from the heat and fold in the vegetables. Cover and leave until cold.

4 Roll out half the pastry thinly to a 12 × 9-inch rectangle. Place on a wetted baking sheet.

5 Stir the reserved blanching water and savory into the cold filling, then spread over the pastry.

6 Roll out the remaining pastry to a slightly larger rectangle than the first. Fold in half lengthwise. Cut through the double thickness of the pastry six times at 2-inch intervals along the folded edge. Unfold the pastry and place over the top of the filling. Seal the edges firmly.

7 Brush the pastry with beaten egg, then bake in a preheated oven at 425°F for 30 minutes.

SPICED POTATO AND CAULIFLOWER PASTRIES

SERVES 4

2 tablespoons corn oil	1½ cups tiny cauliflower flowerets
1 onion, finely chopped	⅔ cup diced potatoes
2 garlic cloves, crushed	⅓ cup vegetable stock
1 teaspoon ground turmeric	12 ounces frozen wholewheat puff pastry, thawed
1 teaspoon ground coriander	
2 teaspoons ground cumin	beaten egg, to glaze
1 tablespoon mango chutney	

1 Heat the oil in a large saucepan, add the onion, garlic and spices and cook for 4–5 minutes, stirring.

2 Add the mango chutney, cauliflower flowerets and potatoes, stir in the stock and cook for 15–20 minutes or until the liquid has evaporated. Let cool.

3 Roll out the pastry on a lightly floured surface and cut out four 7-inch rounds. Divide the filling among the rounds, placing it on one half of each round. Brush beaten egg around the edges of the rounds and fold the pastry over the filling to encase. Seal the edges, then flute.

4 Place on a greased baking sheet and brush with egg. Bake in a preheated oven at 400°F for 20–25 minutes or until golden. Serve hot or cold.

TO MICROWAVE

Place the oil, onion and garlic in a medium bowl. Cover and cook on HIGH for 3 minutes. Stir in the spices, recover and cook on HIGH for a further minute. Add the mango chutney, cauliflower and potatoes with ¼ cup of the stock. Cook on HIGH for 10–12 minutes or until tender. Cool. Complete steps 3 and 4.

LIGHT MEALS

The recipes in this chapter are ideal for lunches and suppers, when you want something quick and easy yet tasty and satisfying. Soups are included for serving simply with chunks of crusty bread or toast. For cooking ahead, choose from the wide selection of savory flans and quiches.

COCK-A-LEEKIE SOUP

SERVES 4

1 tablespoon butter	1 bouquet garni
¾ pound chicken (1 large or 2 small chicken portions)	salt and pepper
	6 prunes, pitted and halved
¾ pound leeks	
5 cups chicken bouillon	

1 Melt the butter in a large saucepan, add the chicken and fry quickly until golden on all sides.
2 Cut the white parts of the leeks into four lengthwise and chop into 1-inch pieces. Wash well. Add the white parts to the pan and sauté for 5 minutes or until soft.
3 Add the stock and bouquet garni and season to taste. Bring to a boil and simmer for 30 minutes.
4 Shred the green parts of the leeks, then add to the pan with the prunes. Simmer for a further 30 minutes.
5 To serve, remove the chicken from the pan and cut the meat into large pieces, discarding the skin and bones. Put the meat in a warmed soup tureen and pour over the soup.

PEA SOUP

SERVES 6

¼ cup butter	2 large mint sprigs
1 small onion, finely chopped	salt and pepper
	2 large egg yolks
2 pounds fresh peas, hulled	⅔ cup heavy cream
5 cups chicken bouillon	mint sprig, for garnish
½ teaspoon superfine sugar	

1 Melt the butter in a large saucepan, add the onion and cook for 5 minutes or until soft. Add the peas, bouillon, sugar and mint sprigs. Bring to a boil and cook for about 30 minutes.
2 Pass the soup through a fine sieve or purée in a blender or food processor. Return to the pan and season to taste.
3 Beat together the egg yolks and cream and add to the soup. Heat gently, stirring, but do not boil.
4 Transfer to a warmed soup tureen and garnish with mint before serving.

MUSHROOM SOUP
SERVES 4

2 tablespoons butter	1 cup finely chopped, mushrooms
¼ cup all-purpose flour	salt and pepper
1¼ cups chicken bouillon	1 tablespoon lemon juice
1¼ cups milk	2 tablespoon light cream
1 tablespoon chopped parsley	

1 Place all the ingredients, except the lemon juice and cream, in a large saucepan. Bring to a boil, whisking continuously. Cover and simmer for 10 minutes.
2 Remove from the heat and add the lemon juice and cream, stirring well.
3 Pour into a tureen or individual dishes, and serve immediately with Melba toast.

HARVEST VEGETABLE SOUP
SERVES 4

2 tablespoons butter	salt and pepper
3 cups diced carrots	½ bay leaf
1 medium onion, sliced	6 tablespoons all-purpose flour
2 medium potatoes, peeled and diced	2 cups milk
1 small sweet green pepper, chopped	1 cup shredded Cheddar cheese or Monterey Jack
¼ cup lentils	croûtons, for garnish

1 Melt the butter and fry the carrots, onion, potatoes and green pepper until soft.
2 Add 2 cups water, the lentils, salt and pepper to taste and the bay leaf and simmer for 30 minutes.
3 Mix the flour with a little of the milk and gradually stir in the rest. Stir well into the soup until it thickens. Simmer for 5 minutes, then stir in ¾ cup cheese.
4 Pour into a serving dish, sprinkle with the remaining cheese and garnish with croûtons. Serve immediately.

——— VARIATION ———
Vegetable and Oatmeal Broth
Substitute 3 tablespoons medium oatmeal and 2 cups chopped rutabaga for the lentils and potatoes.

QUICK WINTER SOUP

SERVES 4–6

4 medium carrots, roughly chopped	1 slice of wholewheat bread, crusts removed
2 small white turnips, roughly chopped	½ teaspoon salt
2 small potatoes, peeled and roughly chopped	2 teaspoons sugar
2 leeks or 1 small onion, roughly chopped (optional)	pepper
1 medium tart apple, peeled, cored and chopped	4 chicken bouillon cubes, crumbled

1 Put all the prepared vegetables in a blender or food processor with the apple and bread and blend until finely minced.
2 Transfer to a large saucepan and add 5 cups water. Bring slowly to a boil, then add the salt, sugar and pepper and the bouillon cubes. Simmer for 45–60 minutes.

—————— **VARIATION** ——————
Curried Winter Soup
Stir in a little curry powder to taste with the seasoning, sugar and bouillon cubes.

LIMA BEAN AND BACON SOUP

SERVES 2–3

1 cup hulled lima beans	1¼ cups vegetable stock
1½ cups hulled peas	salt and pepper
1 large onion, chopped	2 broiled Canadian bacon slices, crumbled, for garnish
2 cups milk	

1 Put the beans, peas and onion in a large saucepan and add the milk and stock. Bring to a boil, then simmer for 20 minutes or until the beans are tender.
2 Let cool slightly, then purée one third of the soup in a blender or food processor. Add to the remaining soup, then season to taste. Reheat gently. Serve hot, garnished with chopped bacon.

—————— **TO MICROWAVE** ——————
Cook the vegetables, milk and stock in a large bowl on HIGH for 20–25 minutes, stirring occasionally. Complete step 2, reheating on HIGH for 2–3 minutes.

—————— **VARIATION** ——————
Use frozen vegetables when fresh lima beans and peas are not available.

MULLIGATAWNY SOUP

SERVES 6

¼ cup butter	1 tablespoon tomato paste
1 medium onion, finely chopped	2 tablespoons mango chutney
⅔ cup finely chopped carrot	6¼ cups beef bouillon
⅔ cup finely chopped rutabaga	1 teaspoon dried mixed herbs
1 small dessert apple, peeled, cored and finely chopped	pinch of ground mace
	pinch of ground cloves
2 bacon slices, finely chopped	salt and pepper
	⅓ cup long grain rice
¼ cup all-purpose flour	⅔ cup heavy cream
1 tablespoon mild curry paste	

1 Melt the butter in a large saucepan, add the onion, carrot, rutabaga, apple and bacon and fry for 5–10 minutes or until lightly browned.

2 Stir in the flour, curry paste, tomato paste and chutney. Cook for 1–2 minutes before adding the bouillon, herbs and spices. Season to taste.

3 Bring to a boil, skim, cover and simmer for 30–40 minutes. Sieve the soup or purée in a blender or food processor.

4 Return the soup to the pan, bring to a boil, add the rice and boil gently for about 12 minutes or until the rice is tender.

5 Adjust the seasoning. Stir in the cream, reserving a little for garnish. Heat gently, without boiling, then pour into a warmed soup tureen or individual bowls and swirl with cream.

CREAM OF ONION SOUP

SERVES 4

2 tablespoons butter	salt and pepper
3 cups thinly chopped onions	4 teaspoons cornstarch
	3 tablespoons light cream
2½ cups milk	parsley sprigs, for garnish

1 Melt the butter in a saucepan, add the onions, cover and cook gently for about 5 minutes or until softened, shaking the pan occasionally to prevent browning.

2 Add the milk and 1¼ cups water, season to taste and bring to a boil, stirring. Reduce the heat, cover and simmer for about 25 minutes or until the onion is tender.

3 Mix the cornstarch to a smooth paste with 3 tablespoons water, stir into the soup and bring to a boil. Cook gently for a few minutes or until slightly thickened, stirring. Add the cream, adjust the seasoning and reheat without boiling. Garnish with parsley sprigs.

CURRIED PARSNIP SOUP

SERVES 6

3 tablespoons butter	6¼ cups chicken bouillon
1 medium onion, sliced	salt and pepper
6 cups diced peeled parsnips	⅔ cup light cream
1 teaspoon curry powder	mild paprika, for garnish
½ teaspoon ground cumin	

1 Melt the butter in a large saucepan, add the onion and parsnip and sauté for about 3 minutes.
2 Stir in the curry powder and cumin and cook for a further 2 minutes.
3 Add the bouillon, bring to a boil, reduce the heat, cover and simmer for about 45 minutes or until the vegetables are tender.
4 Cool slightly, then transfer the vegetables to a blender or food processor, using a slotted spoon. Add a little bouillon and blend to a smooth purée.
5 Return the vegetable pureé to the pan. Season to taste, add the cream and reheat gently, without boiling. Serve sprinkled with paprika.

CULLEN SKINK

SERVES 4

one ¾-pound smoked haddock	knob of butter
1 medium onion, chopped	salt and pepper
2½ cups milk	chopped parsley, for garnish
1½ pounds potatoes	

1 Put the haddock in a medium saucepan, just cover with 4 cups boiling water and bring to a boil again. Add the onion, cover and simmer for 10–15 minutes or until tender. Drain off the liquid and reserve.
2 Remove the bones from the haddock and flake the flesh, then set aside. Return the bones and strained stock to the pan with the milk. Cover and simmer for a further hour.
3 Meanwhile, peel and roughly chop the potatoes, then cook in boiling salted water for about 20 minutes or until tender. Drain well, then mash.
4 Strain the liquid from the bones and return it to the pan with the flaked fish. Add the mashed potato and butter and stir well to give a creamy consistency. Season and garnish.

--- **TO MICROWAVE** ---

Put the haddock, onion and 2½ cups boiling water in a large bowl. Cover and cook on HIGH for 10 minutes or until the haddock is cooked. Drain off the liquid and reserve. Remove the bones from the haddock and flake the flesh, then set aside. Return the bones and strained stock to the bowl with the milk, cover and cook on HIGH for 20 minutes. Meanwhile, complete step 3. Strain the liquid from the bones and return it to the bowl with the flaked fish. Add the mashed potato and butter and stir well to give a creamy consistency. Season, garnish and serve.

HADDOCK AND CORN CHOWDER

SERVES 4–6

2–4 tablespoons butter	salt and pepper
1 pound potatoes, peeled and cut into ½-inch dice	½ pound fresh haddock fillets
2 medium onions, thinly sliced	½ pound smoked haddock fillets
½ teaspoon chili powder	2 cups cream-style corn
2½ cups fish or vegetable stock	¼ pound cooked shelled shrimp
2½ cups milk	chopped parsley

1 Melt the butter in a large saucepan. Add the vegetables and the chili powder and stir over a moderate heat for 2–3 minutes.

2 Pour in the stock and milk and season to taste. Bring to a boil, cover and simmer for 10 minutes.

3 Meanwhile, skin the fresh and smoked haddock fillets and divide the flesh into bite-size pieces, discarding all the bones.

4 Add the haddock to the pan with the corn. Bring back to a boil, cover and simmer until the potatoes are tender and the fish begins to flake apart. Skim the surface of the soup.

5 Stir in the shrimp with plenty of parsley. Adjust the seasoning and serve.

DEVONSHIRE CRAB SOUP

SERVES 6

2 tablespoons butter	1¼ cups chicken bouillon
1 small onion, finely chopped	1 teaspoon anchovy paste
1 celery stalk, chopped	salt and pepper
½ cup long grain rice	2 tablespoons brandy
2½ cups milk	⅔ cup heavy cream
½ pound frozen or canned crab meat, drained and flaked	chopped parsley, for garnish

1 Melt the butter in a large saucepan, add the onion and celery and cook for 10 minutes or until soft. Add the rice and milk, cover and cook for 15 minutes or until the rice is cooked. Cool slightly.

2 Pass the soup through a sieve or purée in a blender or food processor. Return to the pan with the crab meat. Add the bouillon and anchovy paste, season to taste and reheat.

3 Add the brandy and cream and heat gently without boiling. Transfer to a warmed soup tureen, sprinkle with chopped parsley and serve very hot.

COOK'S TIP

Melba toast makes a good accompaniment to many soups, including the one above. To make it, simply toast bread slices lightly on both sides, cut off the crusts, then, holding the toast flat, slide a knife between the toasted edges to split the bread. Cut each piece into triangles and toast under the broiler, untoasted side uppermost, until golden and the edges curl. Watch closely to prevent burning.

SPAGHETTI BOLOGNESE

SERVES 4

2 tablespoons butter or margarine	1 garlic clove, finely chopped
3 tablespoons olive oil	1 bay leaf
2 bacon slices, finely chopped	1 tablespoon tomato paste
½ pound lean ground beef	⅔ cup dry white wine
1 small onion, minced	⅔ cup beef bouillon
1 small carrot, finely chopped	salt and pepper
1 small celery stalk, finely chopped	1–1½ pounds fresh or dried spaghetti

1 Melt the butter or margarine with the oil in a saucepan, add the bacon and cook for 2–3 minutes or until soft.
2 Add the ground beef and cook for a further 5 minutes or until lightly browned.
3 Add the onion, carrot, celery, garlic and bay leaf. Stir and cook for 2 minutes. Add the tomato paste, wine and bouillon. Season to taste.
4 Bring to a boil, then simmer, uncovered for 1–1½ hours, stirring occasionally.
5 Cook the spaghetti in a large saucepan of boiling salted water for about 10 minutes for dried pasta, 3 minutes for fresh.
6 Drain the spaghetti well and turn into a warmed serving dish. Top with the sauce and serve immediately.

PAN HAGGERTY

SERVES 4

2 tablespoons butter	1 cup shredded Cheddar cheese or Monterey Jack
1 tablespoon vegetable oil	salt and pepper
3 cups thinly sliced potatoes	
2 medium onions, thinly sliced	

1 Heat the butter and oil in a large heavy-based skillet. Remove the pan from the heat and pour in layers of potatoes, onions and grated cheese, seasoning well with salt and pepper between each layer, and ending with a top layer of cheese.
2 Cover and cook the vegetables gently for about 30 minutes or until the potatoes and onions are almost cooked.
3 Uncover and brown the top of the dish under a hot broiler. Serve straight from the pan.

COOK'S TIP
Choose firm-fleshed potatoes for this dish, such as California Long Whites or Round Reds, as they will keep their shape and not crumble into mash at the end of the cooking time.

RED FLANNEL HASH

SERVES 4

1 pound potatoes, scrubbed	1 teaspoon garlic salt
salt and pepper	1 cup diced cooked beets
½ pound salt beef or corned beef, chopped	2 tablespoons chopped parsley
1 medium onion, finely chopped	¼ cup butter or margarine

1 Cook the potatoes in their skins in lightly salted boiling water for about 20 minutes or until tender.
2 Drain the potatoes, leave until cool enough to handle, then peel off the skins with your fingers. Dice the flesh.
3 Put the diced potatoes in a large bowl, add the beef, onion, garlic salt, beets and parsley and toss to combine. Add pepper to taste.
4 Heat the butter or margarine in a heavy-based skillet until very hot. Add the hash mixture and spread evenly with a fish slice or spatula.
5 Lower the heat to moderate and cook the hash, uncovered, for 10–15 minutes. Break up and turn frequently with the slice or spatula, so that the hash becomes evenly browned. Serve hot.

SPICY SCOTCH EGGS

SERVES 4

2 tablespoons butter or margarine	salt and pepper
1 onion, minced	4 hard-cooked eggs, shelled
2 teaspoons medium-hot curry powder	all-purpose flour, for coating
1 pound bulk pork sausage	1 egg, beaten
1 cup finely shredded sharp Cheddar cheese	1–1½ cups dried breadcrumbs
	vegetable oil, for deep frying

1 Heat the butter or margarine in a small saucepan, add the onion and curry powder and fry gently for 5 minutes or until soft.
2 Put the sausage and cheese in a bowl, add the onion and season to taste. Mix with your hands to combine the ingredients well.
3 Divide the mixture into four equal portions and flatten out on a floured board or work surface.
4 Place an egg in the center of each piece. With floured hands, shape and mold the sausage around the eggs. Coat lightly with more flour.
5 Brush each Scotch egg with beaten egg, then roll in the breadcrumbs until evenly coated. Chill for 30 minutes.
6 Heat the oil in a deep-fat fryer to 325°F. Carefully lower the Scotch eggs into the oil with a slotted spoon and deep-fry for 10 minutes, turning them occasionally until golden brown on all sides. Drain and cool on kitchen paper towels.

COLD BEEF IN SOUR CREAM

SERVES 4

2 tablespoons vegetable oil	1 teaspoon Dijon mustard
1 pound lean rump steak in a thin slice, cut into thin strips	2 teaspoons chopped fresh thyme or ½ teaspoon dried
salt and pepper	1 green dessert apple, cored and thinly sliced
1 medium onion, finely chopped	⅔ cup dairy sour cream
2 cups thinly sliced button mushrooms	1 tablespoon lemon juice
	crisp lettuce, to serve

1 Heat the oil in a large skillet. When hot, add the steak in a shallow layer and cook over a high heat until browned, turning occasionally. Do not crowd the pan; the meat should remain pink in the center.

2 Transfer the beef to a bowl using a slotted spoon. Season to taste.

3 Reheat the fat remaining in the pan, add the onion and fry until golden brown. Add the mushrooms, mustard and thyme and fry over a high heat for 1 minute. Add to the beef, cover and leave to cool.

4 Combine the apple with the sour cream and lemon juice.

5 To serve, line a shallow dish with crisp lettuce. Combine the beef mixture with the sour cream, adjust the seasoning and pile into the center of the lettuce.

CASHEW STUFFED MUSHROOMS

SERVES 4

8 medium flat mushrooms	1 tablespoon chopped fresh oregano or ½ teaspoon dried
1 tablespoon olive oil	2 teaspoons tomato paste
2 small onions, finely chopped	2–3 tablespoons grated Parmesan cheese
2 garlic cloves, crushed	
½ cup unsalted cashews, chopped	

1 Remove the stalks from the mushrooms, chop and set aside. Bring a large saucepan of salted water to a boil, add the mushroom caps and cook for 30–60 seconds. Drain, set aside and keep warm.

2 Heat the oil in a medium saucepan, add the onions and garlic and fry gently for 3–5 minutes or until the onions have softened. Stir in the mushroom stalks, cashews and oregano. Cook for 3–5 minutes or until the nuts begin to brown. Stir in the tomato paste.

3 Arrange the mushroom caps on a lightly oiled baking sheet. Divide the topping mixture among them and sprinkle over the Parmesan cheese.

4 Bake in a preheated oven at 375°F for 10–15 minutes or until golden.

TO MICROWAVE

Complete step 1. Place the oil, onion and garlic in a bowl, cover and cook on HIGH for 2½–3 minutes. Add the chopped mushroom stalks, cashews and oregano. Cover and cook on HIGH for 2–3 minutes. Stir in the tomato paste. Arrange four mushrooms in a circle on a plate, fill with topping and sprinkle with Parmesan. Cook on HIGH for 3–4 minutes, rearranging occasionally. Repeat with the remaining four mushrooms. Broil to brown, if liked.

GARLIC MUSHROOM PARCELS

SERVES 4–6

1 tablespoon olive oil	pepper
1 onion, finely chopped	¼ cup cream cheese
1–2 garlic cloves, crushed	6 sheets of frozen filo pastry, thawed
2 cups chopped button mushrooms	2 tablespoons butter, melted
1 tablespoon chopped fresh thyme or 1 teaspoon dried	

1 Heat the oil in a medium saucepan, add the onion and garlic and cook gently for 3–5 minutes or until the onion has softened. Add the mushrooms, thyme and pepper to taste. Cook for 5–6 minutes, stirring.

2 Drain off any excess juices and add the cheese, stirring continuously until the cheese has melted. Cook for a further 2 minutes, then leave to cool.

3 To make the parcels, lay the first sheet of filo pastry lengthwise on a work surface. Brush with butter, then lay a second sheet on top. Brush with butter, then cut into eight equal strips.

4 Place 1 teaspoon of the cooked filling in one corner of a strip of pastry. Fold this corner over to make a triangle, encasing the filling. Continue to fold in the shape of a triangle, brushing with a little extra melted butter just before the final fold. Repeat to make 24 parcels. Place on a greased baking sheet.

5 Bake in a preheated oven at 400°F for 10–15 minutes or until golden brown and crisp, turning the parcels over halfway through cooking. Serve hot or cold.

TORTILLA

SERVES 4

2 tablespoons olive oil	5 eggs, beaten
2 cups thinly sliced potatoes	salt and pepper
1 Bermuda onion, thinly sliced	1 tablespoon chopped fresh parsley or 2 teaspoons dried
1 sweet red pepper, chopped	

1 Heat the oil in a skillet, add the potatoes, onion and pepper and fry gently for 20–25 minutes or until the potatoes are golden and cooked.

2 Pour the beaten egg into the pan, season to taste and sprinkle over the parsley.

3 Cook the tortilla over a gentle heat for 7–10 minutes or until golden. Carefully invert the tortilla onto a plate, then slide it back into the skillet to cook the other side for a further 3–5 minutes.

4 Turn the tortilla onto a warmed serving plate.

TO MICROWAVE

Place the oil, potatoes, onion and pepper in a shallow 8-inch dish. Cover and cook on HIGH for 7–10 minutes or until tender, rearranging occasionally. Pour in the beaten eggs, season to taste and sprinkle over the parsley. Cover and cook on HIGH for 3–4 minutes or until almost set. Carefully invert the tortilla onto a plate, then slide back into the dish and cook on HIGH for a further 2–3 minutes or until almost set. Complete step 4 as above.

FARMHOUSE CAULIFLOWER SOUFFLÉS

SERVES 8

2 cups small cauliflower flowerets	1 cup milk
salt and pepper	1 tablespoon whole grain mustard
3 tablespoons butter	1 cup shredded sharp Cheddar cheese
3 tablespoons all-purpose flour	4 eggs, separated

1 Grease eight individual ramekin dishes.
2 Put the cauliflower in a saucepan and just cover with boiling salted water. Cover and simmer until tender, then drain.
3 Meanwhile, prepare a white sauce. Put the butter, flour and milk in a saucepan. Heat, whisking continuously, until the sauce thickens, boils and is smooth. Simmer for 1–2 minutes, then add the mustard and season to taste.
4 Turn the sauce into a blender or food processor. Add the cauliflower and blend to an almost smooth purée.
5 Turn into a large bowl and let cool slightly. Stir in the cheese with the egg yolks.
6 Whisk the egg whites until stiff but not dry and fold into the sauce mixture. Spoon into the dishes.
7 Bake in a preheated oven at 350°F for 25 minutes or until browned and firm. Serve at once.

TO MICROWAVE

The sauce can be prepared in the microwave. Put the butter, flour and milk in a medium bowl. Cook on HIGH for 4–5 minutes or until boiling and thickened, whisking frequently. Add the mustard and season.

OMELETTE ARNOLD BENNETT

SERVES 2

¼ pound smoked haddock	3 eggs, separated
¼ cup butter	salt and pepper
⅔ cup heavy cream	½ cup shredded Cheddar cheese

1 Put the fish in a saucepan and cover with water. Bring to a boil, then simmer gently for 10 minutes. Drain and flake the fish, discarding the skin and bones.
2 Put the fish in a saucepan with half the butter and 2 tablespoon cream. Toss over a high heat until the butter melts, then let cool.
3 Beat the egg yolks in a bowl with 1 tablespoon cream. Season to taste and stir in the fish mixture. Stiffly whisk the egg whites and fold in.
4 Heat the remaining butter in an omelette pan or small skillet. Pour in the egg mixture and cook gently until beginning to set but still fairly fluid. Do not fold over. Slide the omelette onto a heatproof serving dish.
5 Mix together the cheese and remaining cream and pour over the omelette. Put under a preheated broiler until golden and bubbling. Serve immediately.

CHICKEN EGGAH

SERVES 4–6

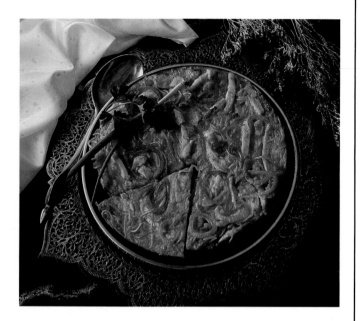

SMOKED HADDOCK GOUGÈRES

SERVES 4

8 chicken thighs	6 eggs
2½ cups chicken bouillon	¼ cup butter or margarine
2 teaspoons ground cumin	1 medium onion, sliced
¼ teaspoon chili powder	1 garlic clove, crushed
salt and pepper	2 teaspoons mild paprika
¼ pound Chinese egg noodles	

1 Put the chicken thighs in a large saucepan, then add the chicken bouillon, cumin and chili powder and season to taste. Simmer for 30 minutes or until the chicken is tender.
2 Remove the chicken from the pan and set aside. Add 5 cups water to the pan and bring to a boil. Add the noodles and boil for about 5 minutes, or according to the packet instructions, until tender. Leave to drain thoroughly in a colander or sieve.
3 Remove the chicken flesh from the bones and discard the skin. Cut the meat into small strips.
4 Using kitchen scissors, cut the cooked, drained egg noodles into short lengths.
5 Beat the eggs lightly in a large bowl, then add the noodles and chicken and stir gently to mix. Melt the butter or margarine in a large heavy-based skillet, add the onion, garlic and paprika and fry gently for about 5 minutes.
6 Pour in the egg mixture and stir lightly with a fork. Cook over a moderate heat for 15 minutes or until set and golden brown underneath.
7 Turn the eggah out on to a plate, then slide back into the pan so that the underside is uppermost. Cook for a further 15 minutes or until golden brown. Serve hot.

7 tablespoons butter	2 tomatoes, peeled, seeded and cut into strips
1¼ cups all-purpose flour	
3 eggs, beaten	salt and pepper
1 pound smoked haddock	lemon juice, to taste
1 medium onion, chopped	1 tablespoon fresh white breadcrumbs
1¼ cups milk	
2 teaspoons capers	2 tablespoons shredded Cheddar cheese
2 hard-cooked eggs, shelled and chopped	chopped parsley, for garnish (optional)

1 To make the choux pastry, put 6 tablespoons butter and 7 fluid ounces water in a saucepan and bring to a boil. Add 1 cup of the flour, then beat well until the mixture leaves the sides of the pan. Cool for 5 minutes, then gradually beat in the eggs.
2 Using a ½-inch plain tube, pipe the mixture in two circles (one on top of the other) inside each of four 1-cup ovenproof dishes. Bake at 425°F for 25 minutes or until risen and golden brown.
3 Meanwhile, poach the haddock for 10 minutes. Drain, flake the flesh and discard the skin and bones.
4 Melt the remaining butter, add the onion and fry for 5 minutes. Add the remaining flour and cook, stirring, for 1–2 minutes. Off the heat, blend in the milk. Bring to a boil, stirring, then simmer for 3 minutes until thick.
5 Stir in the capers, eggs, fish and strips of tomato. Add salt, pepper and lemon juice to taste.
6 Spoon the mixture into the center of the cooked gougères. Mix together the breadcrumbs and cheese, sprinkle on top and return to the oven for 10 minutes.

HADDOCK AND MUSHROOM PUFFS

SERVES 4

14 ounces puff pastry, thawed if frozen	4 teaspoons capers, chopped
1 pound haddock fillets, skinned	1 tablespoons chopped fresh chives or 1 teaspoon dried
8-ounce can creamed mushrooms	salt and pepper
1 teaspoon lemon juice	1 egg

1 Roll out the pastry on a lightly floured surface to a 16-inch square. Using a sharp knife, cut into four squares, trim the edges and reserve the trimmings.

2 Place the squares on dampened baking sheets. Divide the fish into four and place diagonally across the pastry squares.

3 Combine the creamed mushrooms with the lemon juice, capers and chives. Season to taste. Mix well, then spoon over the pieces of haddock fillet.

4 Brush the edges of each square lightly with water. Bring the four points of each square together over the filling and seal the edges to form an envelope-shaped parcel.

5 Decorate with pastry trimmings and make a small hole in the center of each parcel. Chill in the refrigerator for 30 minutes.

6 Beat the egg with a pinch of salt and use to glaze the pastry. Bake in a preheated oven at 425°F for about 20 minutes or until the pastry is golden brown and well risen. Serve hot.

--- **VARIATION** ---

Angler Fish and Mushrooms Puffs

Substitute angler fish (or any other white fish) for the haddock in the above recipe.

MOCK CRAB

SERVES 2

1 hard-cooked egg, shelled	1 cup shredded Monterey Jack cheese
1 tablespoon butter	2 cooked chicken breast fillets, skinned and finely chopped
½ teaspoon prepared English mustard	
a few drops of anchovy essence	lettuce leaves, sliced tomato and cucumber, for garnish
pepper	

1 Separate the egg yolks from the whites, sieve the yolks and chop the whites. Reserve a little of the egg yolk and mix the remainder with the butter, mustard, anchovy essence and pepper to taste.

2 Mix in the cheese with a fork so that it is evenly blended but as many shreds as possible of the cheese remain separate.

3 Mix in the chicken lightly, then taste and adjust the seasoning. Cover and leave in a cool place for at least 2 hours for the flavors to develop.

4 Serve on a small bed of lettuce, in crab shells if available, garnished with the reserved egg yolk, chopped egg white and a little sliced tomato and cucumber.

--- **COOK'S TIP** ---

This was a popular Victorian luncheon dish, cleverly invented to deceive the eye and even the palate. The 'crab' is in fact finely shredded chicken and grated cheese, and the fishy disguise is made all the more convincing with anchovy flavoring.

LEEKS IN CHEESE SAUCE

SERVES 4

8 medium leeks	1 cup shredded Cheddar cheese
¼ cup butter	salt and pepper
5 tablespoons all-purpose flour	8 thin slices of ham
2½ cups milk	fresh breadcrumbs

1 Put the whole leeks in a saucepan of boiling salted water and boil gently for 20 minutes or until soft. Drain and keep warm.

2 Meanwhile, melt three-quarters of the butter in a pan, stir in the flour and cook gently for 1 minute, stirring. Remove the pan from the heat and gradually stir in the milk. Bring to a boil and continue to cook, stirring, for about 5 minutes, then add ¾ cup cheese and season to taste.

3 Wrap each leek in a slice of ham, place in an ovenproof dish and coat with sauce. Top with breadcrumbs and the remaining cheese. Dot with the remaining butter and brown under a preheated broiler.

VARIATION

Asparagus in Cheese Sauce
When in season, asparagus would make an interesting substitute for the leeks in the above recipe.

MACARONI AND BROCCOLI CHEESE

SERVES 2

3 ounces wholewheat macaroni	¾ cup shredded Cheddar or Red Leicester cheese
salt and pepper	1½ cups broccoli flowerets
2 tablespoons butter	1 tablespoon wholewheat breadcrumbs
¼ cup all-purpose flour	
1¼ cups milk	

1 Cook the macaroni in 5 cups boiling salted water for 15 minutes, then drain.

2 Put the butter, flour and milk in a saucepan. Heat, whisking continuously, until the sauce boils, thickens and is smooth. Simmer for 1–2 minutes.

3 Remove the pan from the heat, add most of the cheese and stir until melted. Season to taste.

4 Cook the broccoli in boiling water for 7 minutes or until tender. Drain well.

5 Put the broccoli in the base of a 4-cup heatproof serving dish. Cover with the macaroni and cheese sauce. Sprinkle with the remaining cheese and the breadcrumbs. Brown under a preheated hot broiler.

TO MICROWAVE

Put the macaroni in a large bowl. Pour over boiling water to cover the pasta by about 1 inch. Cover and cook on HIGH for 4 minutes. Stand for 3 minutes. Put the butter, flour and milk in a medium bowl and cook on HIGH for about 4 minutes, until boiling and thickened, whisking frequently. Complete step 3. Cook the broccoli in a large bowl in 3 tablespoons water on HIGH for 3½ minutes. Drain well. Complete step 5.

ZUCCHINI QUICHE

SERVES 4

1½ cups all-purpose flour	3 eggs
salt and pepper	⅔ cup heavy cream
½ cup butter or margarine	2 teaspoons chopped fresh basil
1 cup shredded Cheddar cheese	finely grated rind of 1 lime (optional)
1 egg yolk, beaten	a little egg white
¾ pound zucchini	

1 To make the dough, sift the flour into a bowl with a pinch of salt. Cut in the butter or margarine.

2 Stir in the cheese, then the egg yolk. Gather the mixture together with your fingers to make a smooth ball of dough. Wrap the dough and chill for 30 minutes.

3 Meanwhile, prepare the filling. Trim the zucchini, then cut into ¾-inch chunks. Plunge into boiling salted water, bring back to a boil, then simmer for 3 minutes. Drain and set aside.

4 Beat the eggs lightly with the cream. Stir in the basil, lime rind (if using) and season to taste. Set aside.

5 Roll out the chilled dough and use to line a 9-inch loose-bottomed flan pan. Chill for 15 minutes.

6 Prick the base of the dough with a fork, then line with foil and baking beans. Stand the pan on a preheated baking sheet and bake blind in a preheated oven at 400°F for 10 minutes.

7 Remove the foil and beans and brush the flan shell with egg white. Return to the oven for 5 minutes.

8 Stand the zucchini chunks upright in the flan shell and slowly pour in the egg and cream mixture. Return to the oven for 20 minutes.

CAULIFLOWER AND STILTON FLAN

SERVES 4–6

1½ cups plus 2 tablespoons all-purpose flour	1 cup milk
¼ teaspoon salt	pepper
½ cup butter	⅔ cup crumbled Blue Stilton cheese
1 pound cauliflower flowerets	¼ cup shredded Cheddar cheese
2 cups chopped onion	

1 Sift 1½ cups flour and the salt into a bowl. Add 6 tablespoons of the butter and cut in until the mixture resembles fine breadcrumbs. Add a little water and bind to a dough. Chill in the refrigerator for about 10 minutes.

2 Roll out the dough on a lightly floured surface and use to line a 9-inch flan dish or ring placed on a baking sheet. Chill again for 10–15 minutes.

3 Prick the base of the dough with a fork, then line with foil and baking beans and bake blind in a preheated oven at 400°F for 10–15 minutes or until set. Remove the foil and beans.

4 Cook the cauliflower flowerets in boiling salted water for 4–5 minutes or until just tender. Drain well and cool.

5 Melt the remaining butter in a pan, add the onion and cook for about 5 minutes or until soft, then stir in the 2 tablespoons flour. Cook gently for 2 minutes, stirring. Remove the pan from the heat and gradually stir in the milk. Bring to a boil and continue to cook, stirring, until the sauce thickens, then add pepper to taste.

6 Sprinkle the Stilton evenly over the base of the flan. Arrange the cauliflower on top. Spoon over the onion sauce and sprinkle with the Cheddar cheese.

7 Bake in the oven at 375°F for 25–30 minutes or until golden and bubbly. Serve hot.

TARTE À L'OIGNON

SERVES 4–6

¼ cup butter	¼ cup milk
5 cups thinly sliced onions	⅔ cup light cream
6 ounces frozen pie dough, thawed	salt and pepper
2 eggs	pinch of grated nutmeg

1 Melt the butter in a large skillet, add the onions, cover and cook gently for 20 minutes.
2 Roll out the dough on a lightly floured surface and use to line an 8-inch flan dish or ring placed on a baking sheet.
3 Beat together the eggs, milk and cream until smooth. Season to taste and add the nutmeg.
4 Pour a little of the egg mixture into the pie shell. Add the onions, then pour in the remaining egg mixture.
5 Bake in a preheated oven at 400°F for 30 minutes or until golden brown and set.

SPICED PEPPER AND ONION FLAN

SERVES 4

1½ cups plus 2 tablespoons all-purpose flour	2 tablespoons butter
salt	1 teaspoon ground cumin
6 tablespoons shortening	⅔ cup milk
1 tablespoon vegetable oil	⅔ cup plain yogurt
2 onions, thinly sliced	2 egg yolks
1 sweet red pepper, sliced	2 tablespoons grated Parmesan cheese

1 To make the dough, sift 1½ cups flour and a pinch of salt into a bowl. Add the shortening and cut in until the mixture resembles breadcrumbs. Bind to a manageable dough with cold water. Knead until smooth.
2 Roll out the dough on a lightly floured surface and use to line an 8-inch plain flan ring placed on a baking sheet.
3 Chill for 15–20 minutes, then line with foil and baking beans. Bake blind in a preheated oven at 400°F for 10–15 minutes or until set but not browned. Remove the foil and baking beans.
4 Heat the oil in a skillet, add the sliced onions and pepper, reserving a few slices for garnish, and sauté for 4–5 minutes. Put into the flan shell.
5 Melt the butter in a saucepan, stir in the 2 tablespoons flour and the cumin. Cook for 2 minutes, stirring, then remove from the heat and gradually stir in the milk and yogurt. Bring to a boil, stirring briskly, and simmer for 2–3 minutes. Beat in the egg yolks.
6 Pour the sauce over the onion and pepper and sprinkle with Parmesan. Cook in the oven at 375°F for 35–40 minutes. Serve hot garnished with sweet pepper slices.

HOT CRAB AND RICOTTA QUICHES

SERVES 6

1½ cups all-purpose flour	⅔ cup milk
salt and pepper	1 cup flaked crab meat
6 tablespoons shortening	1 cup crumbled Ricotta cheese
2 eggs	2 tablespoons grated Parmesan cheese
⅔ cup light cream	

1 To make the dough, sift the flour and a pinch of salt into a bowl. Add the shortening and cut in until the mixture resembles fine breadcrumbs. Add enough cold water to bind to a manageable dough and knead until smooth.

2 Roll out the dough on a lightly floured surface and use to line six 3½-inch fluted, loose-bottomed, flan pans. Line with foil and baking beans and bake blind in a preheated oven at 400°F for 10–15 minutes. Remove the foil and baking beans.

3 Meanwhile whisk the eggs, cream and milk together in a bowl and add the crab meat, Ricotta, Parmesan and plenty of salt and pepper. Pour into the flan cases.

4 Reduce the oven temperature to 375°F and bake the quiches for 35 minutes or until golden.

VARIATION

Make one large quiche instead of six individual ones, if preferred. You will need to use an 8-inch flan dish or ring.

SMOKED HADDOCK FLAN

SERVES 4–6

1¾ cups all-purpose flour	1 small bunch of scallions, chopped
salt and pepper	2 eggs, hard-cooked, shelled and quartered
6 tablespoons shortening	
¾ pound potatoes, peeled	2 tablespoons butter
¾ pound smoked haddock	1 cup shredded Cheddar cheese
1¼ cups milk	

1 To make the dough, sift 1½ cups of the flour into a bowl with a pinch of salt. Cut in the shortening. Add cold water to bind to a dough and knead until smooth.

2 Roll out the dough and use to line an 8-inch flan dish or ring placed on a baking sheet. Bake blind at 400°F for 10–15 minutes or until set.

3 Cook the potatoes in boiling salted water for about 20 minutes or until tender, then drain and mash. Set aside. Place the fish in a saucepan with the milk, bring to a boil, then simmer for 15 minutes.

4 Strain the milk into a bowl. Remove the skin and bones from the fish and flake the flesh. Place in the flan shell.

5 Plunge the chopped scallions into a pan of boiling water, blanch for 1 minute, then drain. Sprinkle the onions over the fish and cover with the eggs.

6 Melt the butter in a saucepan, stir in the remaining flour and cook gently for 1 minute, stirring. Remove from the heat and gradually stir in the reserved milk. Bring to a boil and cook, stirring, until the sauce thickens. Season.

7 Spoon the sauce into the flan shell and pipe potato across the top in a lattice design. Sprinkle with cheese and bake in the oven for about 25 minutes or until brown. Serve hot.

SPINACH AND SHRIMP QUICHE

SERVES 4–6

1¾ cups wholewheat flour	⅔ cup milk
salt and pepper	¼ pound cooked shelled shrimp
½ cup butter	5 ounces frozen chopped spinach, thawed and drained
1 egg, beaten	

1 Sift the flour into a bowl with a pinch of salt, add the butter and cut in until the mixture resembles fine breadcrumbs. Stir in enough cold water to bind to a manageable dough and knead until smooth.

2 Roll out the dough on a lightly floured surface and use to line an 8-inch flan ring placed on a baking sheet. Line with foil and baking beans and bake blind in a preheated oven at 400°F for 20 minutes or until set. Remove the foil and beans.

3 Mix the egg, milk, shrimp and spinach, season well and pour into the flan shell.

4 Bake in the oven at 350°F for about 40 minutes, until just set. Serve hot.

CURRIED BACON FLAN

SERVES 4–6

1½ cups all-purpose flour	1 teaspoon curry powder
salt and pepper	3 eggs, beaten
6 tablespoons shortening	⅔ cup plain yogurt
2 tablespoons butter	½ pound tomatoes, peeled and thinly sliced
1 cup sliced celery heart	
12 bacon slices, diced	

1 To make the dough, sift the flour and a pinch of salt into a bowl. Add the shortening and cut it in until the mixture resembles fine breadcrumbs. Add enough cold water to bind to a manageable dough and knead until smooth.

2 Roll out the dough on a lightly floured surface and use to line an 8½-inch, loose-bottomed French fluted flan pan. Line with foil and baking beans and bake blind in a preheated oven at 400°F for 10–15 minutes or until set.

3 Melt the butter in a small skillet, add the celery and bacon and sauté until golden brown. Stir in the curry powder and cook for 2 minutes.

4 Blend the eggs with the yogurt, add the pan ingredients, season to taste, and turn into the flan shell. Top with tomato slices.

5 Bake in the oven at 375°F for about 25 minutes or until golden brown and set. Serve hot or cold.

FETA CHEESE PUFFS WITH BASIL

MAKES 8

1½ cups crumbled Feta cheese	pepper
⅔ cup plain yogurt	14 ounces frozen puff pastry, thawed
2 tablespoons chopped fresh basil or 1 teaspoon dried	beaten egg
	basil leaves, for garnish

1 Mix the crumbled cheese with the yogurt, chopped basil and pepper to taste. (Don't add salt as the cheese adds sufficient.)

2 Roll out the pastry thinly on a lightly floured surface and cut out sixteen 4½-inch rounds. Fold and re-roll the pastry as necessary.

3 Place half the rounds on two dampened baking sheets. Spoon some of the cheese mixture into the center of each one.

4 Brush the pastry edges with egg. Cover with the remaining rounds, pressing the pastry edges together to seal. Make a small slit in the top of each pastry puff.

5 Brush with beaten egg. Bake in a preheated oven at 425°F for about 15 minutes or until well browned and crisp. Serve warm, garnished with basil.

──── COOK'S TIP ────

Feta is a Greek cheese made from goat's or ewe's milk. Vacuum packs, which tend to be rather salty, are available at some supermarkets, but the best Feta (sold loose in brine) is found in Greek and Middle Eastern stores.

CREAMY HAM AND LEEK PIES

SERVES 4

¼ cup butter	2 tablespoons chopped fresh parsley or 2 teaspoons dried
4 cups thickly sliced leeks	1 teaspoon grated nutmeg
1½ cups sliced carrots	salt and pepper
½ cup all-purpose flour	¾ pound puff pastry
1¼ cups vegetable stock	beaten egg, to glaze
1¼ cups milk	
½ pound cooked ham, diced	

1 Melt the butter in a large saucepan, add the leeks and carrots and sauté for 5 minutes. Stir in the flour and cook, stirring continuously, for 1 minute.

2 Gradually stir in the stock, then add the milk. Cook over a medium heat, stirring, until the mixture comes to a boil and thickens. Stir in the ham, parsley and nutmeg. Season to taste, then let cool.

3 Roll out the pastry on a lightly floured surface to ¼ inch thick. Use a 1½-cup individual pie dish as a template to cut out four lids for the pies.

4 Divide the ham and leek filling between four 1½-cup individual pie dishes. Dampen the edges of the dishes with water. Cut the remaining trimmings of pastry into thin strips and place around the rim of each dish. Moisten the strips and lay a lid over each pie. Press the edges to seal, trim and flute.

5 Make a small cut in the top of each pie and brush with beaten egg to glaze. Bake in a preheated oven at 425°F for 25–30 minutes or until golden brown.

CORNISH PASTIES

SERVES 6

3½ cups all-purpose flour	1 cup diced rutabaga
salt and pepper	1 medium onion, chopped
1 cup butter	½ teaspoon dried mixed herbs
1 pound top round steak, cut into small pieces	1 egg, beaten
1 cup diced potatoes	

1 To make the dough, sift the flour into a bowl with a pinch of salt. Set aside 2 tablespoons butter. Cut the rest into the flour mixture until the mixture resembles fine breadcrumbs. Add enough cold water to bind to a manageable dough and knead until smooth.

2 Put the meat, potato, rutabaga and onion in a bowl. Mix in the herbs and season to taste.

3 Divide the dough into six equal pieces. Roll out each piece on a lightly floured surface to an 8-inch circle.

4 Spoon some of the filling onto half of each dough circle and top with a little of the remaining butter.

5 Brush the edges of the dough with water, then fold over and seal the edges firmly together.

6 Place the pasties on a baking sheet and brush with beaten egg. Bake in a preheated oven at 425°F for 15 minutes. Reduce the heat to 325°F and cook for a further 1 hour. Serve warm or cold.

CHICKEN PARCELS

SERVES 4

1 tablespoon butter	1 teaspoon lemon juice
1 small onion, chopped	½ pound boneless cooked chicken, chopped
2 medium carrots, diced	salt and pepper
1 tablespoon wholewheat flour	13 ounces frozen puff pastry, thawed
1 teaspoon mild curry powder	beaten egg, to glaze
1¼ cups chicken bouillon	

1 Melt the butter in a large saucepan, add the onion and carrots, cover and cook for 4–5 minutes or until the onion is transparent. Stir in the flour and curry powder and cook, stirring, for 1 minute. Remove from the heat and gradually stir in the bouillon. Bring to a boil, stirring continuously, then simmer for 2–3 minutes or until thickened.

2 Reduce the heat, add the lemon juice and chicken and season to taste. Let cool.

3 When the chicken mixture is cool, roll out the pastry on a lightly floured surface to a 14-inch square. Using a sharp knife, cut into four squares.

4 Place the pastry squares on dampened baking sheets, then spoon the chicken mixture onto the pastry, leaving a border round the edges. Brush the edges of each square lightly with water. Fold each square in half and seal and crimp the edges to make a parcel.

5 Make two small slashes in the top of each parcel. Brush with beaten egg to glaze.

6 Bake in a preheated oven at 425°F for 15–20 minutes or until the pastry is golden brown. Serve hot or cold.

PISSALADIÈRE

SERVES 6

CHILI PIZZA FINGERS

SERVES 6

1 cup all-purpose flour	½ pound tomatoes, peeled and sliced
salt and pepper	
¼ cup butter or margarine	2 tablespoons tomato paste
⅓ cup vegetable oil	1 teaspoon chopped herbs (marjoram, thyme or sage)
3 cups finely sliced onions	
2 garlic cloves, crushed	anchovy fillets and ripe olives, for garnish

1 To make the dough, sift the flour and a pinch of salt into a bowl. Add the butter or margarine and cut in until the mixture resembles fine breadcrumbs. Add about 2 tablespoons water and mix until it forms a smooth dough. Wrap and chill in the refrigerator for 15 minutes.

2 Roll out the dough on a lightly floured surface and use to line an 8-inch plain flan ring placed on a baking sheet. Line with foil and baking beans and bake blind in a preheated oven at 400°F for 20 minutes. Remove the foil and beans.

3 Meanwhile, make the filling. Heat the oil in a large saucepan, add the onions and garlic and sauté for 10 minutes or until very soft but not brown.

4 Add the tomatoes to the pan and continue cooking for 10 minutes or until the liquid has evaporated. Stir in the tomato paste and herbs and season to taste.

5 Turn the mixture into the flan shell. Brush with a little oil and cook in the oven at 400°F for 20 minutes.

6 To serve, garnish the pissaladière with a lattice of anchovy fillets and the ripe olives. Serve either hot or cold.

½ pound lean ground beef	2 cups wholewheat flour
½ teaspoon chili powder	⅓ cup medium oatmeal
1 garlic clove, crushed	1 tablespoon baking powder
1 medium onion, chopped	
1 small sweet green pepper, chopped	salt and pepper
	¼ cup butter or margarine
1 cup sliced mushrooms	1 egg, beaten
1½ cups chopped peeled tomatoes	¼ cup milk
	1 tablespoon tomato paste
8-ounce can red kidney beans, drained	6 ounces Mozzarella cheese, thinly sliced
⅔ cup beef bouillon	

1 First prepare the topping. Put the ground beef, chili powder and garlic in a saucepan and sauté for 3–4 minutes, stirring occasionally. Add the onion, green pepper and mushrooms and fry for a further 1–2 minutes. Stir in the tomatoes, red kidney beans and beef bouillon. Bring to a boil, then simmer for about 15 minutes or until most of the liquid has evaporated, stirring occasionally.

2 Meanwhile, combine the flour, oatmeal, baking powder and a pinch of salt in a bowl. Cut in the butter or margarine. Bind to a soft dough with the egg and milk, then knead lightly until smooth.

3 Roll out the dough to a 10×7-inch rectangle. Lift on to a baking sheet, then spread with tomato paste. Pile chili mixture on top and cover with cheese.

4 Bake at 400°F for about 30 minutes or until golden and bubbling. Cut into fingers.

PASTA WITH PEAS AND HAM IN CREAM SAUCE

SERVES 4

10–12 ounces tagliatelle	1 cup frozen peas, cooked
½ cup butter	¼ cup light cream
1 large onion, sliced	1 cup shredded Cheddar cheese
¼ pound ham, cut into thin strips	salt and pepper

1 Cook the tagliatelle in boiling salted water for about 10 minutes or until tender, but not soft. Drain well.

2 Meanwhile, melt the butter in a pan, add the onion and cook for about 3 minutes or until soft. Add the ham and peas and cook for a further 5 minutes.

3 Add the drained tagliatelle to the pan, stir well and add the cream and most of the cheese. Toss gently, season to taste and serve at once, sprinkled with the remaining cheese.

VARIATION

Spaghetti with Peas and Ham in Cream Sauce Substitute spaghetti for the tagliatelle in the above recipe.

BACON CAKES

MAKES 8

7 bacon slices	⅔ cup milk
2 cups self-rising flour	1 tablespoon ketchup
pinch of salt	a dash of Worcestershire sauce
2 tablespoons butter	milk, to glaze
¾ cup shredded Cheddar cheese	

1 Cook three bacon slices under a preheated broiler until crisp, then cut into small pieces.

2 Sift the flour and salt together into a bowl, add the butter and cut in until the mixture resembles fine breadcrumbs. Add all but 1 tablespoon of the cheese and the crumbled bacon.

3 Mix the milk, ketchup and Worcestershire together and add to the dry ingredients. Mix to a soft dough, roll out to a 7-inch circle, brush with milk and cut into eight wedges.

4 Arrange the wedges on a buttered, floured baking sheet in a circle with edges overlapping. Sprinkle with the remaining cheese.

5 Bake in a preheated oven at 400°F for 30 minutes. Cut the remaining bacon in half and roll up. Place the rolls on a skewer and broil until crisp. Use to garnish the bacon cakes.

FISH CAKES WITH HERBS

SERVES 4

10 ounces haddock, skinned and boned	1 tablespoon chopped chives
1 tablespoon lemon juice	1 tablespoon chopped parsley
1 tablespoon Worcestershire sauce	¾ pound potatoes, cooked and mashed
1 tablespoon horseradish sauce	1 cup wholewheat breadcrumbs
½ cup milk	

1 Put the fish in a blender or food processor with the lemon juice, Worcestershire and horseradish and blend to a purée. Transfer to a bowl and stir in the milk, chives, parsley and potatoes.

2 Shape the mixture into four fish cakes and coat with breadcrumbs.

3 Cook under a preheated moderate broiler for 5 minutes on each side or until browned. Serve immediately.

────────── **VARIATION** ──────────

Cod Fish Cakes with Herbs

The above fish cakes are equally good made with cod instead of haddock.

CHICKEN LIVER SKEWERS

SERVES 4

2 small oranges	1 sweet green pepper, roughly chopped
1 cup unsweetened orange juice	1 cup chopped onion
1 teaspoon chopped fresh tarragon or ½ teaspoon dried	4 cups beansprouts
1 pound whole chicken livers, thawed if frozen	1 small bunch of chives, chopped
2 slices of bread, crumbed	salt and pepper

1 Finely grate the rind of one of the oranges. Place in a saucepan with the orange juice and tarragon and simmer for 2–3 minutes or until reduced by half.

2 Cut the tops and bottoms off both oranges, then remove the peel by working around the oranges in a spiral.

3 Divide the oranges into segments by cutting through the membranes on either side of each segment.

4 Cut the chicken livers in half and toss lightly in the breadcrumbs. Place in a lightly greased broiler pan and cook under a preheated broiler for 2 minutes on each side.

5 Thread the pepper and onion onto four oiled kabob skewers alternately with the livers.

6 Place the skewers in the broiler pan and spoon over a little of the reduced orange juice. Broil for 2–3 minutes on each side, turning and basting occasionally.

7 Meanwhile, steam the beansprouts for 2–3 minutes. Warm the orange segments in a separate pan with the remaining reduced orange juice.

8 Mix the beansprouts with the chives and season to taste. Arrange on a warmed serving dish. Top with the skewers and spoon over the orange segments and juice.

JANSSON'S TEMPTATION

SERVES 6

4 medium baking potatoes	salt and pepper
two 2-ounce cans anchovy fillets, soaked in milk for 20 minutes and drained	1 large onion, finely chopped
2 tablespoons butter or margarine	2 cups light cream
	2 tablespoons chopped parsley, for garnish

1 Peel the potatoes and cut into very thin matchstick strips. Cut the anchovies into thin strips.
2 Arrange half of the potato strips in a layer in the bottom of a well-buttered ovenproof dish. Sprinkle with a little salt and plenty of pepper.
3 Arrange the strips of anchovy and chopped onion over the potato layer, then top with the remaining potato. Sprinkle with salt and pepper as before.
4 Pour half the cream slowly into the dish, then dot with the remaining butter. Bake in a preheated oven at 350°F for 30 minutes. Add the remaining cream and bake for a further 1 hour or until the potatoes feel tender when pierced with a skewer. Cover the dish with foil if the potatoes show signs of over-browning during cooking. Serve hot, sprinkled with the parsley.

--- **COOK'S TIP** ---

In Sweden, this dish is usually served as an appetizer, but it is easily substantial enough to serve as a main course. To refresh the palate, follow with a crisp green salad tossed in a sharp oil and vinegar dressing.

SALMON KEDGEREE

SERVES 6

¾ pound salmon	salt and pepper
⅔ cup dry white wine	1½ cups long grain rice
2 small onions, chopped	¼ cup butter
1 carrot, sliced	1½ teaspoons English dry mustard
1 celery stalk, chopped	3 eggs, hard-cooked, shelled and quartered
1 tablespoon lemon juice	cayenne, to finish
6 peppercorns	celery leaves or parsley sprigs, for garnish
1 bouquet garni	

1 Put the salmon in a saucepan and pour in the wine and enough water to cover the fish. Add half of the chopped onions, the carrot, celery, lemon juice, peppercorns, bouquet garni and 1 teaspoon salt. Bring slowly to a boil, then remove from the heat. Cover tightly and cool.
2 Cook the rice in boiling salted water until tender.
3 Meanwhile, remove the salmon from the liquid and flake the flesh, discarding the skin and any bones. Strain the cooking liquid and reserve.
4 Melt half the butter in a large skillet, add the remaining onion and fry gently for about 5 minutes or until soft. Drain the rice thoroughly, then add to the onion with the remaining butter. Toss to coat, then stir in the mustard.
5 Add the flaked salmon and the hard-cooked eggs and a few spoonfuls of the strained cooking liquid to moisten. Heat through. Shake the pan and toss the ingredients gently so that the salmon and eggs do not break up.
6 Transfer to a warmed serving dish and sprinkle with cayenne to taste. Garnish and serve immediately.

SHRIMP RISOTTO

SERVES 4

1 small onion, thinly sliced	½ sachet saffron strands
1 garlic clove, crushed	salt and pepper
4 cups chicken bouillon	½ pound shelled shrimp
1 cup long grain brown rice	½ cup frozen petits pois
½ cup small button mushrooms	12 cooked shell-on shrimp, for garnish

1 Place the onion, garlic, bouillon, rice, mushrooms and saffron in a large saucepan or Dutch oven. Season to taste. Bring to a boil and simmer, uncovered, for 35 minutes, stirring occasionally.

2 Stir in the shrimp and petits pois. Cook over a high heat for about 5 minutes or until most of the liquid has been absorbed, stirring occasionally.

3 Taste and adjust the seasoning, then turn into a warmed serving dish. Garnish with the whole shrimp and serve immediately.

QUICK CHICKEN AND MUSSEL PAELLA

SERVES 4–6

¼ cup olive oil	5½ cups boiling chicken bouillon
about 1 pound boneless chicken meat, skinned and cut into bite-size cubes	1 teaspoon mild paprika
1 onion, chopped	½ teaspoon saffron powder
2 garlic cloves, crushed	salt and pepper
1 large sweet red pepper, sliced into thin strips	two 6-ounce jars mussels, drained
3 tomatoes, peeled and chopped	lemon wedges, cooked shelled shrimp and fresh mussels (optional), for garnish
2 cups risotto rice	

1 Heat the oil in a large, deep skillet, add the cubes of chicken and fry over a moderate heat until golden brown on all sides. Remove from the pan and set aside.

2 Add the onion, garlic and sweet red pepper to the oil remaining in the pan and fry gently for 5 minutes or until softened. Add the tomatoes and fry for a few more minutes or until the juices run, then add the rice and stir to combine.

3 Pour in 4 cups of the boiling bouillon (it will bubble furiously), then add half the paprika and the saffron powder. Season to taste. Stir well and add the chicken.

4 Simmer, uncovered, for 30 minutes or until the chicken is cooked through, stirring frequently during this time to prevent the rice from sticking. When the mixture becomes dry, stir in a few more tablespoons of boiling bouillon. Repeat as often as necessary to keep the paella moist.

5 To serve, fold in the mussels and heat through. Taste and adjust the seasoning, then garnish with lemon wedges, shrimp, mussels and a sprinkling of paprika.

SPAGHETTI ALLA CARBONARA

SERVES 4

4 eggs	¾ pound spaghetti
⅔ cup light cream	1½ cups shredded Cheddar cheese
2 tablespoons butter	salt and pepper
½ pound bacon slices, chopped	2 tablespoons chopped parsley

1 Beat together the eggs and cream. Heat the butter in a skillet, add the bacon and fry until crisp.

2 Meanwhile, cook the spaghetti in boiling salted water for about 8 minutes or until tender, but not soft. Drain and add it to the bacon in the skillet.

3 Cook for 1 minute, stirring all the time. Remove from the heat and add the egg mixture. Mix well. (The heat of the spaghetti will be enough to cook the eggs).

4 Stir in 1 cup cheese and season to taste. Transfer to a warmed serving dish and serve immediately, sprinkled with the parsley and remaining cheese.

MACARONI CHEESE

SERVES 4

6 ounces short-cut macaroni	salt and pepper
3 tablespoons butter	1½ cups shredded sharp Cheddar cheese
¼ cup all-purpose flour	2 tablespoons fresh breadcrumbs
2½ cups milk	
pinch of nutmeg, or ½ teaspoon prepared mustard	

1 Cook the macaroni in boiling salted water for 10 minutes, then drain well.

2 Meanwhile melt the butter in a saucepan, stir in the flour and cook gently for 1 minute. Remove from the heat and gradually stir in the milk. Bring to a boil and continue to cook, stirring, until the sauce thickens, then remove from the heat, add the nutmeg or mustard and season to taste. Stir in 1 cup of the cheese and the macaroni.

3 Pour into an ovenproof dish and sprinkle with the remaining cheese and the breadcrumbs.

4 Place on a baking sheet and bake in a preheated oven at 400°F for about 20 minutes or until golden and bubbling.

TUNA AND PASTA IN SOUR CREAM

SERVES 4

½ pound pasta spirals or shells	2 tablespoons malt vinegar
salt and pepper	7-ounce can tuna, drained and flaked
1 teaspoon vegetable oil	4 eggs, hard-cooked, shelled and finely chopped
2 tablespoons butter	
⅔ cup dairy sour cream	4 tablespoons chopped parsley
1 teaspoon anchovy essence	

1 Cook the pasta in plenty of boiling salted water to which the oil has been added, for about 15 minutes or until *al dente* (tender but firm to the bite). Drain well.

2 Melt the butter in a deep skillet and toss in the pasta. Stir in the sour cream, anchovy essence and vinegar.

3 Add the tuna and egg to the pan with the parsley. Season well and warm through over a low heat, stirring occasionally. Serve immediately.

PASTA BAKE

SERVES 4

1 pound lean ground beef	¼ pound wholewheat spaghetti rings
1 sweet red pepper, sliced	1¼ cups plain yogurt
1 onion, chopped	1 egg, beaten
1 cup sliced button mushrooms	½ cup all-purpose flour
1-pound can tomatoes	2 tomatoes, sliced, and chopped fresh parsley, for garnish
1 teapoon hot pepper sauce	
salt and pepper	

1 Put the ground beef in a saucepan and fry gently in its own fat, until turning brown. Drain off any fat. Add the pepper, onion, mushrooms, tomatoes with their juice and hot pepper sauce. Season to taste and simmer gently for 10 minutes.

2 Meanwhile, cook the pasta in boiling salted water for about 10 minutes or until tender, but not soft. Drain well and place in a 7-cup ovenproof dish. Top with the beef mixture.

3 Beat together the yogurt, egg and flour until smooth and pour over the ground beef. Bake in a preheated oven at 350°F for 40 minutes. Serve hot, garnished with tomatoes and chopped parsley.

SESAME CHICKEN PITAS

SERVES 4

2 tablespoons sesame oil	2 cups beansprouts
1 onion, sliced	1 tablespoon dark soy sauce
⅔ cup tiny broccoli flowerets	2 tablespoons toasted sesame seeds
1 sweet red pepper, diced	4 large pita breads
½ pound cooked chicken breast, sliced into thin strips	

1 Heat the oil in a large skillet, add the onion and stir-fry for 2 minutes. Add the broccoli and pepper and cook for 3–4 minutes, stirring frequently.
2 Add the chicken strips to the pan, stir well, then add the beansprouts and soy sauce. Continue to cook for 2–3 minutes. Sprinkle over the sesame seeds and stir to combine. Remove from the heat and keep warm.
3 Cut through a long side of each pita bread and open the cavity to form a pocket. Place the pita breads on a baking sheet. Bake in a preheated oven at 400°F for 5–10 minutes to heat.
4 Using a slotted spoon, fill each pita pocket with the chicken mixture. Serve immediately.

——— TO MICROWAVE ———

Put the oil and onion in a medium bowl. Cover and cook on HIGH for 2–2½ minutes. Add the broccoli and sweet pepper, re-cover and cook on HIGH for 2–2½ minutes. Add the chicken, beansprouts and soy sauce, stir and cook on HIGH for 2–2½ minutes. Stir in the sesame seeds. To warm the pita breads, place on a double thickness of kitchen paper towels and cook on HIGH for 1–1½ minutes or until warm. Complete step 4.

PAN BAGNA WITH AVOCADO

SERVES 6–8

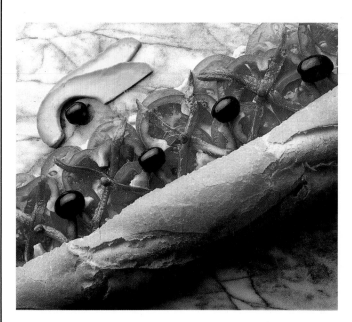

2 ripe avocados	two 14-inch French loaves
1 tablespoon lemon juice	½ pound tomatoes, sliced
1 tablespoon vegetable oil	1 small sweet green pepper, sliced into thin rings
garlic salt and black pepper	a few capers and pitted ripe olives
2-ounce can anchovies, drained	

1 Halve the avocados and remove the stones. Mash the flesh with the lemon juice and oil and season to taste with garlic salt and pepper. Cut the anchovies into thin strips.
2 Halve the loaves lengthwise. Pull out and discard some of the crumb. Spread the bases with the avocado mixture and top with tomatoes and pepper. Arrange the anchovy strips in a lattice pattern on top and sprinkle with capers and olives. Position the top of the loaf over the filling to make a sandwich, cut the loaf in chunks and serve.

CHICKEN TACOS

SERVES 6

6 Mexican taco shells	salt and pepper
2 tablespoons butter or margarine	shredded lettuce
1 medium onion, chopped	1 cup shredded Cheddar cheese, grated
1 pound cooked chicken meat, diced	hot pepper sauce
4 tomatoes, peeled and chopped	

1 Put the taco shells in the oven to warm according to the instructions on the packet.

2 To make the filling, melt the butter or margarine in a skillet, add the onion and fry for about 5 minutes or until soft but not colored. Stir in the chicken and half the tomatoes, season to taste and heat through.

3 Spoon 1–2 tablespoons filling into each shell. Add a little lettuce, the remaining tomatoes and the cheese with a few drops of hot pepper sauce. Serve immediately.

CRISPY STUFFED POTATO SKINS

SERVES 4–6

4 medium baking potatoes, scrubbed and pricked	vegetable oil, for deep frying
1½ cups shredded sharp Cheddar cheese	½ cup fresh breadcrumbs
3 tablespoons chopped chives or 1 tablespoon dried	FOR THE DIPPING SAUCE 2 tablespoons chopped chives or 2 teaspoons dried
salt and pepper	1¼ cups dairy sour cream

1 Place the potatoes on a baking sheet and bake in a preheated oven at 425°F for 1–1½ hours.

2 Cut each potato in half and scoop out the flesh, taking care not to break the skins. Chop the flesh into chunks and place in a medium bowl. Add 1 cup of the cheese and 2 tablespoons of the chopped fresh chives or 2 teaspoons dried. Season to taste and cover with foil to keep warm.

3 Heat the oil in a deep fat fryer to 375° and deep-fry the potato skins in batches for 3–4 minutes or until crisp. Drain well and arrange, hollow side up, on a baking sheet.

4 Spoon the potato mixture into the skins. Mix the remaining cheese, chives and breadcrumbs together and sprinkle over each stuffed potato skin. Put under a preheated broiler until golden. For the dipping sauce, stir the chives into the sour cream and serve with the stuffed potato skins.

TO MICROWAVE

Place the potatoes on a double thickness of kitchen paper towels. Cook on HIGH for 10–15 minutes, rearranging. Stand for 5 minutes. Complete steps 2–4.

SALADS

Needing little or no accompaniment, these salads are complete meals on their own, combining cooked meats, fish, eggs or cheese with dried beans, grains and vegetables as well as more usual salad ingredients. They are the perfect choice for a summer lunch or buffet for family or friends.

CRAB SALAD

SERVES 2

1 tablespoon lemon juice	2 ounces pasta shells, cooked
1 tablespoon mayonnaise	pepper
1 tablespoon plain yogurt	lettuce, shredded
½ pound cooked crab meat, thawed if frozen	cucumber and lemon slices, for garnish
½ cucumber, diced	
2 tomatoes, peeled and cubed	

1 Mix together the lemon juice, mayonnaise and yogurt.
2 Combine the dressing with the remaining ingredients, except the lettuce and garnish. Serve the crab salad on a bed of shredded lettuce, garnished with cucumber and lemon slices.

CHEF'S SALAD

SERVES 4

½ pound cooked ham	6 small tomatoes, halved, or 2 large tomatoes, quartered
½ pound cold cooked chicken	3 scallions, finely chopped
½ pound Emmenthal cheese	French or blue cheese dressing, to serve
1 Iceberg lettuce	
2 eggs, hard-cooked, shelled and quartered	

1 Using a sharp knife, cut the ham and chicken into fine strips and set aside. Remove any rind from the cheese. Carefully cut the cheese into small dice. Wash the lettuce under cold running water and pat it dry.
2 Finely shred the lettuce leaves, or leave them whole, and use to line an oval serving dish.
3 To serve, arrange the meat and cheese alternately around the edge of a large dish. Add the egg and tomatoes and sprinkle over the finely chopped scallions. Serve the dressing separately.

PORK AND MUSHROOM SALAD

SERVES 6

two ¾-pound pork tenderloins	10 green olives, pitted and chopped
vegetable oil	⅔ cup dairy sour cream
knob of butter	¼ teaspoon dry mustard
½ pound small button mushrooms	salt and pepper
juice of ½ lemon	1 teaspoon chopped marjoram or mint
1 small onion, finely sliced	lemon wedges, for garnish
1 small sweet green pepper, finely shredded	

1 Cut the pork into ½-inch slices on the diagonal, then cut each slice into neat strips.

2 Heat a little oil and the butter in a large skillet, add half the pork and fry quickly to brown and seal the meat. Repeat with the remaining meat, then return all to the pan. Lower the heat and cook slowly for 10–15 minutes or until very tender. Using a slotted spoon, lift the meat out of the pan and leave to cool.

3 Add the mushrooms to the pan with ¼ cup water and the lemon juice. Cook, stirring, for 1–2 minutes. Using a slotted spoon, remove from the pan and cool.

4 Put the onion and green pepper in a pan of cold water, bring to a boil, then simmer for 1–2 minutes. Drain and cool under cold running water. Stir into the pork with the cooled mushrooms and the olives.

5 Mix the sour cream with the mustard, season to taste and stir into the pork. Cover and chill for at least 3 hours.

6 Stir the salad well before serving sprinkled with marjoram or mint and garnished with lemon wedges.

DEVILED DUCKLING SALAD

SERVES 6

two 3-lb oven-ready ducklings	1 tablespoon mild curry paste
salt	salt and pepper
⅔ cup dairy sour cream	½ cup cashews
⅓ cup mayonnaise	¾ pound fresh apricots, pitted and thickly sliced
1 tablespon clear honey	chicory leaves, to serve

1 Cut away any surplus fat from the ducklings, then wipe them with a damp cloth. Pat dry.

2 Prick the birds all over with a sharp fork or skewer and sprinkle generously with salt. Place the ducklings, breast-side down, side by side, on a wire rack or trivet in a large roasting pan.

3 Roast in a preheated oven at 350°F for about 1¾ hours or until the birds are really tender, basting occasionally. Half-way through the cooking time, turn the birds over so they are standing breast-side up.

4 Meanwhile, prepare the dressing. In a large bowl, mix together the sour cream, mayonnaise, honey and curry paste. Season and stir in the cashews and apricots.

5 While the ducklings are still warm, strip off the crisp breast skin and reserve. Remove the meat from the bones.

6 Coarsely shred the meat, discarding all the remaining skin, fat and bones. Fold the shredded duckling meat into the dressing, cover and chill for 2–3 hours.

7 Using a pair of kitchen scissors, cut the reserved duckling skin into strips and quickly crisp it further under a hot broiler.

8 To serve, spoon the duckling salad down the center of a large flat platter, then arrange the crisp duck skin over the top. Serve on a bed of chicory leaves.

CHICKEN AND GRAPE SALAD

SERVES 4–6

3 pound roasting chicken	3 tablespoons clear honey
1 onion	⅔ cup heavy cream
1 carrot	1½ cups seedless green grapes, halved
1 bay leaf	⅓ cup seedless raisins
6 peppercorns	salt and pepper
2 eggs	lettuce and mild paprika, for garnish
⅓ cup lemon juice	

1 Put the chicken in a large saucepan with the onion, carrot, bay leaf and peppercorns, cover with water and poach for about 50 minutes or until tender. Let cool in the stock.

2 Remove the chicken from the stock and cut all the meat off the bones, discarding the skin. Cut the meat into bite-size pieces.

3 Beat the eggs with ¼ cup lemon juice and the honey. Put in the top of a double boiler or in a heatproof bowl standing over a saucepan of hot water and heat gently, stirring, until thick. Cover with damp baker's parchment and leave to cool.

4 Whip the cream until softly stiff and fold into the cold lemon mixture.

5 Add the remaining lemon juice to the grapes, then combine with the chicken, raisins and sauce.

6 Serve garnished with lettuce and paprika.

SMOKED CHICKEN AND AVOCADO SALAD

SERVES 4–6

2 pounds smoked chicken	½ teaspoon green peppercorn mustard
9 tablespoons olive oil	2 ripe avocados
juice of 1 lemon	salt and pepper
1 teaspoon bottled grated horseradish	sprigs of fresh cilantro and lemon slices, for garnish

1 Remove all the meat from the chicken carcase, taking care to cut thin, even slices which will look attractive in the finished dish.

2 To make the dressing, whisk together the oil, lemon juice, horseradish and mustard. Add the chicken and coat in the dressing. Cover and leave for 30 minutes to 1 hour.

3 Halve the avocados and remove the stones. Peel off the skin, then cut the flesh lengthwise into thin, even slices.

4 Arrange the chicken and avocado slices alternately on a flat, round plate, overlapping around the rim.

5 Chop any remaining oddly-shaped pieces of chicken and avocado and toss them together. Pile this mixture into the center of the plate.

6 Season the dressing remaining in the bowl and brush over the avocado slices to prevent discoloration.

7 Garnish the center of the salad with fresh cilantro and lemon slices, and serve immediately with the dressing.

CHICKEN WITH CURRIED LEMON MAYONNAISE

SERVES 4

3 pound broiler-fryer chicken	2 celery stalks, finely chopped
⅔ cup dry white wine	¾ cup thick mayonnaise
1 strip of lemon rind	2 tablespoons apricot jam
bouquet garni	finely grated rind and juice of 1 lemon
6 black peppercorns	1 sweet red or green pepper, diced
salt and pepper	2 red-skinned dessert apples
1 tablespoon butter	⅔ cup heavy cream
1 small onion, chopped	lettuce, to serve
1 tablespoon curry powder	

1 Put the chicken in a deep saucepan with the wine, enough water just to cover, the strip of lemon rind, bouquet garni, peppercorns and a good pinch of salt. Cover and simmer for 1–1¼ hours or until the chicken is tender, then leave to cool in the liquid for about 2 hours.

2 Remove the chicken from the liquid. Strain the liquid into a saucepan, then boil until reduced to a few tablespoons. Cool for 5 minutes. Meanwhile, remove the chicken from the bones and dice the meat, discarding all skin.

3 Melt the butter, add the onion and curry powder and fry for 5 minutes or until soft. Add the celery and fry for 2 minutes, stirring. Cool for 10 minutes.

4 Add the onion and celery to the mayonnaise with the apricot jam, grated lemon rind and juice and the diced pepper. Thin with the reduced cooking liquid. Season.

5 Core and dice or slice the apples. Whip the cream until thick, then fold into the mayonnaise with the apples and chicken. Chill for 30 minutes. Serve on a bed of lettuce.

BEEF AND OLIVE SALAD

SERVES 4

1 pound rolled lean brisket	1 pound green beans
1 bay leaf	salt and pepper
6 peppercorns	3 tablespoons soy sauce
1 large bunch of scallions	4 teaspoons lemon juice
12 ripe olives	

1 Put the beef, bay leaf and peppercorns in a small saucepan and add enough water to cover. Bring to a boil, cover and simmer gently for about 1 hour or until the meat is tender. Leave to cool in the cooking liquid for about 2 hours.

2 Slice the scallions diagonally into thick pieces. Quarter and pit the olives. Trim and halve the green beans. Cook the beans in boiling salted water for 5–10 minutes or until just tender. Drain well, rinse under cold running water and drain again thoroughly.

3 Drain the beef and trim off the fat. Slice thinly and cut into 1½-inch long shreds.

4 Put the beef in a bowl, add the scallions, olives, beans, soy sauce and lemon juice. Toss well together, then season with pepper. (The soy sauce should provide suffcient salt.) Cover and chill in the refrigerator for about 30 minutes before serving.

AVOCADO AND LEMON SALAD WITH OMELETTE RINGS

SERVES 4–6

4 eggs	1 teaspoon coriander seeds
½ cup shredded Cheddar cheese	⅓ cup olive or vegetable oil
salt and pepper	3 tablespoons lemon juice
2 tablespoons butter or margarine	2 ripe avocados
1 teaspoon black peppercorns	parsley sprigs, for garnish (optional)

1 Put the eggs in a bowl with the cheese and 1 tablespoon water. Season to taste and whisk together.
2 Melt a quarter of the butter or margarine in an omelette pan or small non-stick skillet. When foaming, pour in a quarter of the egg mixture. After a few seconds, push the set egg mixture into the center of the pan and tilt the pan to allow the egg to run to the edges. Cook until just set.
3 Brown the omelette under a preheated hot broiler. Turn out onto a plate. Repeat with the remaining egg mixture to make another three omelettes.
4 While the omelettes are still warm, roll them up loosely. Wrap in wax paper and let cool.
5 Meanwhile, crush the peppercorns and coriander seeds coarsely with a pestle and mortar, or with the end of a rolling pin in a strong bowl.
6 Whisk together the oil, lemon juice and crushed spices and season to taste. Halve, stone and peel the avocados, then slice thickly into the dressing. Toss gently to coat.
7 Slice the rolled omelettes thinly. Arrange the omelette rings and avocado slices in individual serving plates. Spoon over the dressing and garnish with sprigs of parsley, if liked. Serve immediately.

CHEESE AND ENDIVE SALAD

SERVES 4

2 large heads of endive, trimmed	⅓ cup vegetable oil
1 cup cubed Monterey Jack or Cheddar cheese	3 tablespoons white wine vinegar
1 sweet green pepper, chopped	1–2 teaspoons soft light brown sugar
2 celery stalks, chopped	1 small garlic clove, crushed
1 cup sliced radishes	salt and pepper
2 tablespoons beef bouillon	1 cup walnut halves

1 Chop the endive coarsely. Place the cheese cubes in a salad bowl with the endive. Add the pepper, celery and radishes and mix together.
2 Place the bouillon, oil, vinegar, sugar and garlic in a screw-topped jar, season to taste, and shake well to combine. Pour over the salad and stir in the walnuts.

CHEDDAR CHEESE AND APPLE SALAD

SERVES 4

½ bibb lettuce	2 dessert apples, peeled, cored and diced
⅔ cup dairy sour cream	
3 tablespoons milk	2 cups diced Cheddar cheese
1 teaspoon lemon juice	2 canned pineapple rings, coarsely chopped
1 teaspoon confectioners' or superfine sugar	4 orange slices and 8 ripe olives, for garnish
¼ teaspoon salt	

1 Tear the lettuce leaves into bite-size pieces and use to cover the base of a serving dish.
2 Combine the sour cream with the milk, lemon juice, sugar and salt.
3 Add the apples, cheese and pineapple to the sour cream mixture and toss lightly together. Pile on to the lettuce and garnish with orange slices and olives.

GOAT'S CHEESE WITH PEAR AND WALNUT SALAD

SERVES 2

a few lettuce leaves, such as Iceberg and radicchio, torn into pieces	½ cup chopped walnuts
	½ bunch of watercress
¼ pound goat's cheese, halved into 2 discs	2 tablespoons lemon juice
	3 tablespoons vegetable oil
2 ripe pears, cored and cut into chunks	

1 Arrange the lettuce on two serving plates and top with the goat's cheese. Mix together the pears, walnuts and watercress.
2 Blend the lemon juice and oil together, add to the pear mixture and toss to coat. Spoon onto the cheese to serve.

VARIATION

Caerphilly with Pear and Walnut Salad
If you prefer not to use goat's cheese, Caerphilly makes a delicious substitute, as do other white cheeses, such as Lancashire, Wensleydale or white Stilton.

WHOLE WHEAT BRAZIL NUT SALAD

SERVES 4–6

½ cup dried black-eye peas, soaked in cold water overnight	3 tablespoons chopped mint
1 cup whole wheat grain, soaked in cold water overnight	salt and pepper
	½ cucumber, diced
⅓ cup plain yogurt	1½ cups chopped peeled tomatoes
2 tablespoons olive oil	1 cup Cheddar cheese grated
3 tablespoons lemon juice	1 cup Brazil nuts chopped

1 Drain the beans and place in a saucepan of water. Bring to a boil and simmer gently for 1½ hours or until tender.
2 Meanwhile, drain the whole wheat and place in a saucepan of water. Bring to a boil and simmer gently for 20–25 minutes or until tender. Drain, rinse well with cold water and cool for 30 minutes. When the beans are cooked, drain and cool for 30 minutes.
3 Whisk the yogurt and olive oil together with the lemon juice and mint. Season to taste.
4 Put the whole wheat, beans, cucumber, tomatoes, cheese and Brazil nuts in a bowl. Pour over the dressing and mix well.
5 Garnish and chill before serving.

WINTER SALAD

SERVES 4–6

1 dessert apple, cored and chopped	½ teaspoon sugar
1 head of celery, sliced	¼ cup light cream
1 cooked beet, peeled and sliced	2 teaspoons white wine vinegar
2 heads endive, trimmed and sliced	salt and pepper
1 punnet of garden cress	3 eggs, hard-cooked, shelled and cut into wedges
½ teaspoon prepared English mustard	

1 Lightly mix the apple, celery, beet and endive together with the cress in a large salad bowl.
2 To make the dressing, whisk the mustard, sugar, cream and vinegar together. Season to taste. Pour over the salad and toss together so that everything is coated in the dressing. Add the eggs, then serve at once.

BEAN, CHEESE AND AVOCADO SALAD

SERVES 4

1 cup dried red kidney beans, soaked in cold water overnight	1 small onion, finely chopped
⅓ cup olive oil	2 celery stalks, finely chopped
juice and finely grated rind of 1 lemon	2 tomatoes, peeled and chopped
¼ teaspoon hot pepper sauce	1 ripe avocado
salt and pepper	celery leaves, for garnish
1½ cups diced Edam cheese	

1 Drain the kidney beans and rinse under cold running water. Put in a saucepan, cover with fresh cold water and bring to a boil. Boil rapidly for 10 minutes, then simmer for 1–1½ hours or until tender.

2 Drain the beans and put in a bowl. Add the oil, lemon juice and rind and hot pepper sauce. Season to taste. Toss well, then leave until cold.

3 Add the cheese, onion, celery and tomatoes to the beans and toss again to mix the ingredients together. Cover and chill.

4 When ready to serve, cut the avocado in half and remove the stone. Peel and chop the flesh into chunky pieces. Fold the avocado pieces gently into the bean salad and taste and adjust the seasoning. Garnish and serve.

MIXED BEAN SALAD

SERVES 4

1 pound fresh lima beans	1 tablespoon lemon juice
salt and pepper	1-pound can red kidney beans, drained and rinsed
½ pound green beans	
1 tablespoon vegetable oil	2 cups cubed Cheddar cheese
⅔ cup plain yogurt	chopped parsley, for garnish
1 tablespoon mild whole grain mustard	

1 Hull the lima beans and cook in boiling salted water for 10 minutes. Add the green beans and continue to cook for 5–10 minutes or until both are tender.

2 Meanwhile, mix together the oil, yogurt, mustard and lemon juice. Season to taste and beat until well blended.

3 Drain the cooked beans and, while still hot, combine with the kidney beans and dressing. Let cool.

4 Toss in the cubes of cheese and garnish with chopped fresh parsley just before serving.

── TO MICROWAVE ──

Put the lima beans in a small bowl with 2 tablespoons water. Cover and cook on HIGH for 10–12 minutes or until tender. Put the green beans and 1 tablespoon water in a small bowl, cover and cook on HIGH for 4–5 minutes or until tender, stirring once. Complete steps 2, 3 and 4.

INDEX

A

anchovies: cheese and anchovy broiled chicken breasts, 72
Jansson's temptation, 160
angler fish: angler fish and mushroom puffs, 149
angler fish and mussel skewers, 104
angler fish with lime and shrimp, 103
fricassee of angler fish with cilantro, 103
asparagus: asparagus in cheese sauce, 150
marinated turkey with asparagus, 83
turkey breast with asparagus, 77
avocado: avocado and lemon salad, 170
bean, cheese and avocado salad, 173
pan bagna with avocado, 164
smoked chicken and avocado salad, 168

B

bacon: bacon and apple pie, 52
bacon and liver roulades, 51
bacon cakes, 158
bacon chops in cider, 50
bacon chops with gooseberry sauce, 51
bacon in cider with sage and onion dumplings, 53
curried bacon flan, 154
lima bean and bacon soup, 139
spaghetti alla carbonara, 162
turkey and bacon kabobs, 83
barbecued spareribs, 47
bean salad, mixed, 173
beef: beef and chestnut casserole, 12
beef and olive salad, 169
beef and red bean gratin, 18
beef and spinach curry, 16
beef crumble, 40
beef in cider, 13
beef in stout, 14
beef in wine with walnuts, 12
beef 'moussaka', 18
beef olives, 8
beef stew with dumplings, 13
beef Wellington, 20
bitkis, 9
boeuf stroganoff, 15
boiled beef and carrots, 11
chili pizza fingers, 157
Chinese beef and vegetable stir-fry, 10
club steaks with mustard, 6
cold beef in soured cream, 145
Cornish pasties, 156
cottage pie, 28
curried mince and apple bake, 17
ground beef with peas, 16
Hungarian goulash, 15
Italian-style meatballs, 10
meat and potato pie, 19
meat loaf with onion sauce, 20
Mexican beef tortillas, 14
minced beef kabobs with horseradish relish, 9
pasta bake, 163
spaghetti bolognese, 143
spiced beef, 11
steak and kidney pie, 19
steak with cream sauce, 7
steak with port, 7
steamed beef and tomato pudding, 17
Stilton steaks, 6
strips of beef in whisky sauce, 8
biryani, vegetable, 131
bitkis, 9
Brazil nuts: whole wheat Brazil nut salad, 172
bread: pan bagna with avocado, 164
broccoli: chicken and broccoli pie, 74
macaroni and broccoli cheese, 150
buckwheat and lentil casserole, 132

C

cabbage: cabbage and hazelnut rolls, 123
pot roast of pork and red cabbage, 42
stuffed cabbage parcels, 48
Canadian pork and veal pie, 49
cashew stuffed mushrooms, 145
cauliflower: cauliflower and zucchini bake, 124
cauliflower and Stilton flan, 151
farmhouse cauliflower soufflés, 147
spiced potato and cauliflower pastries, 136
cheese: bean, cheese and avocado salad, 173
Caerphilly with pear and walnut salad, 171
cauliflower and Stilton flan, 151
Cheddar cheese and apple salad, 171
cheese and anchovy broiled chicken breasts, 72
cheese and endive salad, 170
cheese soufflé, 121
cheesy smoked salmon roulade, 115
creamy cod bake, 95
crispy stuffed potato skins, 165
farmhouse cauliflower soufflés, 147
feta cheese puffs with basil, 155
fresh tagliatelle with leek and Roquefort sauce, 127
goat's cheese with pear and walnut salad, 171
Grandma's cheese pudding, 120
haddock and caraway cheese soufflé, 95
hot crab and ricotta quiches, 153
hot fish terrine with Gruyère sauce, 111
leeks in cheese sauce, 150
macaroni and broccoli cheese, 150
macaroni cheese, 162
mock crab, 149
pan haggerty, 143
pasta and mushrooms baked with two cheeses, 125
ratatouille pasta bake, 128
spinach and ricotta crêpes, 129
spinach and Stilton crêpes, 129
Stilton steaks, 6
tagliatelle with cheese and nut sauce, 127
zucchini, Parmesan and tomato bake, 121
chef's salad, 166
chick-peas, baked potatoes with, 124
chicken: boned stuffed squabs, 76
cheese and anchovy broiled chicken breasts, 72
chicken and broccoli pie, 74
chicken and grape salad, 168
chicken and red currant curry, 71
chicken eggah, 148
chicken julienne, 67
chicken Kiev, 73
chicken parcels, 156
chicken pot pies, 74
chicken supremes in wine and cream, 73
chicken tacos, 165
chicken thighs with spicy tomato sauce, 65
chicken Véronique, 67
chicken with apricots and brandy, 68
chicken with curried lemon mayonnaise, 169
chicken with lemon and almonds, 68
chicken with mushrooms and bacon, 69
chicken with saffron, 70
chicken with tarragon sauce, 70
cock-a-leekie soup, 137
Cornish caudle chicken pie, 64
Coronation chicken, 75
deviled squabs, 75
gingered Japanese chicken, 66
golden baked chicken, 63
honey barbecued chicken, 72
lemon and turmeric chicken, 69
mock crab, 149
quick chicken and mussel paella, 161
sesame chicken pittas, 164
shredded chicken with mushrooms and walnuts, 66
smoked chicken and avocado salad, 168
spiced chicken, 71
spiced roast chicken, 64
stir-fried chicken with zucchini, 63
stoved chicken, 65
chicken liver see liver
chili: chili lamb and coconut curry, 38
chili pizza fingers, 157
chili pork and beans, 42
steamed mullet with chili sauce, 102
vegetable chili, 133
Chinese beef and vegetable stir-fry, 10
club steaks, 6
cock-a-leekie soup, 137
cod: cod fish cakes with herbs, 159
cod in a spicy yogurt crust, 96
cod in cream and celery sauce, 94
cod with coriander in cream, 93
creamy cod bake, 95
fish Wellington, 107
fisherman's hot pot, 110
fisherman's pie, 118
Spanish cod with peppers, tomatoes and garlic, 96
Tandoori cod, 93
corn: haddock and corn chowder, 142
corned beef: red flannel hash, 144
Cornish caudle chicken pie, 64
Cornish pasties, 156
Coronation chicken, 75
cottage pie, 28
couscous, 133
crab: crab salad, 166
Devonshire crab soup, 142
hot crab and ricotta quiches, 153
crêpes: curried shrimp, 119
spinach and ricotta, 129
spinach and Stilton, 129
cullen skink, 141
curries: beef and spinach curry, 16
chicken and red currant curry, 71
chicken with curried lemon mayonnaise, 169
chili lamb and coconut curry, 38
Coronation chicken, 75
curried bacon flan, 154
curried eggs, 135
curried beef and apple bake, 17
curried parsnip soup, 141
curried shrimp crêpes, 119
curried winter soup, 139
Indonesian fish curry, 107
quick turkey curry, 81
vegetable curry, 130
Cyprus stuffed peppers, 123

D

Danish roast loin of pork, 41
Devonshire crab soup, 142
duck: deviled duckling salad, 167
duck julienne en croûte, 86
duck with Cumberland sauce, 86
duck with mango, 87
duckling roulades with peaches, 85
duckling with brandy and green peppercorn sauce, 85
duckling with green peas, 84
roast duck with apple stuffing, 84
sweet and sour duck joints, 87
tropical duck, 87

E

Eastern lamb kabobs, 31
eggs: avocado and lemon salad with omelette rings, 170
chicken eggah, 148
curried eggs, 135
omelette Arnold Bennett, 147
sausage and egg pie, 54
spicy Scotch eggs, 144
tortilla, 146
eggplants: beef 'moussaka', 18
lamb and eggplant moussaka, 38
stuffed eggplants, 120
endive: cheese and endive salad, 170

F

fish: fish cakes with herbs, 159
fish in spicy sauce with tomatoes, 108
fish Wellington, 107
fisherman's hot pot, 110
fisherman's pie, 118
Italian fish stew, 108
Mediterranean fish stew with aïoli, 109

tomato fish bake, 110
see also cod, salmon *etc.*
flounder, mushroom-stuffed, 99

G

game pie, 89
gammon *see* bacon, ham
goose: roast goose with apples and prunes, 91
goulash, Hungarian, 15
gray mullet: gray mullet cooked in lemon and red wine, 102
steamed mullet with chili sauce, 102
ground beef with peas, 16

H

haddock: cullen skink, 141
fish cakes with herbs, 159
fish mousses with cilantro and tomato sauce, 111
haddock and caraway cheese soufflé, 95
haddock and corn chowder, 142
haddock and mushroom puffs, 149
haddock au gratin, 94
haddock in a spicy yogurt crust, 96
haddock in cream and leek sauce, 94
Indonesian fish curry, 107
omelette Arnold Bennett, 147
smoked haddock flan, 153
smoked haddock gougères, 148
hake: hot fish terrine with Gruyère sauce, 111
halibut Creole, 97
ham: baked ham, 49
creamy ham and leek pies, 155
glazed gammon steaks, 50
pasta with peas and ham in cream sauce, 158
veal and ham pie, 25
haricot beans, Southern, 134
harvest vegetable soup, 138
herring: herring in oatmeal, 112
stuffed herring, 113
Hungarian goulash, 15

I

Indonesian fish curry, 107
Italian fish stew, 108
Italian liver, 55
Italian squid stew, 115
Italian stuffed tomatoes, 122
Italian-style meatballs, 10

J

Jansson's temptation, 160
Jerusalem artichoke gratin, 122

K

kabobs: angler fish and mussel skewers, 104
chicken liver skewers, 159
Eastern lamb kabobs, 31
lamb kabobs in spicy yogurt dressing, 40
ground beef kabobs with horseradish relish, 9
turkey and bacon kabobs, 83
kedgeree, salmon, 160
kidneys: creamed kidneys in wine, 59
kidney and mushroom sauté, 60
kidney sauté, 57
kidneys à la crème, 59
kidneys in batter, 58
kidney toad in the hole, 55

steak and kidney pie, 19
veal and kidney pie, 25

L

lamb: blanquette d'agneau, 37
braised shoulder of lamb with apricot stuffing, 32
brown ragout of lamb, 35
chili lamb and coconut curry, 38
crown roast, 31
crumb-topped lamb chops, 45
Eastern lamb kabobs, 31
guard of honour, 31
honeyed lamb noisettes, 29
lamb and eggplant moussaka, 38
lamb and maître d'hôtel butter, 36
lamb and orange casserole with choux dumplings, 35
lamb and watercress bake, 39
lamb crumble, 40
lamb cutlets reform, 28
lamb fillet with red currant sauce, 29
lamb in tomato sauce with herb bread, 33
lamb kabobs in spicy yogurt dressing, 40
lamb noisettes with red wine sauce, 30
lamb steaks with caper sauce, 27
lamb with cherries, 34
Lancashire hot pot, 36
minted lamb burgers with cucumber, 30
Oriental lamb, 34
Parson's 'venison', 33
portmanteau lamb chops, 26
rolled stuffed breasts of lamb, 32
shepherd's pie, 28
spiced lamb, 37
spiced lentil bake, 39
tangy chops, 27
Lancashire hot pot, 36
lasagne, vegetable, 126
leeks: cock-a-leekie soup, 137
creamy ham and leek pies, 155
fresh tagliatelle with leek and Roquefort sauce, 127
leek and macaroni gratin, 125
leeks in cheese sauce, 150
likky pie, 53
lentils: buckwheat and lentil casserole, 132
spiced lentil bake, 39
spinach and lentil roulade, 129
lima bean and bacon soup, 139
lima bean and tuna gratin, 118
liver: bacon and liver roulades, 51
calf's liver with green grapes and Madeira, 61
chicken liver skewers, 159
chicken livers in sherry cream sauce, 58
Italian liver, 55
lamb's liver and mushrooms, 57
liver goujons with orange sauce, 56
liver in stroganoff sauce, 56
liver sauté, 57

M

macaroni: leek and macaroni gratin, 125
macaroni and broccoli cheese, 150
macaroni cheese, 162
wholewheat macaroni bake, 128
mackerel: broiled mackerel with sage sauce, 114
mackerel parcels, 113

smoked mackerel soufflé, 114
stuffed mackerel, 113
meat and potato pie, 19
meat loaf with onion sauce, 20
meatballs, Italian-style, 10
Mediterranean fish stew with aïoli, 109
Mexican beef tortillas, 14
mixed bean salad, 173
mixed vegetable ring, 135
mock crab, 149
moong dal and spinach, 131
moussaka, lamb and eggplant, 38
mousses, fish with cilantro and tomato sauce, 111
mullet *see* gray mullet
mulligatawny soup, 140
mushrooms: cashew stuffed mushrooms, 145
chicken with mushrooms and bacon, 69
garlic mushroom parcels, 146
haddock and mushroom puffs, 149
kidney and mushroom sauté, 60
lamb's liver and mushrooms, 57
mushroom soup, 138
mushroom-stuffed flounder, 99
pasta and mushrooms baked with two cheeses, 125
pork and mushroom salad, 167
pork tenderloin with white wine and mushrooms, 46
shredded chicken with mushrooms and walnuts, 66
sweetbreads with mushrooms and white wine, 61
veal scallops in mushroom sauce, 21
mussels: angler fish and mussel skewers, 104
mussels and clams with tomatoes, 117
mussel and onion stew, 116
quick chicken and mussel paella, 161

N

noodles: chicken eggah, 148
pasta and mushrooms baked with two cheeses, 125

O

oatmeal: vegetable and oatmeal broth, 138
omelettes *see* eggs
onions: cream of onion soup, 140
meat loaf with onion sauce, 20
pissaladière, 157
sausage popovers with onion sauce, 52
spiced pepper and onion flan, 152
tarte à l'oignon, 152
Oriental lamb, 34
oxtail: braised oxtail, 62
orange oxtail stew, 62

P

paella, quick chicken and mussel, 161
pan bagna with avocado, 164
pan haggerty, 143
parsnip soup, curried, 141
Parson's 'venison', 33
pasta, 125–8, 162–3
pasta and mushrooms baked with two cheeses, 125
pasta bake, 163
pasta bake, ratatouille, 128
pasta with peas and ham in cream sauce, 158
peas: duckling wih green peas, 84

pasta with peas and ham in cream sauce, 158
pea soup, 137
peppers: Cyprus stuffed peppers, 123
pork chops with peppers, 44
Spanish cod with peppers, tomatoes and garlic, 96
spiced pepper and onion flan, 152
spiced veal with peppers, 23
pheasant: pheasant au porto, 91
pheasant breasts with vermouth, 90
pheasant with chestnuts, 90
roast pheasant with herby forcemeat balls, 89
pies: bacon and apple, 52
Canadian pork and veal, 49
chicken and broccoli, 74
chicken parcels, 156
chicken pot pies, 74
Cornish caudle chicken, 64
Cornish pasties, 156
creamy ham and leek, 155
feta cheese puffs with basil, 155
fish Wellington, 107
game pie, 89
haddock and mushroom puffs, 149
likky pie, 53
sausage and egg, 54
sour cream salmon, 106
spiced potato and cauliflower pastries, 136
steak and kidney, 19
veal and ham, 25
veal and kidney, 25
pissaladière, 157
pitas, sesame chicken, 164
pizza fingers, chili, 157
plaice: fish medallions with dill sauce, 112
stuffed plaice with lemon sauce, 99
pork: barbecued spareribs, 47
Canadian pork and veal pie, 49
chili pork and beans, 42
crumb-topped pork chops, 45
Danish roast loin of pork, 41
fruity stuffed pork chops, 44
gourmet pork rolls, 48
honeyed spareribs, 47
likky pie, 53
parceled pork, 45
pork and mushroom salad, 167
pork with cider and coriander, 46
pork scallops with juniper, 43
pork fillet with white wine and mushrooms, 46
pork in plum sauce, 43
pork chops with peppers, 44
pot roast of pork and red cabbage, 42
roast pork with apples, 41
stuffed cabbage parcels, 48
sweet and sour pork, 47
potatoes: baked potatoes with chick-peas, 124
cabbage and hazelnut rolls, 123
crispy stuffed potato skins, 165
cullen skink, 141
fisherman's hot pot, 110
fisherman's pie, 118
Jansson's temptation, 160
Lancashire hot pot, 36
meat and potato pie, 19
pan haggerty, 143
red flannel hash, 144
shepherd's pie, 28
special parsley fish pie, 109

spiced potato and cauliflower
pastries, 136
tortilla, 146

Q

quiches and savory flans:
cauliflower and Stilton flan, 151
courgette quiche, 151
curried bacon flan, 154
hot crab and ricotta quiches, 153
pissaladière, 157
smoked haddock flan, 153
spiced pepper and onion flan,
152
spinach and shrimp quiche, 154
tarte à l'oignon, 152
quick winter soup, 139

R

rabbit: rabbit casserole with cider
and mustard, 88
rabbit casserole with sage
dumplings, 88
ratatouille: ratatouille pasta bake,
128
spaghetti with ratatouille sauce,
126
red flannel hash, 144
red kidney beans: bean, cheese and
avocado salad, 173
beef and red bean gratin, 18
chili pork and beans, 42
chipolatas and beans, 54
rice: shrimp risotto, 161
quick chicken and mussel paella,
161
salmon kedgeree, 160
vegetable biryani, 131

S

salmon: cheesy smoked salmon
roulade, 115
fish medallions with dill sauce,
112
salmon kedgeree, 160
salmon with fennel sauce, 106
salmon with herb sauce, 105
sour cream salmon pie, 106
summer poached salmon, 105
sausages and bulk sausage: sausages
and beans, 54
kidney toad in the hole, 55
sausage and egg pie, 54
sausage popovers with onion
sauce, 52
spicy Scotch eggs, 144
toad in the hole, 55
scallops in creamy basil sauce,
116
Scotch eggs, spicy, 144
seafood stir-fry, 119
sesame chicken pittas, 164
shrimp: angler fish with lime and
shrimp, 103
curried shrimp crêpes, 119
mousselines of sole with shrimp,
98
shrimp risotto, 161
spinach and shrimp quiche, 154
shepherd's pie, 28
skate with capers, 103
sole: mousselines of sole with
shrimp, 98
sole bonne femme, 97
sole 'stewed' in cream, 98
soufflés: cheese, 121
farmhouse cauliflower, 147
haddock and caraway cheese,
95
smoked mackerel, 114
soups, 137–42
Southern baked beans, 134

spaghetti: spaghetti alla carbonara,
162
spaghetti bolognese, 143
spaghetti with peas and ham in
cream sauce, 158
spaghetti with ratatouille sauce,
126
turkey Tetrazzini, 81
Spanish cod with peppers, tomatoes
and garlic, 96
spinach: beef and spinach curry, 16
creamy cod bake, 95
moong dal and spinach, 131
spinach and lentil roulade, 129
spinach and shrimp quiche, 154
spinach and ricotta crêpes, 129
spinach and Stilton crêpes, 129
trout stuffed with spinach and
walnuts, 101
squabs: boned stuffed squabs, 76
casseroled with cider and apple,
92
deviled squabs, 75
squid stew, Italian, 115
sweetbreads: creamed
sweetbreads,
60
sweetbreads with mushrooms
and white wine, 61

T

tacos, chicken, 165
tagliatelle: fresh tagliatelle with
leek and Roquefort sauce, 127
pasta with peas and ham in cream
sauce, 158
tagliatelle with cheese and nut
sauce, 127
tagliatelle with seafood and
champagne sauce, 117
Tandoori cod, 93
terrine, hot fish with Gruyère
sauce, 111
toad in the hole, 55
tomatoes: chicken thighs with spicy
tomato sauce, 65
fish in spicy sauce with tomatoes,
108
fish mousses with cilantro and
tomato sauce, 111
Italian stuffed tomatoes, 122
lamb in tomato sauce with herb
bread, 33
mussels and clams with
tomatoes, 117
pissaladière, 157
Spanish cod with peppers,
tomatoes and garlic, 96
steamed beef and tomato
pudding, 17
tomato fish bake, 110
zucchini, Parmesan and tomato
bake, 121
tortilla, 146
Mexican beef tortillas, 14
trout: baked trout with cucumber
sauce, 101
baked trout with hazelnuts and
dill, 100
trout in cream, 100
trout stuffed with spinach and
walnuts, 101
tuna: lima bean and tuna gratin,
118
tuna and pasta in sour cream,
163
veal with tuna fish mayonnaise,
26
turkey: casseroled turkey in red
wine, 80
marinated turkey with
asparagus, 83

quick turkey curry, 81
roast turkey, 76
roast turkey with lemon stuffing,
77
stuffed turkey legs, 82
turkey and bacon kabobs, 83
turkey balls with cranberry and
orange sauce, 82
turkey breast with asparagus, 77
turkey scallops with cranberry
and coconut, 79
turkey scallops with damsons,
78
turkey scallops with hazelnut
cream sauce, 78
turkey scallops with plums, 78
turkey in spiced yogurt, 80
turkey julienne, 67
turkey sauté with lemon and
walnuts, 79
turkey sauté with orange and
walnuts, 79
turkey Tetrazzini, 81

V

veal: blanquette de veau, 37
Canadian pork and veal pie, 49
escalopes fines herbes, 21
fricassée of veal, 23
sautéed veal with zucchini and
grapefruit, 22
spiced veal with peppers, 23
veal and ham pie, 25
veal and kidney pie, 25
veal cobbler, 22
veal scallops, 24
veal scallops in mushroom sauce,
21
veal in Marsala, 24
veal with tuna mayonnaise, 26
vegetable and oatmeal broth, 138
vegetable biryani, 131
vegetable chilli, 133
vegetable curry, 130
vegetable hot pot, 132
vegetable jalousie, 136
vegetable lasagne, 126
vegetarian medley, 130
vegetarian roast, 134
venison scallops with red wine, 92

W

whiting: special parsley fish pie,
109
whole wheat Brazil nut salad, 172
winter salad, 172

Y

yogurt: cod in a spicy yogurt crust,
96
haddock in a spicy yogurt crust,
96
lamb kabobs in spicy yogurt
dressing, 40
turkey in spiced yogurt, 80

Z

zucchini: cauliflower and
zucchini bake, 124
zucchini, Parmesan and tomato
bake, 121
zucchini quiche, 151
sautéed veal with zucchini and
grapefruit, 22
stir-fried chicken with
zucchini, 63